Frederic Franklin

ALSO BY LESLIE NORTON

Léonide Massine and the 20th Century Ballet
(McFarland, 2004)

Frederic Franklin

A Biography of the Ballet Star

LESLIE NORTON
with FREDERIC FRANKLIN

McFarland & Company, Inc., Publishers
Jefferson, North Carolina, and London

LIBRARY OF CONGRESS CATALOGUING-IN-PUBLICATION DATA

Norton, Leslie, 1952–
Frederic Franklin : a biography of the ballet star /
Leslie Norton with Frederic Franklin.
p.   cm.
Includes bibliographical references and index.

ISBN-13: 978-0-7864-3051-2
softcover : 50# alkaline paper ∞

1. Franklin, Frederic, 1914–   2. Ballet dancers — Biography.
3. Ballet.   4. Ballet Russe de Monte Carlo — History.
I. Franklin, Frederic, 1914–   II. Title.
GV1785.F755N67   2007   792.802'8092 — dc22   2007020399

British Library cataloguing data are available

On the cover: Frederic Franklin in *Don Quixote* (1955), a Ballet Russe de Monte Carlo
production *(photograph by Maurice Seymour, courtesy of Ronald Seymour)*

Manufactured in the United States of America

*McFarland & Company, Inc., Publishers
Box 611, Jefferson, North Carolina 28640
www.mcfarlandpub.com*

To all of my friends in the Ballet

F.F.

Table of Contents

Preface and
Acknowledgments

Frederic Franklin: A Biography of the Ballet Star chronicles many key eras in twentieth century ballet. This book is in eight chapters, each covering a different period in Franklin's long career. Franklin was one of the great ballet stars of the twentieth century. His performing career reached its peak with the Ballet Russe de Monte Carlo, with whom he danced from 1938 to 1957. During this time, such stellar choreographers as Bronislava Nijinska, Agnes de Mille, George Balanchine, and Sir Frederick Ashton created leading roles for him in their ballets, and he formed a legendary partnership with Alexandra Danilova. World War II cut the company off from its original home base in Europe after its first season. However, if the Ballet Russe was a stranger to London and Paris during most of its existence, its dancers and repertory were familiar in Chicago, Boston, Kansas City, St. Louis, Milwaukee, San Francisco, Cleveland, Seattle, Portland, Los Angeles, Houston, Toronto, Ottawa and Montreal, not to mention countless small towns en route to these metropolises. Since they gave millions of Americans their first exposure to this art form, Franklin and his colleagues were of vital importance in the flowering of a native, American ballet tradition.

As a performer, Franklin took the stage by storm. He was the most generous of artists, giving endlessly of himself to audiences. The steps which he danced might hardly have had names, or cost him years of work in the studio, since he laid his mastery of them in the service of expression. Franklin had charisma in spades — small wonder that he became something of a matinee idol.

When he left the Ballet Russe, Franklin became artistic director of the National Ballet, the first major company in the nation's capital. The company was highly acclaimed in New York and in other major cities across America. When the company fell on hard financial times and folded in 1974, Franklin began freelancing, doing what he probably does better than anyone else in the world. He has been pivotal in enhancing both the standards and prestige of America's regional ballet companies. He has revived an astonishing number of historically significant Petipa, Ballet Russe and Americana works, thus enriching the repertories of these companies and greatly contributing to the preservation of important ballets. An evangelist for dance, Frederic has inspired generations of dancers through his teaching, coaching and directing. Professionally, he has engendered universal love and respect.

This is a book about the life and times of Frederic Franklin. As a biographical subject he is in many ways ideal, for when one studies his work within the context of the many different eras through which he lived, Franklin serves as a unifying thread through decades of the development of art in the West. He is a man who has not only remained for years at the vanguard of dance but has also been an integral part of the cultural history of the twentieth and twenty-first centuries. Even the seemingly superficial anecdotes that one will find in this book have been included in the hope that they may provide glimpses of what it was like to be a ballet dancer and a balletgoer over the years. In the same vein, this book includes detailed analyses of the major ballets in which Franklin danced. The study thus integrates discussion of Fred's lifetime experiences with multifaceted perspectives on his art.

To see Franklin staging ballets is to enjoy a rare pleasure — the pleasure of seeing someone who appears completely attuned to his world. He is at home and in his element, even under the most stressful of circumstances. In his 1997 revival of *Coppelia* for American Ballet Theatre, Kevin McKenzie assigned him six casts of principals to rehearse, and he had only ten days to stage the entire ballet. He could never rehearse the six couples all together because their schedules were so complicated. With more energy than many people half his age, Franklin simply rolled up his sleeves and got to work. Against nearly insurmountable odds, he successfully pulled off what is known among company members as the "Ballet Theatre Miracle." The necessity of having to work in so disjointed a fashion provokes no complaint from him; he seems, if anything, to find the enforced variety refreshing to the spirit. He keeps his sense of humor and is unfailingly gracious to his dancers. There are people who have worked closely with him for ten years or more and have yet to see him lose his temper or hear him raise his voice in anger.

To this day, even in his nineties, he projects his prodigious energy forward, filling his calendar with performances and stagings. Repose is neither considered in the present nor planned for in the future. He still dances principal character roles for American Ballet Theatre and very recently staged an important Sir Frederick Ashton revival for the Royal Ballet, pausing only for a quick trip to Buckingham Palace, where he was awarded a Commander of the British Empire medal by the queen herself.

As a person, Franklin has a special quality of the spirit — a quality of richness and joie de vivre that he has communicated and passed along to everyone he has ever met. In the end, true artistry has everything to do with character. Beyond the beauty or cleverness or power of what a dancer delivers physically on the stage or in the studio, what reaches us is the essence of a person. It is the quality of his heart that makes Frederic Franklin so exceptional a human being, and this must be the ultimate subject of a biography on Freddie.

Writing this book has been a labor of love, albeit long and arduous. Public and private collections on Frederic Franklin exist in abundance, but they are scattered. Comprehensive research has required dozens of trips to New York, as well as the usual delays for travel funds and interlibrary loan requests. At present, the most extensive and complete Franklin resources are concentrated in the Jerome Robbins Dance Division, New York Public Library at Lincoln Center, in the NYPL Newspaper Archives and, of course, in Mr. Franklin's vast personal collection. To the many archivists and librarians who have assisted me, I owe an unpayable debt. Special thanks are reserved for the peerless staff of the Jerome Robbins Dance Division and for Phil Karg in particular.

I am indebted to photographers Myra Armstrong, Jack Vartoogian, Charles Green, Nan Melville, Donald Saddler, William Ausman, Sandy Underwood, Philip J. Gershong, and Roy Round for allowing permission to use their stunning photographs. Thanks as well to Ron Seymour for permission to use the photos of Maurice Seymour, to Avivah and Gabriel Pinski for permission to reproduce the photographs of Fred Fehl, to the Museum of the City of New York for permission to reproduce the photos of Marcus Blechman, to British Ceremonial Arts for the videotape still of the investiture, and to Kelly Ryan, Director of Press and Public Relations at American Ballet Theatre, for permission for all photographs of American Ballet Theatre productions. Ballerina Virginia Johnson was kind enough to donate photos from her own personal collection. Nancy Reynolds gave permission for two photographs taken by her late husband, Brian Rushton.

Victoria Morgan, Artistic Director of Cincinnati Ballet, and Marcello Angelini, Artistic Director of Tulsa Ballet Theatre, allowed me to pester them, month after month, with questions. They were extremely generous with their time in their interviews with me, and their memories of Frederic Franklin have been enormously helpful. Similarly, Nancy Reynolds, founder of The Balanchine Foundation, gave me some invaluable updating on the impressive activities of this institution, which will be of great interest to the reader. My hat is off to Susan Morgan, who did most of the photo reproductions in this book. The late George Verdak graciously allowed me the use of his private dance history archives in Indianapolis. Thanks to Tatiana Massine Weinbaum, who secured permission for me to view her father's films, now housed in the Jerome Robbins Dance Division of the New York Public Library.

Without the assistance of Hamilton College's Information Technology Services, the technical difficulties in translating draft software would have been nearly insurmountable. The expertise, kindness and patience of the ITS staff have been extraordinary.

Finally, thanks to Bill Ausman, the dearest friend of our subject, Freddie. Bill did a close reading of my drafts, page by page, and his insights were always thoughtful and on target. It was Bill who wrote the photo captions for this book, thus ensuring the most accurate and thorough descriptions possible.

No acknowledgment would be complete without a big "thank you" to the person who inspired this book. At the time that I had completed my first draft, Mr. Franklin did not know me from Adam. I sent the first draft to Cincinnati Ballet's Victoria Morgan and was thrilled when she gave me access to Freddie's telephone number. Next came the dreaded task of phoning Mr. Franklin to ask if I could send the manuscript and obtain some personal interviews. One Sunday morning, in great fear and trepidation, I summoned forth the courage to make that call. When Fred picked up the hook, I was very shaky and breathless: "May I have the honor of speaking with Mr. Frederic

Franklin?" I squeaked. From the other end, Freddie boomed, "Speak up, Darling. I can hardly hear you!" I took a deep breath, managed to be audible, and the results have been far more inspiring than I had ever dreamed of. While I am still in awe of Mr. Franklin, it is impossible to remain afraid of a man who is so kind and generous to everyone. Freddie's wonderful comments are the very heart and soul of this book, as the reader will quickly see.

· 1 ·

Finding Ballet in a Roundabout Way

When he was a seven-year-old boy, Frederic Franklin happened to see a girl doing an Amazonian warrior dance at his Liverpool dancing school. She did it to the March in Act I of the *Nutcracker*. He liked the dance a lot, and he promptly replicated it step by step, having seen the dance only once. Like the young Mozart, said to be able to write down a long piece of music after just one hearing, Franklin had, and still has, a prodigious memory. And he has much to look back on.

The eldest of three children of Fred Franklin, a refreshment caterer, and his wife Mabel, *née* Brown, Franklin was born in Liverpool on June 13, 1914, into an environment that was sane, sound and commonplace. There were endless debates over the choice of a first name, and a decision had still not been reached when the babe was brought forward to the altar for the christening. So Mr. Franklin just told the questioning priest, "Aw, let's just call him Fred."[1] Fred had two junior siblings, Greta May and John Brown. No member of the family, before young Freddie, had ever "gone on the boards." Although both of his parents were very musical, they were in no way connected with the theatre or any of the arts, and he cannot be said to have had any stage background as a small child. When he was four, his parents took him to see *Peter Pan*, and when he came home, he tried to fly. He said to his parents, "'I know what I am going to do when I am grown up. I am going to be in the theatre.' They made soothing noises, like: 'of course dear,' but I was quite serious. 'Listen,' I told them, 'I am going to be in the theatre.'"[2]

A month later, someone brought a Gramophone into the house. Freddie had never seen one before, and he got up on the chest of drawers and put his head into the great horn, to hear the music. It was Armistice of 1919 and in the excitement, no one noticed him. He stayed up all night, "dancing about" the living room. This became a daily habit. Franklin's parents soon noticed that he had an unusually correct ear for music and picked up very easily any tunes that he heard.

Franklin's aunt belonged to a tennis club and at the end of the season, they always had a dance. That year it happened to take place in the studio of ballet teacher Marjorie Kelly. Seeing his aptitude for dance, Franklin's auntie told Mrs. Kelly that her six-year-old nephew Freddie ought to "have a go" because he liked to "wiggle around the Victrola."[3] When Mabel took her son to see Mrs. Kelly, she offered to take him on as a pupil and reminded Mrs. Franklin that he would need ballet shoes. Here is Franklin's account of their purchase:

> We go to downtown Liverpool and there's a shop, and I went in there, and I said to my mother, "Those are exactly the ones I have to wear." So the next day I went to the class and Mrs. Kelly said, "Freddie, what on earth have you got on your feet?" I said, "They're ballet shoes." Mrs. Kelly cried, "Yes, but they're the wrong kind. They're pointe shoes!" I didn't know any differently. I didn't know there *were* any other ballet shoes.[4]

Thus began Freddie's dance career, holding on to a chair at his first class and copying what the little girls were doing. He was always the only boy in class at Mrs. Kelly's, but he said, "It didn't bother me because I was having a wonderful time." Fortunately, Mrs. Kelly was a very good teacher, so Franklin was well trained from the start. Freddie remembers that, in those days, there were what were known as "Rose-Dance Schools," where the students went around throwing petals on the floor à la Isadora Duncan.[5] Mrs. Kelly was not a teacher of that sort.

Freddie gave his first performance in the same year, 1920. His premiere appearance before the public was as a bunny rabbit at a big function at the Adelphia Hotel in Liverpool. He went out and danced before the large assemblage in his rabbit suit, and when he finished, they gave him a box of chocolates that was as big as he was. Franklin remembered his thought: "'Well, if I go out there and dance and get a box of chocolates every time, I don't mind doing this again.' And that's how it all started."[6]

At the age of ten, Franklin took a two-year hiatus from formal dance lessons. Mrs. Kelly had given him about all that she could, since her school was geared to very young children. Two years later, Mabel Franklin read in the paper about a school that taught elocution, drama and all kinds of dancing. She took him at once to the studio of Mrs. Shelagh Elliott Clarke. When Mabel told Mrs. Clarke that she was Mrs. Franklin, Clarke asked, "Are you the mother of Freddie Franklin? Oh, of course he comes here!"[7]

Apparently, he already had a small name back then in Liverpool.

At the studio of Shelagh Elliott Clarke, Franklin was schooled in ballet, ballroom dancing, tap and musical theatre. But he was also trained in elocution and etiquette, reciting long poems and learning such graces as how to sit properly. It was all a wonderful background for a lad from Liverpool.

While with Miss Clarke, he passed with honors both the elementary and intermediate examinations of the Association of Operatic Dancing, now known as the Royal Academy of Dancing. He went to London for these exams and at his elementary examination, the adjudicators were none other than Edouard Espinosa, Adeline Genée, Tamara Karsavina and Phyllis Bedells. There were forty-three students up for this exam. Freddie was the sole boy, and he was one of only eleven students who passed.

Royal Academy exams, long known for their rigor, were even more exacting back when Freddie was a lad. The barre was from 9:30 a.m. until 12:30, and the center was from 1:30 p.m. to 5:30. Throughout, the students were quizzed extensively on dance theory, responding orally to such commands as "Describe a *plié*."

Frederic Franklin as a bunny rabbit, January 1921, age 6, in his first public recital, at a gala arranged by his teacher Marjorie Kelly at the Adelphi Hotel, Liverpool. Photograph: Collection of Frederic Franklin.

Greek Dancing à la Isadora Duncan. 1927. The Studio School of Dancing and Dramatic Arts, Liverpool, Shelagh Elliott-Clarke and Lesly M. Booth, directors. From left to right: E. Slocombe, B. Phillips, Fred Franklin, L. Frodsham, B. Langley, T. Rae, and B. Cowell. Photograph: Mortath's Pictorial Press Agency, Liverpool, in the collection of Frederic Franklin.

By the time he began studies with Clarke, Freddie was already well known as a child dancer in and around Liverpool, his appearances including incidental dances in plays. By age fifteen, he had earned several medals and diplomas. He began giving ballroom lessons to help support the studio, the lesson fees going to Mrs. Clarke.

The Diaghilev Ballets Russes came to Liverpool in 1929, and that was the first time the fifteen-year-old Franklin saw professional ballet dancers. He fell in love with Alexandra Danilova: "I cut her picture out of the program and put it up on the wall over my bed. She was the most glamorous being imaginable."[8] He never imagined at the time that she was destined to play a monumental role in his life. His next experience of professional ballet was in 1931, when Anna Pavlova's company came to Liverpool. Through a friend, he got an audition with Pianovsky, Pavlova's *maître de ballet*. M. Pianovsky liked him; he told him that if he would go to London and study with Anna Pruzina for six months, he would be taken into the company. At that moment Pavlova herself arrived:

> It was at the Empire Theater in Liverpool, and she entered like a queen, in a black dress, and a huge black hat. Doors flew open, and everyone breathed:
> "Madame!" She came past us and *looked* at me, with great dark eyes in a face like ivory, and I trembled and shook. She went by into her dressing room, and all the doors closed after her.[9]

Pavlova was very strict with the girls in her company; they were chaperoned wherever they went. Right then she was involved in a lawsuit over one of the girls, who had married without her parents' consent — there was a great to-do with the parents over a broken contract. Every day, Pavlova went up to court sessions in London for these tiresome legal squabbles and came back in time to perform in Liverpool. Pavlova and her company returned to London; she danced the season at Golders Green and caught influenza on her way to The Hague, where she died of pneumonia. Franklin has vivid memories of coming home from school and hearing the tragic news from his mother.[10]

Franklin had wide-ranging theatrical interests. He was just a kid interested in any kind of dance, from Lancashire clogging to Hollywood tap dancing. At the time, he was by no means resolutely determined to become a professional ballet dancer, do or die. For one thing, no such profession existed in England in those days. Ninette de Valois's effort to found a native, British ballet was still in its infancy. The only ballet performances to be seen were those of Diaghilev's Ballets Russes and the Pavlova company. After the deaths of Diaghilev and Anna Pavlova in 1929 and 1931, respectively, ballet seemed to be headed for extinction, and critics were already placing wreaths on its tomb. Franklin set his sights on musical comedy.

His father was not in favor of Franklin's going on the stage, but his mother pushed for him. Papa only changed his mind years later, when he finally saw Frederic dance.[11] Freddie plucked up his courage at the age of seventeen and went to London, determined to break into show business:

> At seventeen, it was useless my staying in Liverpool. I couldn't get anything there. So mother got the money from her mother, and they sent me to London. I lived in one room with a gas burner, and I could make tea in the morning. They gave me a kettle and a cup and saucer.[12]

He had no connections in London, but he never doubted that he would find a job. Living in a cold-water flat, eating his dinners at Woolworth's, he made the rounds of the theatrical agencies. This handsome lad had eyes of sapphire blue, golden hair, and a skin of milk-and-roses — he was altogether the round-cheeked English choir boy. He looked fourteen and pretended to be eighteen, wearing a hat to make himself look older.

On one auspicious morning, he spotted an ad in *Variety* that read, "Wanted: A Boy."[13] Franklin responded to the ad. The audition was on the complete opposite end of London, and Franklin had to walk there, not having much money. The only other boy at the audition was Harold Turner, one of the best of the early English *danseurs nobles*. Franklin thought, "I'll never get the job with him here."[14] But Harold was a classical dancer, and the job was for the chorus, with the Lancashire Lads. Franklin was chosen because he could tap and do chorus routines. When his auditioners asked his age, he told them he was eighteen.

The Lancashire Lads was one of the troupes owned by J. W. Jackson. The Lads had been engaged for a revue with Josephine Baker at the Casino de Paris. In Paris, the Lads would be known as the "Jackson Boys." As soon as Freddie went for his passport, he got caught in the foolish lie about his age. Mr. Jackson apparently thought him worth the trouble, as he put up the required five hundred–pound bond to take a minor out of the country. At the Casino de Paris, he was thrown into the show immediately, wearing shoes that didn't fit, "dying of fright, learning the dances between numbers in the dressing-room."[15]

In the 1930s, the Casino de Paris was the most respectable of the music halls in Paris. It had been bought in 1929 by Henri Varna and Oscar Dufrenne. Audiences at the Casino de Paris tended less toward foreigners than those of the Folies Bergère and the Moulin Rouge, and it emphasized singing and dancing more than nudity, although there was still plenty of the latter. This was the era of the "grand revue," which meant a profusion of ostrich feathers, naked women, monumental sets and spectacular transformation scenes.

Franklin's first revue featured Josephine Baker as mistress of ceremonies. It was called *Paris qui remue*, which can roughly be translated as "Paris which Bustles," but is perhaps better interpreted as "Swinging Paris." The Jackson Boys were ten in number. Complemented by the "Original Sixteen Jackson Girls," they did tap routines and were a back up for Baker in other numbers. Just why the Jackson girls were "Original" while the Jackson boys were not has never been explained.

By 1931, Josephine Baker had changed her image. As a nineteen year old in 1925, she had courted frenzy with her *"Danse Sauvage,"* performances of the Charleston in the nude, and an outrageous number in which her sole article of clothing was a hip-slung girdle of bananas. At twenty-four, after two years of training in singing and dancing, she no longer had to rely on shock value to please her audiences. In the words of Phyllis Rose, "The diamond-in-the-rough of 1925 had been polished and placed in a 1930 Cartier setting."[16] In marked contrast to the caricatured negritude of the 1925 poster for the *Revue Négre*, the only racial allusion in the poster for the 1930–31 Casino de Paris show was a slight caramelizing of Baker's skin. It seems to represent her complete transformation from a black novelty act to a glamorous music-hall star.

As a publicity stunt for *Paris qui remue*, producer Henri Varna bought Josephine a leopard. The star and the leopard — Chiquita — became inseparable. She bought him a diamond collar which was sold years later for $20,000.[17] Variously cited in the press as a panther, a tiger and a jaguar, Chiquita became the darling of the news media.

Little is known about what exactly the Jackson Boys and the Original Sixteen Jackson Girls did in this revue. Franklin remembers only that they tapped and sang and that he went down into the pit to play the piano for one of the numbers. The revue itself centered around the 1931 Colonial Exposition in Paris, an enormous celebration of France's colonial empire. Despite its title, the revue had little to do with Paris, swinging or not. It made a whirlwind tour of Martinique, Algeria, Indochina and equatorial Africa.

One of the most elaborate sketches, "Ounawa," starred Baker and her feline familiar, Chiquita. Set in the equatorial jungle, it concerned an African girl in love with a French colonist. During the sketch, Baker sang for the first time *"J'ai deux amours."* The song expressed her claim to have two loves — her country and Paris. So ecstatically was it received that it eventually became Baker's signature song. There is no calculating how many times she had sung it by the time of her death forty-five years later.

One number in which Franklin and his fellow Jackson Boys appeared took place toward the end of the revue. Backed up by this bevy of young men in tuxedos, Baker sang *"Dis-nour Josephine."* The Jackson Boys sang of her return from her voyages and asked if Paris seemed changed to her. She declared herself charmed with all the cities of the world but added, "there's only one Paris." *Paris qui remue* was a solid hit, running for over one year and 481 performances.

Josephine Baker —1920s. Given to Franklin when he was in *Paris qui remue* with Ms. Baker at the Casino de Paris in 1931. Photograph: Paris Watery, in the collection of Frederic Franklin.

Franklin signed on to do the next revue, which was to star the legendary Mistinguette, who was known as "the Sarah Bernhardt of the Music Hall." Born Jeanne Bourgeois, Mistinguette befriended a revue writer when she was a teenager. They met on the train, and she saw him regularly en route to her violin lessons. Once he sang for her a little ditty called "Miss Tinguette" and recommended the title as a good stage name. With a slight modification, Jeanne Bourgeois took his advice.

Her career began at a very seedy nightclub called the Eldorado. It catered to a working class audience of "blowsy women and men in greasy caps."[18] She stayed ten years at the Eldorado, from 1897 to 1907. Many years later she wrote, "I went there as a nobody and left there ripe for stardom." Little by little, Mistinguette had become the queen of the Eldorado, but she now wanted to be a goddess in other spheres. She declared that she "could not rest until the great stages of the Moulin-Rouge and the Folies-Bergère and the Casino de Paris were mine for good."[19]

She had her first success in the big time with a short duet called "La Chaloupée" in La Revue de la Femme at the Moulin Rouge. Performed with Max Dearly, it was an apache dance. Gotten up as two street thugs, the duet was an alternation between caresses and struggles, brutality and sensual tenderness. The number brought the house down and led to an offer to star in an upcoming revue at the Folies Bergère. Her co-star, Maurice Chevalier, would become the great love of her life.

Le Grand Revue des Folies Bergère opened on March 15, 1917. The show-stopping number was "La Valse Renversante," a duet for Mistinguette and Maurice Chevalier. At the time, an exaggerated and dangerous acrobatic dance called the valse reversée was the rage of Paris, hashed up afresh in every new revue, and always causing a furor. However, it was being danced to death. The producers at the Folies Bergère had a sudden inspiration and decided to go the valse reversée one step better. "Valse Renversante" can roughly be translated as "Staggering Waltz." The idea was that the waltz had to be entirely catastrophic. As they danced, Mistinguette and Chevalier got caught up in everything on the stage — chairs, tables, sofas, lamps. When every stick of furniture had gone careening into the wings, there was only one thing left in its normal state of equilibrium — the stage carpet. But the dance had to genuinely live up to its name, so the two stars tripped their feet on the carpet, fell and landed underneath it, and finally rolled up frantically in its folds.[20]

Mistinguette's Casino de Paris days began in 1918 with Laissez-les Tomber, nicknamed the "Ladder Revue" because of a notorious scene in which thirty nudes climbed up and down ladders thirty feet in height. Subsequent Mistinguette revues included Parakiri, Paris qui danse, Paris qui jazz at the Casino and Ça c'est Paris, La Revue Mistinguette and Paris qui tourne at the Moulin-Rogue. In Paris qui tourne (1928), Mistinguette, portraying Madame Dubarry, was beheaded in full view of the audience: "the guillotine came crashing down onto its base. The audience caught their breath. My head had disappeared." Le tout Paris went laughingly to see Mistinguette "lose her head," but the police were not amused: they intervened and forbade the performance of this scene. Mistinguette wrote, "It seems the thing was in bad taste. Very well; the police is always right."[21]

Although Mistinguette's dramatic skits were popular, she is best-remembered for her riveting descents down a long staircase, trailing feathers and draped in jewels, displaying first one profile, then another, showing off legs that she claimed were insured by Lloyds of London. In *Parikiri* she wore 20,000 francs worth of paradise plumes and had to have two dressers escort her to the wings to hold up the jewel-encrusted panniers of her costume. Her close friend Michel Georges Michel described the scene:

> She takes up her position immediately behind the grand staircase, down which are already defiling a procession of every sort of bird: finches, sparrows, ostriches, lyre-birds. Each costume has a feather head-dress a foot or so higher than the one before it. The cheers that greet it go according to the length of the plumes. By the same token, when Mistinguette herself at last appears, in a head-dress that reaches almost up to the flies of the theatre — delirium breaks out.... When at the last bar she takes her bow at the footlights, her highest plumes stretch straight across the orchestra-pit and tickle the heads of the occupants of the front row of the stalls.[22]

Franklin's first exposure to the daunting Mistinguette came with his second revue, *Paris qui brille* (Paris which Glitters). Rehearsals started at the end of Baker's revue. The Jackson Boys went in a week before the opening and didn't come out of the theatre at all. They rehearsed there, slept there, ate there. The Jackson Boys had sixteen numbers with Mistinguette. She wouldn't have the young and pretty Jackson Girls near her.[23]

In Baker's previous revues, Mistinguette had been upset that her place at the Casino

"The Lancashire Lads." The Jackson Boys dressed and posed as boxers from a number in the show at the Casino de Paris. 1931. Frederic Franklin is second from left. From left: Joe, Fred, Paddy, Walter, Seth, Pip, Arthur, Cyril, Bert, Max. Photograph: R. Sobol, Paris, in the collection of Frederic Franklin.

had been taken by an African American, that Baker was walking down the staircase that she had made her own. She was quite vocal in her objections, and word reached Baker that Mistinguette did not want "that little black girl" to use her dressing room.[24] Baker responded by changing behind a makeshift tent thrown up in the hall until she had made her point. Certainly, Baker and Mistinguette were fierce rivals, and they were constantly being compared. Baker held her own.

Paris qui brille opened on October 30, 1931. In addition to the inevitable staircase scene, other scenes depicted Ben Hur's chariot race, a snowstorm and a Roman orgy, all powered by the Jackson Boys and Girls and performed on a revolving stage. The Ben Hur skit featured an equestrian act performed by Mistinguette, who had been coached by a famous circus trainer. The horses were sent onto a moving treadmill operated by a mechanic from a signal box. The brave steeds kept up a brisk trot and must have wondered why they never got anywhere.

During the run of the revue, Freddie got very homesick. Going to the theatre to play the piano and sing when he had time off helped him to shake off the blues. Passing by the orchestra pit on her way to a costume fitting, Mistinguette studied his handsome face closely for the first time. One evening when her partner, musical comedy star Billy Milton, was taken ill, she chose young Franklin to take his place, and from then on, he became the regular understudy. Eight weeks into the run, Mistinguette came into the theatre, ascended her staircase, and asked the Jackson Boys, "Where is ze boy play ze piano?" "Him," said the boys, pointing to Freddie. Franklin will never forget that moment: "She walked all the way up her stairs just to get me." Freddie was to do a regular number with the glamour queen. Franklin protested that he couldn't play the piano well enough, or sing. "Oh Madame, I can't, I really can't," he said. "But I say you can," she replied in her hoarse, gravelly voice.[25] Before he knew it, Franklin was dressed in the best Jackson tails they had on hand. He played "You're Driving Me Crazy" as the piano rose from the pit on hydraulics. Then the piano would be lowered for Mistinguette to get up on it, and Franklin sang with her.

When his Paris engagement was over, Franklin returned to London with one ambition: to get into a West End show. He landed a chorus spot in *The Co-Optimists*, starring Stanley Holloway, but the show folded after only two weeks. With two fellow Jackson Boys, he next appeared in *The One Girl*, starring Louise Brown and Pearl Osgood. Franklin astounded the latter when he learned her entire, intricate tap routine in one viewing, just by watching in the wings. [26] *The One Girl* closed after only three weeks on the road and three weeks in London.

During the run of this show, Franklin heard from one of the Jackson Boys, Carl Hyson, that there was an audition at the Grosvenor House cabaret in Park Lane. Upon arrival, Franklin learned that he would be auditioning for Wendy Toye. Toye was already a big name in dance, even though she was only fifteen. She was trained in ballet by Anna Pruzina, one of Pavlova's teachers, but she danced in every field of entertainment from cabaret and music hall to ballet. With C. B. Cochran (the "English Ziegfeld") adjudicating, Wendy Toye had won the English Charleston Competition. Wendy was now holding auditions for a partner.

Freddie was too poor to afford practice clothes, so he took the audition in street clothes. Wendy had him do a step from a Hungarian character dance and then asked

Fred to wait a few minutes. Unbeknownst to him, she was making a telephone call. Shortly thereafter, into the studio walked Freddie's idol, Anton Dolin. He was doing a vaudeville show with Alicia Markova at Leiscester Square Theatre and arrived wearing a white and red dressing gown in full make up. Here's what transpired:

> He said, "Freddie, show me what you can do," and I said, "Oh my God." And then I jumped a bit and turned. I could turn very well to the left. So I did a lot of *chaîné* turns, and then he said, "Can you go the other way?" "Yes," I said, "but not as well." "Try," he said. So I went. And he said, "Do this," and I did something else. And he said, "Wendy, take him." And he left as imperiously as he had entered.[27]

Dolin first won fame in the leading role of Beau Gosse in Nijinska's 1924 production of *Le Train Bleu* for Diaghilev's Ballets Russes. He left the company in 1925, partly because he could make much more money in revues and music halls, but he returned in 1929 to dance the leading male role in George Balanchine's *Le Bal*. After Diaghilev's death, he became a much-respected teacher and performer on the London scene.

Under the supervision of Dolin, Franklin and Toye danced in cabaret shows at Grosvenor House, Café de Paris, and Café Anglais, London's most exclusive nightclubs at the time. One day, Wendy's mother came to Franklin and said, "Freddie, dear, Mr. Toye and Wendy and I have decided that you are to come and live with us."[28] At the time, Franklin and fellow Jackson Boy Joe Ritchie were living with a "dear landlady" named Mrs. Middleton. While they were "well taken care of,"[29] the Toye's offer was hard to resist. Fred was taken into a beautiful home — the Toyes were a family of wealth and culture — with maids and a car with a liveried chauffeur. More importantly, Mrs. Toye gave him books to read, took him to art galleries and to the theatre, and led him to appreciate classical music.

It was through Wendy Toye that Franklin was introduced to London's ballet world. He befriended Antony Tudor, Hugh Laing, and other members of Marie Rambert's Ballet Club. During their partnership, Wendy Toye and Franklin often danced with the Vic-Wells Ballet — she substituting for Alicia Markova in the Ashton works; he as a hunter in *Swan Lake*, in the czardas in *Coppelia*, and so on.

While Franklin had been in Paris, he had not taken one single ballet lesson for a whole year. Mrs. Toye took him to see Nicholas Legat: "He looked me up and down and said, in his heavy Russian accent, 'Over there is portrait. Please go and have look at it.' There was a painting on a wall, I went and looked at it and came back, and Mr. Legat said to Mrs. Toye, 'I accept him.' He had wanted to see how I moved."[30]

All of the best dancers in London were in Legat's class, and many were Russians, which intimidated Franklin. He stayed at the back of the class for the entire duration of his lessons. Legat habitually played the piano as he taught. Wendy (whom Legat called "Toyitchka") often demonstrated the exercises for him. Franklin soon began to study with other superb teachers — Lydia Kyasht, Lydia Sokolova and Anton Dolin. Until then, he had not yet understood the life of a dancer — the unremitting discipline, day after day, and the need to study harder the better one got.

Dolin thought Freddie had talent and had great faith in him. Not everyone felt that way at the time. Ninette de Valois, the great pioneer of ballet in England and a former soloist with the Ballets Russes, had a chat with Dolin one day. When they got around to discussing Franklin's work, she remarked, "Oh, my dear, yes, I suppose he's got possibilities, but quite impossible for serious ballet. He is just a cabaret dancer. Too dreadful! Such a pity!"[31] But the fact of the matter is that almost all of Britain's native ballet dancers were sporadically employed in cabarets and variety shows. They had to dance in these venues, since neither de Valois nor Marie Rambert could offer them a living wage.

One morning in 1933, Dolin telephoned Mrs. Toye. He had accepted a role in a play called *Ballerina*, even though he knew the script was perfectly dreadful. *Ballerina* was made from a book of the same name by Lady Eleanor Smith. The central role in the play was danced by Eva Brigette Hartwig (who later took the stage name of Vera Zorina). At the beginning of the play, a complete one-act ballet was staged, with Dolin as the male lead and the seventy-year-old ballerina Lydia Kyasht ensconsed on a throne. She gestured regally whilst the boys danced around her with long wigs and butterfly nets. There were four secondary males in the show, including Hugh Laing, whom Fred really befriended for the first time. Much to Laing's disgruntlement, Freddie was named as Dolin's official understudy.

Although Mrs. Toye thought the play might be a good experience for Wendy and Freddie, it didn't work out that way:

> The show was a mad mélange, Dolin's ballet act sharing the bill with Billy Bennett, a marvelous red-nose comedian — one of the vulgarist men I've ever known. Humor is still very broad in the provinces. In the 1930s, it was broader still — and a man in leotard and tights (that looked like flesh-colored underwear) was a hilarious sight to the uninitiated. The audience had a fit every time I came out. "Ow! Look at him!" people would shriek, amid boos and whistles — sprinkled with the most appalling suggestions. I was in Purgatory, but poor Dolin was in sheer Hell — *he* had been a star of Diaghilev's Ballets Russes![32]

Ballerina ran for only six weeks. Undaunted, Dolin next backed and starred in a play called *Precipice*, based on Vaslav Nijinsky and Sergei Diaghilev, with Toye and Franklin in supporting roles. It was an enormous flop and lasted only one week. Having sunk all his savings into *Precipice*, Dolin was in dire financial straits. He called Mrs. Toye and said, "I need the children. I've got fifteen shillings left. You'll have to lend me twenty pounds, and then the children and I are going out on the road."[33] The dancing of Toye and Franklin, Dolin surmised, might help to save his next venture, *King Folly*, another rather vulgar musical starring Billy Bennett. The trio went off to the provinces in high hopes, but *King Folly* was soundly booed in the boondocks. Dolin was on a losing streak.

A major turning point for British ballet had been the establishment of the Vic-Wells Ballet in January of 1931. Ninette de Valois realized that the only place in which an English ballet might be born and nurtured was within a repertory theatre. Anything self-supporting and existing independently would at that time have been utterly impossible. London's Old Vic Theatre offered a solution. Located on the shabby south bank of the Thames, it was nonetheless a remarkable institution. Under the direction of Lilian Baylis, it offered Shakespeare and opera at the lowest possible prices. De Valois managed to persuade Baylis to present ballet as well. Because the Old Vic was already desperately overcrowded, Baylis set her sights on the long-derelict Sadler's Wells in Islington, which had just been rejected as a site for a pickle factory. When Baylis purchased and renovated the theatre, de Valois became director of the Vic-Wells Ballet which, as its name suggests, performed alternately at the two theatres.

The Vic-Wells began with only six dancers. It provided ballets within the plays and operas and curtain-raisers before them. The first independent evening of ballet was given on May 5, 1931. Baylis then decided on ballet once a fortnight through the 1931–32 season.

On January 1932, a special matinee was given at the Sadler's Wells, and Alicia Markova appeared with the company for the first time. When she was eight, Alicia's mother, Eileen, had taken her daughter to a doctor. He took one look at the flat-footed, knock-kneed girl in his consulting room and told Eileen that without urgent ballet lessons she would spend the rest of her life in leg irons and a wheelchair. Eileen enrolled

Anton Dolin — Inscribed photo: "To Freddie from Anton Dolin. 'A big, happy & successful career, Freddie, is my fervent wish and prophecy.'" The photo was probably taken circa 1928, when Dolin was a star with Diaghilev's Ballets Russes. Photograph: Dorothy Wilding, in the collection of Frederic Franklin.

her at once in Thorne Academy, and the following year she won a dance competition. She then began more serious study with the Russian ballerina Seraphina Astafieva, who told Eileen, "You have a race horse."[34]

She was "discovered" by Diaghilev at the tender age of fourteen and was promptly cast in the title role of his 1925 production of *Le Chant du rossignol*. She toured with the Ballets Russes from 1925 to 1929, dancing Papillon in Fokine's *Carnaval*, the Bluebird Pas de Deux in *Aurora's Wedding*, and the title role in Balanchine's *La Chatte*. After the death of Diaghilev, she had known a period of depression and anxiety, but an invitation by Frederick Ashton to appear in one of his ballets restored her confidence and introduced her to the exciting possibilities for English ballet.

Audiences were very excited by Markova's exquisite dancing at the Sadler's Wells, and on the strength of the public interest she aroused, a brief "season" of ballet was planned for the following March with Markova and Dolin as principals. On October 5, 1932, the Vic-Wells presented Act II of *Le Lac des cygnes* with Markova as Odette.

"Danse Moderne"—a pas de deux called "Greys," done to Eric Coates's music by Frederic Franklin and Wendy Toye, from their cabaret act at Grosvernor House, London, 1934. Photograph: Audrey and Leslie Elstob, London, in the collection of Frederic Franklin.

First and foremost, audiences came to see Markova. For the first time, the Vic-Wells had a truly classical ballerina, and de Valois must at once have recognized that if she could secure Markova as a permanent member of her company, she would be able to present some of the great classical ballets.

For the 1933–34 season, Markova signed a contract for the entire year. Her salary was a scant ten pounds per week, but the company was prepared to offer her famous roles in full-length versions of *Giselle, Casse Noisette* and *Le Lac des cygnes*. For two full seasons, Markova was to be the jewel of the Vic-Wells Ballet.

It was an achievement of first-class importance for the Vic-Wells to have staged these full-length ballets and to be able to claim them all as box-office winners. Anton Dolin observed, "No one can ever estimate how much the company owes to Markova. Had it not been for her, I doubt whether the Sadler's Wells Ballet would exist. She and she alone put that company firmly on its feet."[35]

By March of 1935, de Valois knew that Markova would be leaving the company before very long. Her departure had been foreshadowed at a dinner held in her honor in February: "I shall always be grateful to Miss Lilian Baylis and Miss de Valois for helping me," she said, "but I feel the time has come for me to take my art out into the world."[36]

Markova had reigned as prima ballerina of the Vic-Wells from the autumn of 1933 until her departure in May of 1935. Although she was short on cash, she at least knew that her sister Doris would be able to help with the rent, for Doris had a good job as a leading soubrette at the Windmill Theatre.

Tales of the successes of the Vic-Wells Ballet and Markova were beginning to reach the West End of London. Vivian Van Damm, the crusty, cigar-smoking impresario of the Windmill Theatre, was persuaded by Doris to see Alicia at the Vic-Wells, shortly before Markova left. A full house and tumultuous applause met his eyes and ears, and he advised the Windmill's owner, Mrs. Laura Henderson, that they could take advantage of some exciting possibilities.

Laura Henderson was a widow of wealth and connection who purchased an abandoned cinema house called the Windmill Theatre in the West End in 1931. Having no idea how to run a theatre, she hired Van Damm. Van Damm came up with the idea to kick-start business with a nonstop musical revue. After the show's initial success, other London theaters began to copy the Windmill's revue format, and soon Mrs. Henderson was losing her shirt. She suggested to Van Damm that the young women in their revue should do the same.

She managed to persuade Lord Chamberlain Cromers — whose job it was to censor stage productions — that nudity has a respectable precedent in the tableaux and sculptures of classical Greek and Roman antiquity. He granted the Windmill a license under certain conditions. There had to be subdued lighting, and the girls couldn't move. They couldn't smile, and they had to have their front foot forward so that one could not see anything in the region that was known as "the fork."[37]

Henderson and Van Damm's nude revues became runaway hits. There had been nudes in the West End before, but the Windmill became the most famous site for them. Documents at the British Library show that the official discomfort over the tastefully presented titillation went on for years after Mrs. Henderson launched her first "Revudeville" show in 1932. Concerns increased because of opposition mounted later in the decade by the Public Morality Council, led by the bishop of London.[38] This, however, did nothing to deter the crowds from stampeding into the stalls.

The outcome of Henderson and Van Damm's interest in classical dancing was an agreement to tour the Vic-Wells Ballet during the summer of 1935. A short season was scheduled at the Sadler's Wells during the latter half of May, and an association called Van Damm Productions was formed with Henderson and Markova as directors. Lilian Baylis was only too happy for the tour to be arranged in association with her, but only if she was not expected to contribute so much as a brass farthing.[39] It was Mrs. Henderson who agreed to finance the expense of taking a large company on the road.

When the Sadler's Wells season ended, the company gave eight special performances at the Shaftsbury Theatre in the West End before opening the tour at Blackpool. The Vic-Wells tour of the provinces had forty-five dancers and an orchestra of forty. In addition to Markova and Dolin, the principal dancers were de Valois, Harold Turner, Walter Gore and William Chappell. The first Vic-Wells tour was the most important ballet event in the provinces since the death of Diaghilev. The quality of the dancing left provincial audiences at a loss for words. Encouraged by the financial success of the Vic-Wells tour, the overwhelming enthusiasm for ballet in the provinces, and the promise of continuing financial support from Laura Henderson, Markova and Anton Dolin thought seriously of forming their own company in the fall.

And thus, the Markova-Dolin Ballet came into existence. Of course, de Valois was sorry to see them go, but, according to Dolin, "she was generous enough to express a certain satisfaction at realizing that there was now sufficient response in Britain to support two ballet companies."[40] Markova and Dolin recruited thirty-two dancers, all British artists of considerable promise. One of them, as history has recorded, was Frederic Franklin. After the disastrous tours of *Ballerina*, *Precipice* and *King Folly*, he and Wendy had resumed their rounds of cabaret dancing. Franklin says that Dolin came up to him one morning and said, "'Freddie, it's about time you became serious about your art,' and I thought, 'Oh dear...'"[41] But it was the best option he had at the time, and Freddie grabbed it with both feet, so to speak.

Of his work with the company, Dolin recollected, "During the years 1935–37, of great dancing and directing activity as well, Fred was a pillar of strength and without him, on several occasions, I sometimes wonder how the performances would have been possible."[42] Other soloists in the new Markova-Dolin company were Wendy Toye, Molly Lade, Kathleen Crofton, Beatrice Appleyard, Diana Gould, Travis Kemp, Guy Massey and Keith Lester.

The repertory included three new works: *David*, a biblical ballet choreographed by Keith Lester; *Aucassin and Nicolette*, with choreography by Wendy Toye; and *Show Folk*, a burlesque of the circus choreographed by Susan Salaman. Dolin revived his ballet *The Nightingale and the Rose*. The classics included *Giselle*, *Swan Lake*, *Les Sylphides*, *Carnaval*, Act II of the *Nutcracker*, and *Pas de Quatre*, in a new version by Keith Lester.

The company opened in Newcastle on November 11, 1935, with *David*, *Carnaval* and *Nutcracker*. At the end of 1935, Van Damm and Henderson took the Duke of York's Theatre for a year, with the idea of making it a center for British ballet. There, the company gave a Christmas season, with an opening bill consisting of *Show Folk*, *Swan Lake* and the *Nutcracker*. A few nights later, Franklin made his company debut as Harlequin in *Carnaval*, dancing with Markova as Columbine. Michel Fokine told C. W. Beaumont, London's most famous book-seller, that the boy in *Carnaval* had done very well.[43] It was a most auspicious beginning for Franklin's ballet career. Partnering a ballerina of Markova's status was quite an honor. Freddie said, "That was when I really entered the ballet world."[44]

Franklin as Harlequin in Michel Fokine's *Carnaval* with the Markova-Dolin Ballet Company. On the company's opening night, in the opening ballet, he partnered with Alicia Markova (as Columbine) in his first role with a professional ballet company. Newcastle-on-Tyne, 1935. Photograph: Harry Lowe, London, in the collection of Frederic Franklin.

Wendy Toye left the Markova-Dolin Ballet shortly after its inception. Other than *Aucassin and Nicolette*, she was being given no opportunity to choreograph. For years, she had staged and choreographed her own shows, and merely dancing was not enough for her, especially when she was receiving various offers to choreograph new musicals. Plus, her former partnership with Franklin was being thwarted. According to Franklin,

Dolin and Markova saw to it that they were never paired: "They would never have put us together. We were a threat to Markova and Dolin. We were much younger — not that much younger, but it made a difference. We were sort of coming up."[45]

At this time, the de Basil Ballet Russe de Monte Carlo was at its peak of vitality, and both the Ballet Club and the Vic-Wells were maintaining a high level of originality and imagination in their new ballets. Dolin explained the Markova-Dolin programming strategy: "We avoided anything eccentric, obscure or ultra-modern, concentrating mainly on the romantic and poetical type of ballet with a good story and plenty of action, easy to follow and the like. We made an instant appeal to the man on the street."[46] But the repertory was banal in the extreme when compared with the other three companies. The Markova-Dolin company could not stand comparison with the Ballet Russe or the Vic-Wells, which were having concurrent London seasons, and the Markova-Dolin ballet had only a modest success in London. The company did very well in the provinces (where ballet was almost unknown and audiences had had no chance to build up standards), but it was not possible to charge high enough admission rates to meet the heavy cost of ballet performances, and Mrs. Henderson lost a great deal of money in spite of good houses. This would not have mattered if the company had been able to make a profit during long West End seasons, but this was not the case, and losses continue to mount.

After the Christmas season at the Duke of York, the company left London and spent practically the whole of 1936 touring. With the stimulating example of Dolin and Markova before him, Franklin worked harder than ever before on his technique. Dolin officially appointed him as his understudy, and he was given a raise from seven to fifteen pounds per week (actually, a pretty good salary in those days).[47]

One day, on tour in Brighton, Freddie saw the Bluebird costume from *The Sleeping Beauty* in his dressing room and thought the wardrobe mistress had made a mistake. The stage manager knocked and said, "Miss Markova and Mr. Dolin would like to see you on the stage for a 'Bluebird' rehearsal. Put on the costume." Never having once rehearsed the role, he was expected to do a run-through of the entire pas de deux with Markova: "All of the dancers were in the wings, watching to see what would happen. Well, she didn't fall in the pit, and I didn't either. He [Dolin] was testing me to see what would happen under the worst circumstances. I had to get all the way through it. I just had to."[48] Freddie passed the test and got the role. In a subsequent performance, the *Dancing Times* critic wrote, "In Blue Bird he lacks restraint, but as the part is well within his technical ability, he will soon acquire the poise and precision that this role demands."[49]

The British ballet boom was at its height in June of 1936, when three companies were all holding London seasons at the same time. De Basil's Ballet Russe de Monte Carlo was at Covent Garden, René Blum's Ballets de Monte Carlo was at the Alhambra, and the Markova-Dolin Ballet was at Streatham Hill. In the subsequent tour of the provinces, the Markova-Dolin Ballet continued to get full and enthusiastic houses.

As the company could not rent a London theatre during the Christmas season of 1936, the dancers took a short holiday. They opened at the King's Theatre, Hammersmith, early in 1937. At this time, Nijinska joined the company to be *maîtresse de ballet* and to revive *The House Party* (*Les Biches*), choreographed for Diaghilev's Ballets

Frederic Franklin as Janos in *Hungaria*, a ballet by Derra De Moroda. Music selected from Hungarian folk tunes, orchestrated by Miklos Rozsa. Décor: Hadley Briggs. Costumes: Sandor. Markova-Dolin Ballet. 1935. Photograph: Audrey and Leslie Elstob, London, in the collection of Frederic Franklin.

Russes in 1924, and *La Bien-aimée*, choreographed in 1928 for Ida Rubenstein. She was also asked to create a new version of *Nutcracker*.

Franklin has vivid memories of Nijinska's tenure with the company. Wafting the scent of Chanel No. 5, she entered the studio in her standard rehearsal attire: a navy blue smock worn over navy trousers and impeccable white kid gloves which she never removed. According to Franklin, "She was going deaf when she came to us at Markova-Dolin. She would come over and give you the rhythm by [tapping her hand] on [your] shoulder."[50] Nijinska took a particular interest in the development of Freddie. Franklin has acknowledged a real debt of gratitude for the inspiration and encouragement given him by this remarkable artist. She cast him with Dolin and Guy Massey as one of the Young Athletes in *The House Party* and created the Trepak for him in her *Nutcracker*. It suited his style and temperament exactly and won an immediate success.

The company started rehearsals with La Nijinska on January 18, opening at the King's Theatre on March 1. After a two-week season, there followed a tour to Glasgow, Edinburgh, Manchester, Liverpool, Birmingham, and Southsea and a return to the King's Theatre for four weeks beginning May 3.[51]

Ten days before the season at the King's Theatre was due to end, Markova took a fall which hurt her foot and jarred her spine. Synovitis symptoms appeared, and she was told that she needed to take several weeks off. Alicia was able to rejoin the company in the spring of 1937, when it opened its provincial tour following the King's Theatre season. This tour proved to be the last undertaken by the Markova-Dolin company. The curtain for this troupe fell for the last time at the Theatre Royal, Birmingham, in November of 1937, just more than two years after that memorable first night in Newcastle.

Laura Henderson had spent twenty-five thousand pounds on the company and financed twenty-two ballets. The theatregoers of the provinces owed Henderson a great debt for the pioneering work she undertook during those early days of British ballet. So did her dancers: she gave fifty British artists guaranteed work with year-long contracts and salaries that permitted them to save and continue their studies. She gave British dancers something to work for and be proud of, apart from music halls and revues.

Fortunately, Henderson and Van Damm continued to enjoy a thriving business at the Windmill. During the war years, their nude revues became great morale boosters for servicemen and citizens enduring nightly Luftwaffe bombings from the Germans. Even amid the air raid sirens, the Windmill was the one theater in London that remained open throughout the war. Van Damm seems to have regarded the enterprise as something of a joke. He defended any exposed flesh by explaining it was inferior war-time elastic that had contributed to a possible sagging of the girls' costumes.[52] The story of Henderson and Van Damm is now the subject of an acclaimed BBC Films presentation, *Mrs. Henderson Presents*, directed by Stephen Frears and starring Judi Dench and Bob Hoskins.

The folding of the Markova-Dolin Ballet was partly due to finances, but that was not the whole story. The break-up was not without acrimony, for both Franklin and Markova had accepted contracts with a new company being formed by Léonide Massine. It was when she learned that Markova was leaving that Laura Henderson withdrew her support. Markova felt the time was ripe for a change. She was tired of "eight performances a week for two years, mostly traveling," and observed, "So eager was I to establish ballet in Britain that for the past eight years I had never danced abroad.... Anton Dolin and I had been dancing together solidly for more than two years. But perhaps variety is the spice of artistic life."[53]

It was Ballet Russe ballerina Alexandra Danilova who laid the groundwork for Franklin's membership in the new Massine company. She had seen Franklin dance, and she said to Massine, "You'd better go see them because there's a boy there [at King's Theatre]."[54] Franklin was first tempted to desert the company during the 1937 season at the King's Theatre. Almost all of the members of Colonel de Basil's Ballet Russe company came to a Markova-Dolin ballet performance. Sitting in the front row were Léonide Massine, Alexandra Danilova and dancer George Zoritch. Word had just gotten out that Massine was going to leave de Basil to start his own company. Franklin was dismayed, for he had been given practically nothing to dance that night. But Dolin came up to him before the performance and said, "Freddie, you must do something."[55] So Franklin's Trepak from *Nutcracker* was hurriedly inserted between two of the scheduled ballets. Franklin danced it magnificently. Afterwards George Zoritch, who had already signed on as a principal in Massine's company, delivered Franklin a note asking him to call Massine the next morning at 9 a.m. Franklin relates, "I did, terrified; we had about a ten-minute conversation and I signed a premier danseur's contract."[56]

When Anton Dolin got the news that Markova and Franklin had joined Massine, Franklin claims that "he was furious. He hated us."[57] One might expect him to be angry with them for leaving him high and dry, but there was another reason. According to Franklin, Dolin fully expected to be asked to join the new Massine troupe as well. It is highly unlikely that he would have changed the program so Franklin could show Massine his Trepak if Dolin was bound and determined to keep the company going. Why would he orchestrate the defection of his second male dancer? In an interview, Franklin said flatly that Massine did not want Dolin in his new company.[58] In an altogether different version of events, Dolin wrote that Massine had put before him "the most attractive proposals to join the company." He said that he declined because "the best thing for Alicia was to get away on her own."[59] On the surface, it might seem odd that Massine would overlook such an illustrious ballet star as Dolin while assembling his roster of dancers. However, Dolin's flamboyant performing style was quite similar to his own, and Massine may have feared a rival. At any rate, Dolin was in high dudgeon over the whole affair for some time to come.

· 2 ·

"Three Times a Star":
The Ballet Russe de Monte Carlo

In 1938, Léonide Massine was a ballet superstar. He was a brilliant choreographer and a dancer without peer in character roles. He was not a classic virtuoso, but he was a great character dancer, and the force of his theatre personality was as exciting as anything ballet had to offer. He began his career with Diaghilev's Ballets Russes, and created sixteen ballets for that company, including the celebrated *Good-Humoured Ladies*, *Parade*, *La Boutique Fantasque*, and *Le Tricorne*. He would go on to achieve his greatest international fame with the Ballet Russe de Monte Carlo.

Following the death of Diaghilev, René Blum, director of the ballet season in Monte Carlo, had dreams of perpetuating the Diaghilev legacy. In 1931 Blum brought to Monte Carlo the Ballet de l'Opéra Russe, directed by Colonel Wassily de Basil. A Cossack officer with an adventurous career during World War I, de Basil was one of the most improbable people to have had an influence on ballet.

When this company came to Monte Carlo, Blum and de Basil discussed a scheme for merging their mutual resources to form a Russian ballet at Monte Carlo. De Basil did his best to convince Blum of the value of his services, but Blum's offer to make him co-director of the new company was still surprising. The two men differed completely in outlook and temperament — de Basil being the hard-bitten ex–cavalry officer, a Russian émigré with little cultural background, and Blum being the epitome of elegance and artistic refinement. But Blum had little taste for the routine day-to-day administration of a ballet company and was glad to have someone to take this chore off his hands. By the end of 1931, de Basil had signed a contract with Blum, and Boris Kochno and George Balanchine were signed on as artistic collaborator and *maître de ballet*, respectively.

Léonide Massine was invited to Monte Carlo to choreograph a new work called *Jeux d'Enfants*. Although he was only brought in as a guest choreographer, it is quite likely that Léonide was waiting in the wings for Balanchine's position. He not only had a more important name as a choreographer, but he was also a star performer, unlike

Balanchine, who had a permanent knee injury and had just lost a lung in a 1931 bout with tuberculosis. When quarrels arose between Blum and de Basil on the one hand and Balanchine and Kochno on the other at the end of the 1932 season, Massine was offered Balanchine's position as ballet master.

Although he was the company's most celebrated dancer, Léonide had to share the limelight with the three young teens, the "Baby Ballerinas"—Tatiana Riabouchinska, Irina Baronova and Tamara Toumanova (although at seventeen, Riabouchinska wasn't really a "baby"). They were discovered by Balanchine and came from the Paris studios of Olga Preobrajenska, Mathilde Kchessinskaya and Lubov Egorova. All three had dazzling technique and joined the Ballet Russe de Monte Carlo for its first season at the rank of principal. Good copy for journalists, the Baby Ballerinas were a perfect sales pitch for launching the new company. They were guarded by jealous stage mothers whose fierce loyalty to their daughters rivaled those of watchdogs. One of the mothers accosted the new company's prima ballerina, Alexandra Danilova, and said, "You know, it's time for you to retire."[1] Danilova had just turned thirty.

Massine's first new work as ballet master was *Les Présages*, a choreographic interpretation of Tchaikovsky's Fifth Symphony. Unswayed by the dire warnings of Blum and de Basil that the music of a familiar symphony was off-limits to the ballet, Massine forged ahead. *Les Présages* was a triumph with the public and press at Monte Carlo, but it was the London premiere at the Alhambra Theatre in April of 1933 that launched the symphonic ballet controversy that was to rage in full force for years. Some musicians and critics deemed the use of a symphony to accompany a ballet nothing less than a sacrilege, while others contended that ballet should not have to acknowledge musical boundaries.

Massine's second, less controversial, triumph was *Le Beau Danube*, first staged in 1924 for Count Etienne de Beaumont's *Les Soirées de Paris*. This comedy ballet was set in Venice and involved a love triangle between a dashing Hussar (Léonide Massine), an Eldest Daughter (Tatiana Riabouchinska), and a Street Dancer (Alexandra Danilova). Its delightful score of familiar works by Johann Strauss and its spirit of youth, joy and animation delighted audiences and drew spectators who might otherwise have shied away from the ballet. It became a staple of the de Basil company, the perennial closing ballet.

The success of *Les Présages* encouraged Massine to create a second symphonic ballet in the fall of 1933. *Choreartium* was danced to Brahms's Symphony No. 4. Its premiere at the Alhambra in October of 1933 incited one of the most heated polemics in dance history. The use of Tchaikovsky for *Les Présages* was less offensive to conservative music critics because Tchaikovsky was already stigmatized as a ballet composer. But when Massine dared to lay hands on a symphony by Brahms — the Grand Lama of absolute music — some musicians and music lovers were outraged. They revered Brahms's symphonies as though they had been brought down by Moses along with the Ten Commandments and found their appropriation for dance an utter abomination. The heated debate spread quickly in news columns throughout Europe and established Massine as the most avant-garde choreographer of his day.

Massine and the company as a whole enjoyed a brilliant success during the 1933 season. The Ballet Russe de Monte Carlo's historic engagement at the Alhambra, scheduled for three weeks, was extended to nineteen. The Ballet Russe scored a major coup when the powerful American impresario Sol Hurok offered to bring the company to the United States for the first time in December of 1933.

Back in 1933, the marketing of ballet in the United States was viewed as a fool-hardy, if not insane, endeavor. Any American public for ballet would have to be created from scratch. Sol Hurok quickly proved that he was neither foolish nor crazy, but a shrewd gambler. He wagered correctly that de Basil's Baby Ballerinas, who had already captivated western Europe, would be especially appealing to Americans. The company opened in New York to half-empty houses. But the publicity engendered by Massine, Alexandra Danilova and, above all, by the Baby Ballerinas was fantastic. Subsequent New York engagements would be characterized by a great clamor for tickets and long queues waiting for standing room.

Léonide continued to create successful works in the seasons that followed, but by 1936 he was getting restless, and his relationship with de Basil deteriorated rapidly. Massine was resentful that de Basil denied him the title of artistic director when he had undoubtedly earned the right to something more prestigious than his present title of ballet master.

The following year would mark Massine's definitive break with de Basil, culmi-nating in an internationally publicized copyright case. Now determined to establish sole ownership of his ballets, he filed suit against de Basil when the Ballet Russe returned to London in the summer of 1937. Massine claimed to be the owner of the copyright in seventeen of his ballets that had been performed by the Ballet Russe de Monte Carlo and sought a restraining order to prevent de Basil from presenting them.

The news set the dance world ablaze with gossip and speculation. In an open let-ter published in *Dancing Times*, Arnold Haskell chided Massine and de Basil, noting that they were fighting "with a bitterness that is damaging to your work and that enriches the legal profession at our [the audience's] expense."[2] Alexandra Danilova, expecting to be called into court as a witness, wrote to a friend in her very best English: "I do not fear. I will tell the truth, the whole truth and nothing is the truth!"[3]

When Massine and de Basil first became associated in 1932, it was admitted that Massine was the owner of the copyright in eight of these disputed ballets. The remain-ing nine had not yet been brought into existence. As the "author" of these seventeen ballets, Massine asserted that he could claim them under the provisions of the Copy-right Act of 1911. Colonel de Basil's attorney countered that Massine was paid a salary by the colonel to cover his choreographic services. He was therefore under a "contract of service" to de Basil within the provisions of the Copyright Act, so the ballets right-fully belonged to de Basil.[4]

To Massine's dismay, Judge Luxmoore's ruling centered on the commercial rela-tionship between the antagonists. He pointed out that ballet is a composite entity, com-prising music, libretto, scenery and costumes, as well as choreography, and he doubted whether there could be copyright in the mere choreography divorced from these other elements. He held that the agreement between Massine and de Basil was indeed a "con-tract of service." Accordingly, in what would be considered a travesty of justice today, Luxmoore awarded the copyright of all nine ballets composed subsequent to January 1932 to Colonel de Basil. It was not until the Copyright Revision Act of 1976 that choreography was expressly included in the subject matter protected by United States copyright legislation.[5]

Massine now took decisive steps to negotiate for a company of his own. The necessary capital had already been found in the person of Cincinnati businessman Julius Fleischmann, heir to a family fortune from yeast, liquor and coffee. Fleischmann donated $250,000 to the ballet's new sponsoring company, known at first as World Art and later as Universal Art.[6] Julius Fleishmann was an officer of a number of organizations devoted to the arts. He was a director of the Metropolitan Opera and vice-president of its national council, and was a fellow of the Royal Society of the Arts in London. He was a sportsman and yachtsman as well as a cultural leader. In 1928, Julius (known affectionately as "Junky") became the subject of much publicity with the construction of his diesel yacht, *Camargo*. Built at a cost of $625,000, the 225-foot vessel was said at the time to be the largest and costliest pleasure craft ever built in the United States.[7]

The next step for Massine's new venture was the takeover of René Blum's Les Ballets de Monte Carlo. Blum had severed connections with de Basil in 1935 because of the latter's increasing preoccupation with American touring at the expense of concern for the company's Monte Carlo seasons. He then created his own company with Michel Fokine as *maître de ballet*. On 19 November 1937, Blum sold the Ballets de Monte Carlo to Universal Art for $48,000.[8] When sold, the new organization was therefore able to use the title "Ballet Russe de Monte Carlo." Under the new arrangements, Fleischmann was to be president of the board and Massine the year-round artistic director. A Russian-born banker named Sergei Dokouchaiev, who had changed his name to Serge Denham, was appointed as vice-president. Partly from dislike of the colonel and also because of the promising financial future of Massine's company, Sol Hurok announced that as of March 1938, he would abandon further management of de Basil's troupe and become the American manager of the new Ballet Russe de Monte Carlo.

There was a widespread feeling that to run two major Russian ballet companies in competition, splitting the repertoire and leading dancers, would be disastrous for all concerned. Massine was obviously not deterred, for he spent the fall of 1937 gathering a distinguished roster of dancers, some of them defectors from the de Basil company. His principals included our hero, Frederic Franklin, along with Markova, Tamara Toumanova, Nina Tarakanova, Mia Slavenska, Nathalie Krassovska, Serge Lifar, Michel Panaieff, Roland Guerard, Marc Platoff and Igor Youskevitch. In the de Basil line-up were Irina Baronova, Tatiana Riabouchinska, Nina Verchinina, Lubov Tchernicheva, David Lichine, Yurek Shabelevsky, Paul Petroff, Yurek Lazowski and Roman Jasinski. Alexandra Danilova was keeping everyone guessing. According to Franklin, Massine didn't really want her in his new company and only invited her at the insistence of Serge Denham: "He was forty-three and Choura was thirty-five, and he wanted someone who would make him look younger. He really would rather have had [Vera] Zorina."[9]

Léonide gave his last performance with de Basil's troupe on January 30, 1938, at the San Francisco Opera House. It was an emotional farewell, since he had meant so much to this company. Rehearsals for his new troupe began in February at Monte Carlo.

When Franklin first walked into the rehearsal room in Monte Carlo, he found more than a hundred dancers milling about, many of whom were not actually under contract, but had heard that they might be, or hoped that they might be. So many different languages were being spoken that Franklin felt as if he were in the Tower of Babel.[10] Massine sorted things out, winnowing down the field to seventy official company members. The maestro had committed to preparing twenty-four ballets by the time of the Metropolitan Opera House opening in October, so the schedule was grueling. The dancers did, at least, have a few nights off before the Monte Carlo season started. They were free to sample the night life, but *not* free to gamble in the casino, since, technically, they were employees of the principality of Monaco, to whom this diversion is denied. No doubt this rule was ignored by the troupe's more daring spirits.

In March, there was a surprise development — a scheme to bury the hatchet and merge the Massine and de Basil companies. Hurok saw a chance to manage the largest and finest ballet company the world had ever seen. (He had also hatched a plan to oust de Basil in the process.) *New York Times* critic John Martin spread the joyous tidings: "Congratulations are in order more or less all around over the healing of the breach in the Ballet Russe.... With the signing of a treaty of peace last week, there comes into being an enormous new-old company with 110 productions in its repertoire, eighty dancers on its roster, and considerable American money to pay its bills." Martin was delighted to see the end of "a campaign of extermination, which, except for its seriousness, might have been conceived by Gilbert and Sullivan." Philip Richardson of *Dancing Times* was staggered by the enormous pooled resources of the company-to-be: "In fact," he mused, "it almost seems too good to be true."[11] It was.

After lengthy debates, a verbal agreement with de Basil was reached in New York at the St. Regis Hotel. Afterwards, de Basil, whose English was quite poor, returned to Europe. From there, he cabled a power of attorney, which was used to sign an agreement with Hurok and Denham on April 15, 1938. When he received a copy of the contract, de Basil burst into tears because it was so different from what he had understood.

What the contract contained was his agreement to turn over to Universal Art complete legal title to six ballets, to sign over to them his annual twelve-week contract at Covent Garden, and to relinquish in perpetuity the right to use the name "Ballet Russe de Monte Carlo."[12] One cannot fathom what possible advantages de Basil was supposed to gain from signing such a contract. On June 8, de Basil wrote a letter repudiating the contract, claiming that he had been tricked and that if he had known what the contract contained, he would not have allowed it to be signed in his behalf. When Hurok, Denham and Fleischmann arrived in London to confirm the merger, the situation looked desperate for the de Basil contingent, but de Basil's supporters and lawyers found a way out. De Basil would have to be put out to pasture for the time being, with authority handed over to a new board of directors. The new troupe would be given the glamorous title "Educational Ballets Ltd." By using the word "educational," it was hoped that the company could avoid the U.K. entertainment tax. The colonel crawled off to lick his wounds on the outskirts of London.

When the merger was repudiated, Universal Art applied for an injunction to restrain de Basil from producing, performing, authorizing, or advertising any performance of the ballets relinquished in the contract. Justice Morton granted the injunction, but, of course, his ruling didn't make the slightest difference, because it did not apply to the new directors of Educational Ballets Ltd.

In late June, the impassioned "Ballet War" hit London with a bang. Educational Ballets Ltd. and Massine's Ballet Russe de Monte Carlo had rival, concurrent seasons at Covent Garden and the Drury Lane, respectively. Balletomanes eager to see both groups found ways to cope: "It was at this period that a determined balletomane could see a couple of ballets at Drury Lane, and run like the wind to Covent Garden (passing a lot of his fellows performing the same exercise in reverse) and catch the last ballet there, and thus see almost every great dancer in the Western world on the same evening."[13]

Without Hurok's backing, there was no United States tour for Educational Ballets Ltd. Instead they embarked on a long Australian tour and were, incidentally, joined by Anton Dolin as guest artist. Under the new appellation of Covent Garden Russian Ballet, the company opened on September 28, 1938, in Melbourne. By 1939 de Basil was back at the helm again as general director with complete artistic control, and the company was renamed "Original Ballet Russe." Massine's troupe was billed as the "One and Only Ballet Russe de Monte Carlo." The Original remained for most of the war in Latin America; the Monte Carlo settled down in the United States. De Basil's company, depleted by travel and attrition, attempted an American comeback in 1946 and a London season the following year, but the company closed down for good after an unsuccessful British tour in 1952.

Massine was obviously quite taken with Frederic Franklin, because he gave him leading roles in all three of his new ballets that would premiere in Monte Carlo and London. *Gaîté Parisienne* was the first new ballet to go into rehearsal. It is a testament to Franklin's versatility that when choreographing *Gaîté Parisienne*, Massine used him as a model to build every one of the principal male roles. Franklin thought that Massine was testing him, and recalls, "We had what was called a show rehearsal, where people came to watch, and afterwards, Massine asked me what part I wanted to do. I told him, 'Whatever you think I should,' and he said, 'All right: the Baron.'"[14]

Massine created a vivid impression in rehearsals. Diane Menuhin, former Balanchine dancer, gives her impression of him: "Spare and small, dressed in his habitual black Spanish trousers and white shirt, with his strong square head and those enormous blazing eyes, he looked like an exclamation mark and had indeed some of the qualities of that punctuation: a coiled spring, ready to pounce, to shock and surprise." In her memoirs, Agnes de Mille wrote, "He was not gracious; neither was he unpleasant. He was totally, unattainably withdrawn from casual contact, and you could place on this attitude any interpretation you chose. He was Massine and a very impressive figure."[15]

Massine always walked into rehearsal with a mysterious notebook with a reddish-brown leather cover. George Zoritch remembers that Massine's notes on these pages were a "mystical series of strange curlicues, dots and designs understandable only to himself. Pensively looking at the pages, he would lay the book down on the chair beside him." According to Franklin, "nobody was allowed near that notebook." The influence of these notes on his choreography remained a mystery for years, but critic G. B. L. Wilson finally solved the puzzle:

> At first I thought they were the steps for the ballet which he had written—but no, for he sometimes held them upside-down and still stared at them. At last I could restrain myself no longer,

and I asked him. He was charming about it; they were photostats of pages from Feuillet's *Receuil de Danses* of 1704. He told me that he had always used them, they were like a vocabulary of steps for him...."But you often hold them *upside down*," I persisted. "I believe they are really like a talisman to you — something you can look at when you are concentrating." Yes, that was it! With Feuillet in his hand, he had something to look at (or appear to) and so was able to withdraw himself from the turmoil of the rehearsal and think.[16]

According to Franklin, both the role of the Baron and that of the Spirit of Creation in *Seventh Symphony* were to have gone to George Zoritch, a Russian who had trained with Olga Preobrajenska in Paris and danced with the Ida Rubenstein company. However, Zoritch sustained a foot injury and his far too leisurely convalescence (essentially a glorious holiday in Paris) caused him to miss the spring season, and stripped him of the new roles promised him by Massine in 1937. Falling into this role was indeed a lucky break for Franklin, because his success as the Baron launched his career with this company. Had Zoritch danced the role, he would not have gotten such a powerful initial boost.

Of Massine's four new ballets, two premiered in Monte Carlo and two in London. *Gaîté Parisienne* was the first premiere. It was choreographed in a scant two weeks and was christened on April 5, 1938, at the Théâtre de Monte Carlo. Designer Etienne de Beaumont set *Gaîté* at Tortoni's, a fashionable Parisian café of the Second Empire. The Second Empire was also the period of Jacques Offenbach, whose music instantly evokes this era. Massine's music, arranged and orchestrated by Manuel Rosenthal, was culled from the manuscript scores of 150 Offenbach operettas.

The curtain rises on an elegant café. Waiters and scrubwomen move about energetically, tidying up before the evening's business. Then a group of billiard players enter in company with several *cocodettes* (girls of easy virtue). An attractive Flower Girl (Eugenia Delarova) and a fascinating Glove Seller (Nina Tarakanova, then Alexandra Danilova) enter and arrange their merchandise.

Next arrives a boisterous Peruvian (Léonide Massine), carrying two traveling bags full of riches. On the town, he is looking for conquests and is enthralled by the beauty of the Glove Seller. When he approaches her to try on a pair of gloves, a few of the *cocodettes* run off with his bags. He frantically chases after them.

There now appears a young Austrian Baron (Frederic Franklin) in a green military top with a braid across the front. His friends have sung the praises of the lovely Glove Seller. When he sees her, he falls head-over-heels in love, but his rapture is interrupted by the music of a march. Soldiers file in, and they do an ultra-military strut for the benefit of the *cocodettes*. La Lionne (Lubov Rostova) makes an impressive entrance with the Duke (Casimir Kokitch). The Duke begins to flirt with the Glove Seller, much to the dismay of the Baron. Having failed to find a man for the evening, the Flower Girl tries her wiles on the Baron — a wasted effort. La Lionne makes eyes at the Officer (Igor Youskevitch), who abandons his attempt to take up with the Glove Seller.

At this point, the passions which have been generating in the café boil over. The Peruvian, his bags recovered, tries to arrange a rendezvous with the Glove Seller, and the Baron confronts his rival. The Duke and the Officer start fighting over La Lionne. The tension explodes, and soon blows are being exchanged by everyone, including the billiard players and waiters. Finally the waiters chase the patrons out, leaving the café empty. The Glove Seller and the Baron enter, and they dance a romantic waltz. Then a burst of clamorous music heralds the arrival of the cancan girls. They arrive in garish attire, with loud stripes and multi-colored petticoats. The patrons come back to see their dance, and everyone joins in.

Dawn approaches; the guests must leave. Only the Glove Seller and the Baron remain. The Peruvian returns to make one last try for a rendezvous with the Glove Seller. When he sees her in the arms of the Baron, he drops his bags in defeat and falls into a limp pose in the darkening café.

The chief flaw of *Gaîté* is that it is essentially a string of entrées rather than an organic composition. P. W. Manchester put it succinctly: "There is no construction at all. Somebody comes on and does a dance.... And all the way through, either a lot of people come on and do a dance or one person or two people. But there is no actual development of a real story."[17] Yet despite its shortcomings, *Gaîté Parisienne* recaptured the period with great wit and flair and gave Massine the perfect vehicle for utilizing his knack for creating atmospheric color, comic characterization, and superb deployment of massed groupings.

As the Peruvian, Massine provided himself with one of the wittiest roles of his career, and he danced it delightfully. In his boundless zeal to conquer Paris, the Peruvian was absurd yet sympathetic. Conveying his idiosyncrasies required almost Chaplinesque precision, for almost every note of the music was described with a step. No less Chaplinesque was the Peruvian's deep faith in his own irresistible sex appeal. The contrast between belief and actuality projected into his characterization gave the role a touch of poignancy.

It was as the Baron that Franklin made his American debut. After the first two or three performances, Freddie had established himself so firmly in the affection of the audiences at the Metropolitan Opera House that his entrance in *Gaîté* was invariably greeted with applause. Franklin danced the role with authority and intelligence. The chief distinction of his portrayal lay not so much in his dancing as in his acting. *Gaîté* tends toward low comedy, and Franklin's role added a dash of sophisticated elegance to the work. Lillian Moore wrote, "This Baron takes himself very seriously indeed. He has a bit of the dandy about him.... It is particularly interesting to watch him while the dancing of others occupies the centre of the stage; to see the pained and incredulous bewilderment with which he observes the first flirtation of his fickle beloved and to watch the gradual growth of impotent rage against his rivals."[18]

Alexandra Danilova arrived in Monte Carlo only when rehearsals for *Gaîté* were well underway. When she first saw the work she declared, "I will dance this ballet." She was put into the role of the Glove Seller for the American premiere, replacing Nina Tarakanova, who had danced the role in Monte Carlo and London. As one would expect, Tarakanova was not happy to be ousted. When the time came to go to America, she threatened to quit unless she was given the opening night of *Gaîté* at the Met. Danilova warned Denham, "I won't go there unless *I* get the opening night." Denham decided in Danilova's favor, and Tarakanova quit the company in a huff. Franklin believes that the whole ballet was different with Tarakanova as the Glove Seller:

> She was so different from Choura. The costume was different. The whole role was different. The idea was that she was young and naïve, and me too. With Nina it was soft and lovely. With Choura it became a *tour de force*.... Nina should have done the role again. She created it.[19]

Franklin's role as the Baron was the beginning of what would become a legendary partnership with Danilova. Born in Peterhof, Russia, on Nov. 20, 1903, she was accepted by the Imperial Ballet School in 1911 and in 1920 entered the Imperial Ballet company. She and George Balanchine left the Soviet Union in 1924 and joined Diaghilev's Ballets Russes. Danilova and Balanchine lived together as husband and wife until 1931, although they never married.

Danilova's stage presence was remarkable, although she did have limitations. She was a superb classicist, but not a virtuoso — the thirty-two *fouettés* in the "Black Swan Pas de Deux" did not come easily to her. She danced in Balanchine abstractions such as *Danses Concertantes* and *Serenade*, and she could be convincingly tragic as Odette in *Swan Lake* or as the Bride in *Baiser de la fée,* but it was the roles demanding gaiety and bubbly effervescence — what Massine called the "champagne roles" — which enchanted her audiences the most. As Edwin Denby wrote, "Where others look happy, she scintillates. But it is her feminine presence, her air of dancing for the delight of it, that captures the audience's heart."[20]

With Danilova, Franklin said, "the chemistry worked."[21] As a struggling English dancer almost nobody had ever heard of, he was in awe of Danilova and never dreamed that he would have a chance to partner her. One night, he was asked to step in for Massine as the Hussar, partnering Danilova in her famous role as the Street Dancer in *Le Beau Danube*. After the performance, Danilova told him, "You know, for the first time in my life in this ballet I felt nothing." Freddie said, "I was mortified, and I rushed up to the dressing room in a flood of tears." Relations between the two remained strictly formal for years to come. "I called her Madame Danilova for the longest time," Franklin recalled.[22]

Gaîté Parisienne was a huge popular success throughout Europe and America and was also received kindly by the critics. John Martin's review was quite typical: "It is, to be sure, pure foolishness and may have little or nothing to do with Art with a large 'A.' It is nevertheless fresh as a daisy, extraordinarily skillful and inventive."[23] *Gaîté Parisienne* became the signature work of the Ballet Russe de Monte Carlo.

After *Gaîté*'s tremendous success in Monte Carlo, Massine was able to continue rehearsals for another symphonic ballet, *Seventh Symphony*, in an atmosphere of high optimism and excitement. This, the second of the Monte Carlo premieres, was first seen by the public on May 5, 1938. It was danced to Beethoven's Symphony No. 7 in A with set and costume designs by Christian Bérard. Depicting the ballet's theme — no less than the creation and destruction of the world — within the confines of a proscenium stage was rather an ambitious undertaking.

Massine's approach to his theme involved a mixture of Greek mythology and the Bible. The first movement, "The Creation," represents chaos, which gradually takes form. The basic forces of nature and all creatures invested with being are assembled by the Spirit of Creation (Frederic Franklin), a commanding figure in a white Greek tunic. The sky, the earth, and water appear with the sun, and they animate the plants, the birds and the beasts. Among them crawls a serpent, the symbol of evil. Finally man and woman take part in the process of creation. At the climax of the movement, the world has progressed from a formless mass to civilization.

In the second movement, "The Earth," humanity is plunged into despair after the first crime has been committed. To the somber strains of Beethoven's celebrated Allegretto, a procession of mourners appears. As the main theme crests, six men enter from upstage left, bearing the body of a slain youth (Charles Dickson), designated "The Adolescent." As he is moved in a loop from upstage center to center stage, individual figures break out of the group and merge into it again. The ensemble women move in counterpoint to one another as the individual voices of the orchestra enter into a fugato on the main theme. Finally, the ensemble forms a diagonal, and the body is borne off downstage right. Here we see death and grief, the murdered Abel and the martyred Christ, brought together in a single striking image.

The third movement, designated as "The Sky," is an Olympian interlude. It takes place far above the earth amidst the ether, where reign the mythological gods. The ensemble dance to the opening strains of the scherzo, and when the second theme is heard, the Goddess (Alicia Markova) and her mate (Igor Youskevitch) glide in and dance a serene pas de deux. There follows a pas de quatre, two solos and dancing for the entire ensemble.

In the fourth movement, "The Bacchanale and the Destruction," humanity is abandoning itself to an orgy. Bacchantes enter, equipped with long trumpets, grapes, wine, and other accouterments for conducting orgies in ancient Greece. Leading the revelers are Nathalie Krassovska, Nini Theilade and Frederic Franklin. As the orgy reaches a fever pitch, the Fire appears. These dancers immolate the revelers and then form a pyramid upstage right.

Given the epic scale of both theme and music, Bérard wisely chose simplicity in set design as his keynote. In front of all four backdrops was a crosspiece of stone supported at each end by a pair of tall caryatid columns. The crosspiece was draped with red cloth in the second movement and in the fourth, it seemed to have suffered some destruction and now had only one figure at each side instead of a pair.

In the first movement, Massine gave each entity a movement style suited to its nature. Thus the movements given to the sky — traveling *fouettés* — conveyed a quality different from those of the water — low-to-the-ground leaps. The many groups were coherently united by the grand, controlling gestures of the Spirit of Creation. Franklin's strongest memories of the year 1938 are of performing this role, another role that was originally intended for George Zoritch.[24] The Spirit of Creation is a role whose essential nobility demands a depth of interpretation rare in a young artist. Walter Terry wrote, "Franklin, as the Spirit of Creation, gave brilliant focus to the first movement. His powerful, sustained dance action suggested the very generating process of energy, and the clean rhythmic patterns of his movements reflected the order and design of a great creative plan."[25] Franklin remembers, "Massine saw how I was moving. Then it all became big and grand and huge. Yuri [Zoritch] was simply not that kind of dancer. It wouldn't have been big and open. It would have been rather lovely and lyrical and softer."[26]

Massine wrote that he saw the second movement as "the story of man's guilt and despair, symbolized by Cain and Abel."[27] But the pictorial implications of its tableaux bore a clear resemblance to numerous Renaissance paintings of the Descent from the Cross. The grieving woman is surely Mary and a hunched up male must just as certainly be Judas. As a matter of taste, the presence of Christ on the stage of a theatre —

Franklin as the Spirit of Creation in *Seventh Symphony*. 1938. Choreography: Léonide Massine. Ballet Russe de Monte Carlo production. Photograph: Maurice Seymour, courtesy of Ronald Seymour.

even if the word "Jesus" did not appear in program notes — seemed sacrilegious to some viewers in 1938. Other balletgoers were disturbed by the appearance of the Adolescent. Charles Dickson's body was painted a moldy green, making him appear as though he had just been exhumed.[28] However, this movement had extraordinary plastic beauty, and it was a superb match to the music, in terms of both mood and structure.

The third movement was the most classical of the four. Alicia Markova and Igor Youskevitch were superb. Unfortunately, the fourth movement is missing from the only available film of *Seventh Symphony*, but it was apparently quite problematic. As was his wont in symphonic ballets, Massine relied heavily on architectural formations. But the motivations for Massine's mass designs were said to be pallid, ineffectual, bogged down. Moreover, the destruction by fire looked positively silly. The Metropolitan Opera House provided a smoke screen to give realism to many an opera, but in Massine's version, the blazing holocaust was represented by twenty dancers in red who carried red streamers on the end of sticks. They dashed furiously across the stage in order to roast their dissipated colleagues and then made equally furious backstage crossovers in order to give the apocalypse a steady fuel supply. Grace Robert observed, "Many uneven dramatic presentations have been saved by a thrilling last act. The *Seventh Symphony* cannot be counted among that number."[29]

When the reviews came out, there were the usual sermons on the crime of using the music of a symphony for a ballet. Some critics, though, thought Massine was improving his symphonic style with each successive attempt. But even the most positive reviews noted that the fourth movement was ineffectual.

St. Francis was the third new ballet to premiere. Paul Hindemith's score for *St. Francis* was originally commissioned by Diaghilev, but the latter died before Hindemith had finished it. A libretto for the unfinished score was worked out jointly after Hindemith suggested the subject during a chance meeting with Massine in Florence. While there, they went together to study Giotto's frescoes of the life of St. Francis in the great church of Santa Croce. For the next few months, Massine read everything he could find about St. Francis and discovered many of the ingredients for the resulting libretto in a medieval collection called "The Little Flowers of St. Francis." *Nobilissima Visione* (retitled *St. Francis* in America) opened at the Drury Lane in London on July 21, 1938.

Scene One is set in the shop of the merchant Pietro Bernadone (Simon Semenoff). As the shop fills with customers, Francis (Léonide Massine) and his Three Companions (Marcel Fenchel, Roland Guerard, Michel Panaieff) are fascinated by the news of foreign countries, which fills them with a longing for travel and adventure. A Knight (Frederic Franklin) arrives to replenish his wardrobe. Excited by the Knight's splendor, Francis challenges him to a bout of sword-play and is quickly overcome. The Knight invites him to join his train, and Francis puts on helm, breastplate, and gauntlets to take service with the Knight.

Scene Two takes place on a country road. As the soldiers proceed, a band of unarmed travelers approach. The Knight orders his men to rob the party. The male travelers are struck down, the loot seized, and the women carried off. Francis, horrified at this injustice, refuses to obey the Knight's command to resume the march. He throws off his military gear and kneels to pray for guidance. Three allegorical figures — Poverty (Nini Theilade), Obedience (Jeanette Lauret) and Chastity (Lubov Roudenko) — appear, and they lead St. Francis off.

Scene Three is in the house of Pietro Bernadone. A feast has been prepared to celebrate the return of Francis. The guests, including the Three Companions, are drinking and dancing, but Francis remains troubled and moody. A band of beggars enters, pleading for crusts of bread. Overcome by their wretchedness, Francis impulsively gives them the golden vessels on the table. Francis's father is furious, and he strikes his son. Francis accepts his father's anger with meekness. In token of his decision to renounce riches, he takes off his fine clothes and lays them at his father's feet. He leaves the house.

In Scene Four, Francis, clad in rags, now lives as a hermit on a country hillside and has given himself over to meditation. He dances with two olive branches to express his religious ecstasy. He is interrupted by a group of peasants who are fleeing from the savage Wolf of Gubbio (Frederic Franklin). Among the fugitives are the Three Companions, who have also renounced materialism to devote themselves to a life of austerity. The Wolf springs out to attack the villagers, but he is unable to withstand the saint's mystic power. The creature becomes meek and docile and is led away by the country folk. Poverty appears and Francis welcomes her as his bride. With the Three Companions, they celebrate a marriage feast of bread and water.

The last scene shows a landscape with a mountain in the distance. Monks and nuns file in stately procession about Francis. Poverty takes Francis by the hand and slowly leads him up the side of a rock to its peak. When they reach the summit, the monks and nuns turn to face the rock and raise their hands in farewell as the sky blazes with light.

Pavel Tchelitchew combined the characteristics of several medieval periods in his set designs, suggesting a transitional period between the Dark Ages and the pre-Renaissance era. The fifth backdrop, with its distant mountain, was by far the most memorable. Above this precipice appeared six hands with fingers held in obviously symbolic positions. Each hand was actually a visual "letter" in the sign language for the deaf and, together, they spelled out "G-L-O-R-I-A."[30]

Hindemith's music is not in the least "dance music" in the usual sense of the word. It is intensely contrapuntal, and ordinarily the mating of polyphony and dancing is thought to be akin to mixing oil and water. Yet even without a driving rhythm, the score did rise and fall in intensity and texture in exact correspondence to the dramatic situation onstage, and it did have a mood and dignity well-suited to the subject matter.

Both Massine and Hindemith were inspired scholars whose research enabled them to recreate the spirit of a period in modern terms. The choreographic patterns of *St. Francis* were based on a study of Byzantine and Italian primitive artists such as Giotto. Massine dispensed with traditional ballet steps in *St. Francis* and employed instead a flat, angular style vitalized by percussive brittle movements; however, he gave himself the freedom to stray from this style where it suited his purpose. One example is the difference between Franklin's dual roles as the Knight and the Wolf of Gubbio. His solo as the Knight in the first scene was athletic and vigorous, but still flat and angular. The Wolf, introduced as comic relief after the meditation episode, departed from the ballet's signature style as he crouched, circled and leapt in a raucous fashion. The fourth scene owed much to German expressionistic dance in the solo for St. Francis and his pas de deux with Lady Poverty, while the apotheosis was true to the signature style throughout.

Many balletgoers, accustomed to surface glitter, fairy tales and technical virtuosity, were simply puzzled by the asceticism of *St. Francis*. American critics, better-accustomed to the adult, stark and serious work of such modern dancers as Martha

Graham, were generally more receptive to *St. Francis* than were European critics. In his rave review, John Martin called it "one of the most memorable and beautiful dance works of our time." On the other side of the Atlantic, the reaction of Arnold Haskell was more typical: "It suffers from the one unforgivable sin: it is dull."[31]

St. Francis's blend of severe Byzantine angularity with early modern dance makes the work look dated today, but this in no way negates its historical importance. It was passionately conceived and masterfully crafted. Moreover, in its courageous attempt to analyze in terms of movement the process of religious discovery, *St. Francis* deserves a place of honor in the period's all-too-brief list of truly adult ballets.

The company was also saddled with an awful version of the ballet *Coppelia*, a hand-me-down from the René Blum company. Under the circumstances, it is not surprising that Danilova gave stellar and less-than-stellar performances in the leading role of Swanilda. Franklin recalls a performance of the latter sort, after which Massine dressed her down before the entire company:

> Poor Choura; she went on as Swanilda and she was all over the place. She was terrible. And I remember Massine absolutely saying in English, "Choura, as the principal ballerina of this ballet company, from the performance you gave last night ... you can't do those sorts of things here." He [Massine] was practically saying, "You have to go." Mind you, at that time, Mr. Massine didn't want Danilova in the company. He wanted *younger* dancers.[32]

Massine and Danilova simply didn't get along for the most part, perhaps because he envied her ability to "steal the show" in ballets in which he too danced a leading role. At one rehearsal he told Danilova, "You know, you have the worst hands in ballet." And she (according to Franklin) turned around and said, "And you know, Mr. Massine, the same goes for your feet."[33]

The last new production at Drury Lane was Nicholas Sergeyev's masterful new staging of *Coppelia* on September 20, 1938. It was an enormous improvement over the Blum version. After the two-act Vic-Wells production of 1933, this was Sergeyev's second staging of this ballet in the West and the first to include the third act. The score, one of the most outstanding examples of ballet music in any era, was by Léo Delibes, and the designer for the Ballet Russe production was Pierre Roy. The ballet itself is a comic retelling of E. T. A. Hoffman's "The Sandman." (Hoffmann also wrote "The Nutcracker and the Mouse King," upon which the *Nutcracker* is based.)

Coppelia was first presented in 1870 at the Paris Opéra. Little is known about the original choreography of Arthur St. Leon. But in 1884, Marius Petipa restaged it at the Maryinsky Theatre, retaining the most innovative elements from the Paris version, including the tangy flavor of Eastern European folk dances like the czardas and the mazurka. The work was carefully recorded in Stepanov notation.

It is because of the work of Vladimir Stepanov that the glorious Russian ballets of the late nineteenth century that became essential works in ballet companies all over the world have survived. He was an anatomy student who devised a system of dance notation which was adopted by the Imperial Ballet in 1893. His tragic death at age thirty deprived the Russian ballet of an ongoing record of its dance creations, but in his short lifetime, Stepanov made detailed notation of the classics that had their debut at the Maryinsky Theatre.

Nicholas Sergeyev was born in 1876 and graduated from the Imperial Ballet School in 1894. He advanced to the rank of soloist and became régisseur in charge of Stepanov notation. Stepanov's scripts for twenty-one works were taken to the West by Sergeyev after the October Revolution of 1917. Some of these scripts offered only sketchy details, but the majority were complete. They provided the source for authentic restorations of such ballets as *The Sleeping Princess* (*The Sleeping Beauty*) for Diaghilev in 1921 and for productions of *Swan Lake, Giselle, Nutcracker* and *Coppelia* for the Vic-Wells Ballet.

In France and England, Sergeyev was regarded as the hero who enabled performances of the classics in complete form to take place, introducing and preserving a vitally important dance heritage. The influence of Sergeyev's productions and records are likely to continue as the nineteenth century classics maintain their position at the very heart of classical ballet.

Coppelia was destined to have a tremendous impact on Franklin's career over the years. At the Ballet Russe premiere, Franklin danced the "Czardas" with Eugenia Delarova, the wife of Massine. Sergeyev was very fond of Franklin and called him "Freddie Ready." Before rehearsals, he could often be heard calling out, "Where Freddie? Freddie Ready!"[34] The leading roles of Swanilda and Franz were first danced by Danilova (who was superb in the Sergeyev version) and Michel Panaieff. Franklin inherited the role of Franz in the 1939–40 season, alternating with Igor Youskevitch. No one taught Freddie the part of Franz. He simply learned it in the wings from watching Panaieff.

Although it's a very popular ballet today, *Coppelia* did not have much success when the Ballet Russe first performed it in America. Franklin explained, "In 1939, people weren't used to seeing just one ballet — they wanted three. We had to put *Gaîté Parisienne* on afterwards, or people didn't come."[35] By 1944, the *Coppelia* production had been shorn of its last act and relegated to matinees (usually composed of harassed elders accompanied by badly-behaved children who would rather be at the movies).

After an enormously successful London season, the company sailed to America and opened their New York season at the Met with the premiere of *Bogatyri* on October 20, 1938. The de Basil company was having an enormous success with Fokine's colorful Russian epic, *Le Coq d'Or*, and Sol Hurok insisted that the new Ballet Russe needed to have a work of the same ilk. The Bogatyri were half-legendary, half-historic figures of the early Middle Ages who were the loyal servants of St. Vladimir (c. 956–1015), the first Christian ruler of Russia.

In the prologue, the Princess Anastachiuska (Mia Slavenska) is napping in her apartments. She dreams of a frightful ogre succeeded by the vision of a handsome Tartar Prince (George Zoritch). In her dream, she rises and dances with him ecstatically, even though the Tartars are the sworn enemies of her people. When she wakens, her ladies-in-waiting dress her in ceremonial robes. Alyosha Popovitch (Igor Youskevitch) steals in undetected and hides under her bed. Then he crawls out and dances gaily with the princess.

Scene one reveals the Bogatyri standing before the walls of Kiev. Exhorted by their general, Mouromitz (Marc Platoff), they boast of their strength and prowess as they prepare for an expedition against the Tartars. Princess Anastachiuska arrives to bestow her blessings. But suddenly the hideous apparition of her dreams descends from the sky, grabs the princess in his claws and flies away with her to his abode. The Bogatyri make haste to go to her rescue.

Scene two is divided into three sections. In the first, the Tartar Prince takes his ease while his warriors dance with wild abandon. In the second section, the Bogatyri come upon a clearing in a forest glade. The Tartar Princess, Khanja (Nathalie Krassovska), and her companions dance seductively before them in harem suits and transparent veils. For a moment the Bogatyri fall under the spell of these enchantresses, but they recover as they recall their duty: they must have no other thought than the doing of brave deeds in the righting of wrongs. The next section finds us in the Ogre's enchanted garden. The Ogre (Simon Semenoff) and the Ogre Attendants (company losers) stand guard over the Princess Anastachiuska, who is sobbing over her lost freedom. Enter the valiant Bogatyri. Dobryna Nikitisch (Frederic Franklin), the bravest of the brave, challenges the Ogre to single combat and emerges victorious. Anastachiuska has been rescued, and the party returns joyfully to Kiev. Scene three is in the banquet hall of the Kiev palace. Princess Anastachiuska marries her dashing rescuer. The princess and Dobryna lead the assembly in a joyous general dance.

What little praise this ballet received went to designer Nathalie Gontcharova. Her style — neo-primitivism — drew upon Russian folk art for inspiration. Her settings for *Bogatyri* were in the fantastic style of Russian fairytale illustrations and employed Gontcharaova's typical color scheme: blindingly bright with violent contrasts. The most memorable scenic effect was the entrance of the Ogre in the first scene: he first appeared in the form of a curtain, lowered to a point just above the amazed Bogatyri's heads. The head and claws of the monster were cut out so that a stagehand could seize the princess and carry her offstage.

For most critics, the only exciting choreography to be found was in the second scene, where ferocious Tartars flourished their scimitars and Tartar maidens danced with oriental sinuousness. But this choreography was so heavily indebted to Michel Fokine's *Polovetsian Dances* (1909) that it could scarcely be called imaginative. The plaiting of Anastachiuska's hair in the prologue was more than a little derivative of a famous ritual action from the first scene of Bronislava Nijinska's 1923 *Les Noces*. Put simply, this ballet was not one of Massine's better efforts.

Of all the works created for the Ballet Russe de Monte Carlo's first season, only *Bogatyri* could be counted a failure. The story was too complicated, the names of its characters were tongue-twisters and the sets, while lovely, completely dwarfed the dancers. For some reason, Massine remained attached to this ballet, and he revised and simplified it for the next season. The prologue was dropped altogether, and the first two sections of the second scene were consolidated. The virtues of Alyosha Popovitch and Dobryna Nikitisch were merged in the first hero, the enlarged role now danced by Franklin. But the ballet remained an obstinate failure. John Martin could see little improvement in *Bogatyri*'s plot "or what might euphemistically be called its form"; it remained "obscure in story, unimaginative in choreography and swallowed up in scenery." Franklin confirmed that it was "a horrendous ballet." Asked what was wrong with it, he replied, "Everything."[36]

The Ballet Russe production of *Giselle*, first seen in London in July of 1938, was another offering for the New York season. Serge Lifar, director of the Paris Opéra Ballet, had been invited to stage this nineteenth century classic and to dance Albrecht with Markova, Toumanova and Mia Slavenska alternating in the title role. He was also to produce his own *Icare* with new costumes and scenery by Eugène Berman. Franklin related, "Massine never wanted Lifar *near* the company, but they needed another name as a headliner [and] Denham insisted.... The trouble was, Mr. and Mrs. Denham loved him; they were personal friends."[37]

Lifar, who first won fame as a leading dancer in the Diaghilev company, had an "artistic temperament" of truly hyperbolic proportions. He often referred to himself as "*Le Dieu de la Danse*." In 1935, he had been temporarily suspended from the Paris Opéra for refusing to appear in a performance at which the president of the French Republic was present. He explained he could not dance that night because he did not like the backdrop curtain used for his dance.[38]

Franklin tells us that Lifar was a "drooly sort of dancer, fond of flamboyant gestures." George Zoritch recalls Lifar's performance as Albrecht: "on his first entrance, Lifar ran around the stage like a witch aflame, his mouth open, eyes bulging. If that were not grotesque enough, his fingers were spread to their widest and formed claws. I thought any minute he might start to claw Giselle when she finally appeared." And in the second act, "The cape Lifar wore as Albrecht on his second-act entrance trailed behind him. It seemed there was an unending reserve of black velvet in the wings by the time his Albrecht had located Giselle's resting place."[39]

At the ballet's end in the London performances, Markova, beloved by the Brits, received twenty-four curtain calls, all of which Lifar insisted upon sharing. The English audience was quick to express its disapproval and insisted that Alicia appear alone before the curtain. According to Anton Dolin, at one performance, Lifar was forcibly held back by two male dancers while Markova finished her curtain calls solo. Lifar was infuriated and resentful of Markova's success.[40]

When the company landed in New York, Lifar refused to dance with Alicia, insisting that Tamara Toumanova should dance *Giselle* with him. Sol Hurok told a reporter, "I refused to permit him to have his way, and on each occasion he sulked."[41] Toumanova was apparently sulking as well because Markova, rather than she, was scheduled to dance *Giselle* on the coveted opening night. Due to a very mysterious oversight, both Toumanova and Markova had been promised the New York opening night of *Giselle* in their contracts. When this fact leaked out, all of the company members took sides at once. Hurok describes the backstage drama:

> Factionalism was rampant. Pressures of almost every sort were put upon Massine to switch the opening night casting. A threat of possible violence caused me to take the precaution to have detectives, disguised as stage hands, standing by; I eliminated the trap-door and understage elevator, used in this production as Giselle's grave, and gave instructions to have everything loose on the stage fastened down.[42]

The fracas reached a climax on the day of the opening. Toumanova was absent from the rehearsal Massine had scheduled for *Le Tricorne*. Suddenly, Papa Toumanova stormed in, glared at Massine, and slugged him in the face. Franklin was a witness to this incident. He remembers that "Volumes of Russian went back and forth. Then Massine left."[43] As a result of this dispute, Toumanova withdrew from the Ballet Russe at the end of the first American season and made her Broadway debut in the musical comedy *Stars in Your Eyes*, with Ethel Merman and Jimmy Durante.

In his biography on Markova, Dolin states that on the afternoon following the

American premiere, the ballerina found a note in her dressing room which said, "Do not dare to dance Giselle tonight or else." He then gives his version of that fateful second-night performance:

> As the curtain came down on the death of Giselle, Alicia had to be helped to her feet.... Somewhere in the pas de deux with Lifar she had hurt her foot and badly.... No one accused Lifar of dropping her. But there were some who suggested that a partner has many opportunities to set a ballerina down hard, on her pointed toes. From the audience, even from the stage, no one would notice.[44]

In her own memoirs, Markova denies that Lifar deliberately dropped her, maintaining that they simply lost balance in a kneel, and he accidentally rolled on to her foot. But her gracious, diplomatic explanation is simply not corroborated by her contemporaries. Following an interview with Massine, *Collier's* fanned the flames of the sabotage rumor by reporting, "A male dancer, jealous of his partner's success, threatens to drop her on the stage. And carries out his threat on the second night — cleverly, so that the audience never knows, but effectively. The girl faints dead away the moment the curtain falls, another ballerina is hastily hooked into her costume for the second act, and a wrenched foot keeps one of the company's three primas off the program for weeks." In an interview for *Ballet Review*, P. W. Manchester described the episode a bit more bluntly: "He slammed her down."[45]

Undaunted by the scandal he had caused, Lifar continued to enhance his reputation as the "bad boy of ballet." For this season, the Ballet Russe had followed a precedent established by Diaghilev, adding to Act II of *Swan Lake* a pas de trois from Act I. For this production, Serge Lifar danced the role of Prince Siegfried. Lifar, who had excellent reasons for avoiding comparison with other male dancers in the company, insisted that the pas de trois be cut, most particularly the enthusiastically applauded variation danced by Roland Guerard. When Massine and Hurok refused to grant his request, Lifar retaliated by challenging Massine to a duel at dawn the next morning in the sheep meadow of Central Park. Massine responded, "Go take an aspirin, Serge." Having failed to resolve the matter with pistols for two and coffee for one, Lifar threatened to quit. According to the *New York Herald Tribune*, Sol Hurok replied, "The Champlain leaves for Paris on Saturday. Why don't you take it if you can't get along here?" Lifar sailed for Paris on October 22, 1938.[46]

Even after Markova recovered, bad luck plagued her. In Boston, at one performance of *Giselle*, when Markova was ready to change into her second-act costume, she discovered that only the bodice and a single thin layer of tulle remained of it, some rapscallion having slashed away the whole of the inside skirt. The remains of the costume were later found in Mia Slavenska's dressing room, wadded up in the toilet.

Alicia never went anywhere without her famous "basket," which contained backup costumes for all of her major roles. After notifying the management of the incident, she calmly slipped on her spare costume for *Giselle*, Act II, and strolled out of the dressing room, smiling like the Cheshire cat for the benefit of the perpetrators. Freddie has a strong hunch as to who these perpetrators were:

> Now, Tamara was with us. And Mama Toumanova and Tamara Toumanova were very, very close. There was trouble. She protected her daughter from all kinds of things. I think it was getting back at Alicia.... We never knew who did it. But people surmised it was Tamara and her mother.... And Lifar and Toumanova were also very close. Very close.[47]

And what was Frederic Franklin up to while the hornets were buzzing round their nasty nest? Apparently, he was taking daily class, rehearsing, washing his tights, glueing on his slippers (sewing elastic on one's shoes was unheard of back then), pondering his interpretations, reviewing his steps and performing every night in his usual highly-disciplined fashion. What was the matter with this man? Discipline was precisely what made Freddie such a valuable asset to the Ballet Russe, but one senses that he didn't miss out on *all* of the buzz.

Franklin was immensely successful and popular in his roles for the new company's first season. Massine was well-pleased with his new find:

> Massine said, "Franklin does everything the way I want him to do it, he does everything the way I show him." And he pushed me. I shall never forget the day that we were all lined up and he said, "*Schéhérazade*— the Golden Slave — Franklin; *Prince Igor*— the Chief Warrior — Franklin." And I asked, "What is happening? I'm terrified!"[48]

While deeply honored by these new roles, Franklin still had a yen to dance in *Le Tricorne*, even if only in the corps de ballet. He had become friendly with Massine's wife, Eugenia Delarova, and he told her of his wish. The next day, Massine said, "'so Freddie, I understand that you want to be in my *Tricorne*.' And I said, 'Oh any place, anywhere.' And he said, 'Well, how would you like to learn my part?'" When Massine became ill in Rochester, Franklin was told to go on in his stead as the Miller. After he had dressed for the part and was warming up in the wings, Massine walked in. "I'm terribly sorry, Freddie," he said, "but I feel much better now."[49]

The Ballet Russe wasted no time in putting out press releases on their new find, Frederic Franklin. In a release entitled "Hoofer Turns to Ballet," the company publicist wrote, "He can swing a tune on the piano or tap it on the floor, but he would rather do an *entrechat* any time, and that is why he is with the Russian ballet company today." Walter Terry described the essence of Franklin's appeal: "There is no stage grin in the world to match that of Frederic Franklin, for the Monte Carlo's young British star fairly grins with his whole body."[50]

Walter Terry is much to be respected as one of the only dance critics of the era who actually took ballet classes himself. His indoctrination came as a surprise to him:

> I remember the first dance class I ever attended. With a background in swimming, diving, tennis and plenty of "gym" work, I felt pretty cocky, yet after an hour's class, I left the third-floor studio and fell down two flights of stairs because my knees wouldn't hold me up. The next morning I had to roll out of bed and haul myself to a standing posture by grabbing the window sill — my stomach muscles felt as if they had been removed during the night and weak custard substituted for them.[51]

In addition to roles in the world premieres, Franklin showed great ability in the Fokine ballets of the Diaghilev era. In *Schéhérazade*, Franklin was splendid as Zobeide's golden-clad slave, enacting his role with a bestial lust and dancing his variations with animal strength and agility. As the Chief Warrior in the *Polovetsian Dances*, he was acclaimed by the Russians as the equal of such well-known dancers as Adolph Bolm, Léon Woizikowsky and Yurek Shabelevsky. In the 1938–39 season, he also danced the Moor in *Petrouchka* and the King of Dandies in *Le Beau Danube*.

After a cross-country American tour that ended in April of 1939, the Ballet Russe returned to Europe and presented two premieres at the Théâtre de Monte Carlo. *Capric-*

Jeannette Lauret as Zobeide and Frederic Franklin as the Golden Slave in *Schéhérazade*. Ballet Russe de Monte Carlo production. 1938–39. Choreography: Michel Fokine (1910). Music: Rimsky-Korsakov. Décor and costumes: Leon Bakst. Photograph: Maurice Seymour, courtesy of Ronald Seymour.

cio Espagnol premiered on May 4, 1939. It was a suite of Spanish dances choreographed by Massine and the great Spanish dancer Argentinita. They danced the leading roles of the Gypsy Couple with Danilova and Panaieff in the supporting roles of the Peasant Couple.

Rouge et Noir made its world debut on May 11, 1939. It was a symphonic ballet in four movements, danced to Shostakovich's Symphony No.1. This was Henri Matisse's second foray into the ballet world: he had done the set and costume designs for Massine's *Le Chant du rossignol* in 1920.

In the first movement, "Man, symbolizing the poetic spirit, is pursued and overtaken by brutal forces." The forces of Yellow, Red, Blue and Black harass the poetic forces of White (Alicia Markova, Igor Youskevitch). In the second movement, "The men of the city encounter the men of the field and bear them off." The forces of Red (similar to Black but more impish than evil) race across the stage and make mischief. The Leader of the Red Group (Frederic Franklin) performs a solo in the foreground as the ensemble moves in intricate counterpoint. The movement ends with a high pyramid formed by the forces of Red, separating Markova and Youskevitch. The protagonists reach for each other on either side. [52]

The third movement begins with a solo for the ballerina in White: "Woman, parted from man, is tormented in her solitude by an evil spirit." The evil Leader of the Black (Marc Platoff) appears. Desiring White, he throws her into acrobatic lifts indicative of torture and suffering and leaves her prone at stage left. In the last movement, "Man eludes the brutal forces and finds woman again. But joy is short-lived, for in freeing himself from his worldly enemies he is conquered by destiny." Youskevitch is murdered by the combined forces of Black, Red, Blue, and Yellow. Markova falls unconscious across the back of the Leader of the Black in a final tableau.

Matisse devised a drop of a vaulted hall with a canary yellow roof and three white pillars. In the center of the backcloth was an enormous blue isosceles triangle. Matisse's razor-edged design was stunning, but it was definitely meant to be seen from the distance affordable at the Metropolitan Opera rather than the intimate Théâtre de Monte Carlo. For costumes, the dancers wore hooded unitards in their assigned colors. The costumes were intended to depersonalize the dancers, to turn them into quasi-human color symbols. Yet, the corporeality of the dancers was unavoidably accented by the skintight unitards, so revealing that they made some viewers squirm in their seats back in 1939. While Lincoln Kirstein noted that the unitards did show clearly the dancers' lines, he too found them distracting: "Union-suit tights are hard to make look neat, but the line of undergarments shining through continually destroyed the line."[53]

Massine's choreographic intent was to relate the five basic colors not only to the music but also to the philosophical theme of the ballet, which was to be the conflict between the spiritual and the material world. The concept got even more involved when Massine opted to give each movement program notes which gave the audience a plot that didn't always seem to be occurring onstage. From the standpoint of pure movement invention, however, *Rouge et Noir* may be among Massine's finest ballets.

Choreographic highlights included the second-movement solo for Franklin as the Leader of the Red Group and the violent pas de deux for Markova and Platoff in the third movement. Walter Terry wrote, "Frederic Franklin was excellent, first as an ebullient, constantly moving figure and later as the figure distinguished by aggressive strength and, perhaps, by the flavor of evil."[54] The ballet's strongest moment was the exquisite, elegiac solo for Markova which began the third movement.

For the most part, *Rouge et Noir* was favorably received, although critics complained that the program notes gave the ballet a false emotional framework. John Mar-

Left to right: Igor Youskevitch, Alicia Markova, Andre Eglevsky and Fredric Franklin in Léonide Massine's *Rouge et Noir*. 1939. Costumes hand painted by Henri Matisse. Ballet Russe de Monte Carlo production. Photograph: Maurice Seymour, courtesy of Ronald Seymour.

tin decided that it was "a highly symbolic ballet about nothing at all."[55] Despite impressive movement invention, Massine's storyline had left him wide open to the usual charges that symphonic ballets were absurdly histrionic and hackneyed.

Rouge et Noir remained in the repertoire from 1939 to 1942. After an absence of several years, *Seventh Symphony* and *Rouge et Noir* were revived by the Ballet Russe, in

1948 at the Metropolitan Opera and in 1949 at New York City Center, with Markova in her original roles.

By the time of this spring season in Monte Carlo, the political situation in Europe was worsening rapidly. By March of 1939, Hitler's armies had marched into Czechoslovakia, Bohemia and Monrovia. As Massine wrote, "the ballet [*Rouge et Noir*] seemed unhappily only too appropriate to the moment of history through which we were passing, for the spiritual life of the world seemed to be disintegrating rapidly under the brute heel of totalitarianism."[56]

After the Monte Carlo season, the company went on to Paris. They were released for the holidays on July 8, with instructions that some of the dancers were to report to the rehearsal room in the Rue d'Amsterdam on Monday, August 28. During the holiday, Freddie went to England to see his family and then returned to Paris, where Frederick Ashton was rehearsing *Devil's Holiday*. They rehearsed right up until Saturday, September 2, while on the street below them Parisians were panicking and leaving the city.

The Ballet Russe was scheduled to open at Covent Garden on September 4. That opening never took place. On September 1, Nazi troops had marched into Warsaw and bombarded the Polish capital. On September 3, England and France declared war on Germany. The dancers found themselves stranded in Europe, wondering how they would ever reach the United States.

There were enormous logistical difficulties in trying to arrange wartime passage across the Atlantic for dancers of seventeen different nationalities. Visas caused complications, because many of the dancers, being Russian refugees or the children of Russian refugees, traveled on Nansen passports. These were actually travel documents, not official citizenship passports, and each case had to be considered separately on its own merit. For some years, Michel Panaieff had been a resident of France under a Nansen passport. In some cases, France decided that young men who had domiciled there owed the country service. Panaieff was called up, and the Ballet Russe lost one of its finest dancers. Igor Youskevitch faced the same dilemma, but was finally able to secure a Yugoslav passport, arriving in New York late in the season. A promising young dancer named André Eglevsky was hired to replace Panaieff.

Matters became even more tense when the U.S. government ruled in October that American citizens must have first precedence in passages from Europe to America. In New York, panic and despair held sway at the offices of Universal Art, but a cooler head prevailed in the end. It was largely through the innumerable transatlantic cables and telephone calls of Sol Hurok that the Ballet Russe was able to reach this country at all. Dancers left in different groups, in separate boats, Franklin's being among the last to sail.

Massine, now being an American citizen, was among the first to cross the Atlantic, arriving in New York on September 14. Realizing that he might not get all of his former dancers, he immediately began holding auditions for replacements. Auditions yielded six boys and six girls. Several were given contracts, and the others held in readiness as understudies, in case the Europeans failed to arrive.

Fortunately, Franklin's class was not called for military service, so he was able to obtain permission to come to America. At the end of September, Franklin was the only

Frederic Franklin on a rock at Cap d'Antibes, in the south of France, his last holiday before the war. 1939. Photograph: Collection of Frederic Franklin.

member of his group still stranded in Paris. Ports and embassies there were closed, but Fred finally got instructions from Hurok via telegram that he should take the train to neutral Rotterdam, Holland, to await passage to America. In Rotterdam, he was reunited with thirty-three company members, including Franklin, Mia Slavenska and Nathalie Krassovska. Franklin had no money, and he immediately went to the Hotel Rotterdam and cabled Mrs. Toye for ten pounds. She was vastly relieved to finally learn of his where-abouts.

The dancers lived in a cheap, dirty *pension*. To relieve the gloom, Freddie took bal-lerina Tanya Grantzeva out to dance one night at a local nightclub. There, they created such a sensation with their ballroom dancing that the manager plied them with refresh-ments. Soon all of the dancers were showing up at this establishment and dancing for their dinners.[57]

After a long wait, the dancers were told to go to the port on the evening of Octo-ber 12 to set sail on board the *Rotterdam*. Because the English channel was riddled with mines, it took them three days and two nights just to get across. When they arrived at Southampton, Franklin had his luggage packed and said good-bye to everyone. The plan was that he would deboard in England and await passage to America. But the ship's captain told him to stay on — it appears that Hurok had paved the way to go directly to America so he could appear on the opening night at the Met. Thanks to Hurok, the dancers on the *Rotterdam* left England only two weeks after the scheduled departure date. The Ballet Russe de Monte Carlo never set foot in Europe again.

The crossing was unusually rough, and many of the dancers were seasick for almost the whole duration of the fourteen-day voyage. With 1,123 passengers, the ship was crammed to capacity and ran out of food and even drinking water. Franklin related, "I was in the bowels of the ship ... it was horrendous."[58] The *Rotterdam* reached New York at noon on the very day of the October 26 opening. Because of passport irregularities, several of the dancers were detained on Ellis Island overnight and consequently missed the opening. Buses were waiting to whisk the rest off to the Metropolitan.

In through the stage door of the Metropolitan came a chattering horde, laughing and excited. There were many tearful reunions. Massine called a halt to the celebrat-ing, dispatching the dancers to their dressing rooms. "Freddie," he said, "your costumes are upstairs. There's a dress rehearsal." Franklin thought, "My God, we haven't rehearsed it [*Devil's Holiday*] for months!" Exhausted, out of practice, unsteady on his "sea legs," still fighting the effects of prolonged seasickness, Franklin danced the difficult role of the Beggar in *Devil's Holiday* and afterwards, the Baron in *Gaîté* that same evening. He was informed that his partner in *Gaîté* would be Mia Slavenska, who weighed 135 pounds at the time. In-between the two ballets, he had a stiff shot of brandy. "I wouldn't have got through it otherwise," he said.[59]

Three new works premiered at the Met that season — *Devil's Holiday*, *Bacchanale* and *Ghost Town*. *Devil's Holiday* (titled *Le Diabole s'amuse* in Europe) was the end result of a plan to do a ballet about Paganini. Initially, Balanchine was to have choreographed it, but then the project was given to Frederick Ashton. However, it happened that Michel Fokine was already preparing his own ballet about Paganini for the de Basil com-pany by the time Ashton was ready to begin. To avoid competition, a new and rather thin story was concocted for the Ashton work.

The score was arranged by Vincenzo Tommasini, who used the twenty-four Caprices of Niccolò Paganini for his source material. Eugène Berman created five back-drops for *Devil's Holiday*, and his costumes were wonderful, especially the horrible dis-guises of the Devil and his two servants. Several of Berman's designs for *Devil's Holiday* are now on exhibit at New York's Museum of Modern Art.

Paganini, because of his superhuman virtuosity and sinister appearance, was popularly supposed to have been in league with the devil. *Devil's Holiday*, in a prologue and three scenes, concerns the Devil's attempts to meddle in human affairs, especially human love affairs. Disguised as a mortal, the Devil (Marc Platoff) wanders in Venice until he is attracted by a noisy argument at the gate of a shabby but once palatial dwelling. The Old Lord (Simon Semenoff) and his Daughter (Alexandra Danilova) are trying to stave off an angry group of creditors. The Devil pays them what they are owed and even includes some passers-by in his largesse. One of the recipients, a Beggar (Frederic Franklin), is obviously attracted to the Daughter. The Old Lord invites the generous stranger to his daughter's betrothal ball. Seeing an opportunity to make mischief, the Devil invites the Beggar to accompany him.

Scene One takes place at the ball. The Daughter is dancing with her fiancé (George Zoritch). When the Devil enters with the Beggar — now richly dressed — she is smitten by the handsome young man. They dance alone and are discovered by the Devil, who summons the Old Lord, the Fiancé, and the guests. The Daughter is spurned by all of them for her indiscretion. There follows an entr'acte in which the Beggar and the Daughter meet in a dream and dance a pas de deux.

Scene Two is set in the forest, where a party of hunters is celebrating around a fox they have killed. They are scared out of their wits when the dead fox turns into a live Devil. He chases them offstage and dances a merry solo. The Beggar enters in despair over his lost love. To cheer him, the Devil conjures up a Gypsy Girl (Nathalie Krassovska), and the Beggar joins her in her wild and uninhibited dance. The Daughter then enters, and not even the magical spell of the Devil can stop the Beggar from running into her arms. He drives the Devil and the Gypsy Girl away.

In the second entr'acte, the Devil dresses for Carnival, assisted by two servants. Carnival revelers in bizarre disguises enter with the advent of Scene Three. When the Devil arrives on the scene, they become apprehensive. Finally they tear his mask off and are terrified to behold his true identity. However, the clock strikes twelve, and the Devil is compelled to depart. The revelers and main characters resume their merrymaking.

The most striking choreography occurred in the tender pas de deux of the two lovers and the solos devised for the Devil and the Beggar. Franklin's Beggar solo had him circling the stage with a strenuous movement in which he went up on his toes and over onto his knees, followed by a kneeling walk forward — repeated several times. This solo was intended to express the Beggar's lovesickness. During rehearsals, Ashton said, "I don't like that pained, soulful look," and told him to let the emotional expression come through the use of his whole body.[60]

Had this ballet survived for any length of time, the Beggar would have been one of Franklin's greatest roles. Grace Robert believed that "Frederic Franklin had in the Beggar a role that for suitability and charm was not equaled in his repertoire until the advent of *Rodeo*. His forest-scene solo, expressive of the Beggar's frustration and longing, is one of the high points of contemporary ballet." Edwin Denby stated, "Franklin is magnificent."[61]

Franklin even had a hand in choreographing the ballet. At a loss for an ensemble passage in the Carnival divertissement, Ashton asked Freddie to show him something.

All he could think of was that the music at that point in the score sounded somewhat like the Mexican Hat Dance. Wendy Toye had taught him this dance in the early '30s, and he remembered every step. Franklin sheepishly showed him a few steps of the dance. To his amazement, Ashton made them the basis for his ensemble number.[62]

The chief weakness of *Devil's Holiday* is in this Carnival scene, where a rather uninventive divertissement blocks the dramatic momentum generated thus far. But otherwise, the ballet had much to be said for it. The problem was that *Devil's Holiday*, which was to have been seen on September 7 at Covent Garden, needed tightening and never even had a dress rehearsal. If the war hadn't erased that London season, Ashton would surely have been able to make adjustments to the trouble spots. As it was, he never even saw a performance of his own ballet.

The critics were appropriately prepared to make allowances for the ballet's condition. Martin initially wrote that the ballet was not in any state to be subjected to review, but wrote later, "a reasonable interval, however, finds the work just about what it seemed to be at its premiere, namely an extremely weak effort." Walter Terry had more faith in the work: "*Devil's Holiday* deserves a lasting place, but not as it was presented last night."[63] This ballet was seen again in the 1941–42 season and was then dropped. For one thing, it was just too large a production to take on tour.

Bacchanale premiered on November 9, 1939. It was a collaboration between Massine and surrealist artist Salvador Dalí and constituted a curious bringing together of Sigmund Freud, Richard Wagner and King Ludwig II of Bavaria. King Ludwig is remembered for his patronage of the composer Richard Wagner, for his lavish palaces and, mainly, for his insanity. History records that King Ludwig actually "lived" all of Wagner's myths, identifying himself with their legendary heroes to the point of profound delusion. Pronounced insane in 1886, Ludwig committed suicide by drowning himself in the Starnberger See Palace in 1886. His body was not discovered right away. At first his searchers found only an umbrella floating on the water. It was Dalí's idea to put a Freudian interpretation on King Ludwig's identification with Wagnerian heroes and to set the work to the "Venusberg" music from *Tannhäuser*.

The curtain rises on a stunning backdrop of a gigantic swan with outstretched wings and a skull-shaped opening in its breast. Lola Montez (Milada Mladova) emerges from the opening. A parade of weird bacchantes from the pages of psychological case books succeeds her onstage: a fish-headed woman, Graces with strange protuberances, psychopathic nymphs and fauns. Periodically, Sacher Masoch (Marc Platoff, then Frederic Franklin) and his wife (Jeanette Lauret) make appearances in which Masoch gleefully subjects himself to fierce whippings by his wife. In the midst of this madness wanders Ludwig (Casimir Kokitch), seeking some kind of relief from his strange hallucinations.

All the while, a satyr and his dwarf companion, seated in a downstage corner, are imperturbably wool-winding and knitting a sock. Venus (Nini Theilade) appears in a nude-colored unitard. Imagining himself to be Tannhäuser, Ludwig approaches Venus. She then becomes a dragon, and, as Lohengrin, Ludwig kills her. But his strength begins to fail: he falls to the floor near death. The Knight of Death enters in the form of an anthropomorphic umbrella, attended by two men wrapped in opposite ends of a sheet. As Ludwig dies, four large umbrellas planted at the corners of the stage open with stately dignity.

Dalí's principal theoretical contribution to surrealism was his "paranoiac-critical

Frederic Franklin in *Devil's Holiday*. Choreography: Frederick Ashton, later Sir Frederick. Ballet Russe de Monte Carlo production. 1939. Photograph: Maurice Seymour, courtesy of Ronald Seymour.

method," which he defined as the "critical and systematic objectification of delirious associations and interpretations."[64] Dalí saw his method as a means of destabilizing the world, believing everything the viewer saw was potentially something else. *Bacchanale* was a good example of his paranoiac-critical method, relying as it did on the dream-like association of seemingly incongruous images.

Those in the audience who had read a little Freud could see that there were few deviations from the clichés of standard Freudian symbolism, especially in the costuming. The double row of teeth adorning the hoopskirt of Lola Montez encircled her pubic area. Other costume grotesqueries included a woman with a huge, rose-colored fish head, nymphs wearing one-half frilly organdy party frocks and one-half men's underwear, and hyperbolically virile fauns who wore nothing but neckties and sassy red lobsters stitched onto their loincloths. The three Graces had some astonishing "graces" attached to their anatomies. Franklin remembers that one girl's breasts went straight out, another's went straight down and the third girl's went straight up. He recounts, "The girls came on stage [after putting on the costumes for the first time] crying their eyes out. They weren't going to wear them. At first they wouldn't even come out of the dressing rooms." Franklin also told his interviewers that a real dwarf was used in this production, and that she got star treatment: "She came with a limo, and she had a little fur coat." When asked if the dwarf went on tour with them, Franklin replied, "No, we had to find a new one in each city we went."[65]

Throughout *Bacchanale*, the symbolism was less to be pursued to the depth of its psycho-sexual import than to simply be taken in the spirit of zany fun. However, the role of Sacher Masoch (taken over by Franklin after the opening), with its recurrent theme of masochism, offended some viewers who laughed at everything else. John Martin found the roles of Masoch and his wife tasteless because their actions were couched "neither in symbolic nor surrealistic terms." "Elsewhere," he quipped, "Dalí's concern with the libido is likely to go safely over the heads of Little Willie and Grandma alike."[66]

Not surprisingly, *Bacchanale* got mixed reviews. Robert Lawrence called it "pulpy pornography," while other critics admired its brilliant concept and gave it qualified praise. *Bacchanale*'s notoriety and the compelling beauty of Dalí's set ensured its return to the Met for the company's 1940 season. But once the novelty began to fade, it was swept into the dustbins of time: "When the organdy frills grew limp, the slightly obscene costumes of the three Graces receded behind modest veils, and the umbrellas began to miss their cues, 'Bacchanale' faded from the repertoire."[67]

Ghost Town was the first choreographic venture of Marc Platoff. It had a libretto and score by Richard Rodgers, orchestration by Hans Spialek and settings and costumes by Raoul Pène du Bois. It was first performed at the Met on November 12, 1939.

In the prologue, two young hikers discover an old, abandoned mining settlement in the Sierras, and they peer wonderingly at its eerie desolation. They happen upon an aged Prospector (Simon Semenoff), who proceeds to tell them the history of this ghost town.

The next scene is a flashback showing the bustling town in its peak years with children, housewives, dance-hall girls, vigilantes, firemen and rival gangs of miners. A brawl breaks out between the Bright Star Miners and the Comstock Miners. The fire department settles the dispute by hosing down the rival gangs. A Mormon Apostle (Roland Guerard) enters with his five flirtatious wives.

Bonanza King Comstock (Casimir Kokitch) sells Ralston (Frederic Franklin) a mine. In his excitement, Ralston drops the claim papers, and Comstock retrieves them. But Eilley Orum (Mia Slavenska) distracts Comstock and snatches up the papers for herself. A stagecoach arrives with the songstress Jenny Lind (Nini Theilade), who will inaugurate the new opera house.

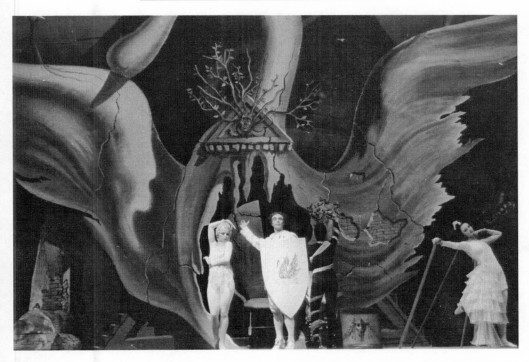

Bacchanale. 1939. Nini Theilade as Venus, Casimir Kokitch as Ludwig II. Choreography: Léonide Massine. Ballet Russe de Monte Carlo production. Photograph: Collection of Frederic Franklin.

Ralston finds gold on his newly purchased claim, and he buys a red coat with big gold buttons to celebrate. Comstock accuses Ralston of claim-jumping. Since he's unable to show the claim papers, Ralston is declared guilty and attacked by the vigilantes. Just when they're fixing to hang him, Eilley intervenes and saves him by producing the papers. Jenny Lind appears and sings "The Last Rose of Summer" to amuse the crowd. Word comes from the assay office that the ore yield has nearly reached the vanishing-point. Panic prevails as the inhabitants prepare to desert the town. Ralston alone believes the town has a future and tries unsuccessfully to persuade Eilley to remain with him.

In the epilogue, we return to the scene of the prologue. The story has been told. As the hikers depart, a prickling chill creeps down their spines as they notice the large gold buttons on the old man's faded red coat.

Ghost Town was yet another attempt to satisfy the clamor for Americana ballets. Although it was hardly an unqualified success, it was at least an improvement over Massine's three essays into Americana — *Union Pacific, The New Yorker* and *Saratoga*. The score for *Ghost Town* left much to be desired. Martin McCall found it "dull and inept." John Martin felt that Rodgers was congenitally unable to make the transition from musical comedy to ballet, and he added, "The sentimental theme song that haunts the heroine makes it almost incumbent upon her sooner or later to burst into some such lyric as 'Ghost Town, I Love You.'"[68]

Like most fledgling choreographers, Platoff made the action too busy and overcrowded at points. Edwin Denby said, "It keeps going all over the place, messes up dances by realistic gestures, by awkward spacing and operatic arm-waving. But there is an exuberant energy in it." John Martin wrote that Platoff "musical-comedy-ized" his subject matter, failing to capture those "rip-snorting, sweaty, raucous days whose picturesqueness lies in their very fleshly malodorousness." But he did praise Platoff's "excellent comedy sense" and thought that he was entitled to "another try and under better conditions. There is every reason to believe he has it in him."[69]

One of the best moments in the ballet was Franklin's dance of jubilation when Ralston finds gold. For Grace Robert, the role of Ralston was "a sort of preliminary sketch for the Champion Roper in 'Rodeo.'"[70] Another highlight was Roland Guerard's portrayal of the Mormon Apostle. His stately, sanctimonious strut was interrupted now and then with twitty and twinkling *entrechats six*, which he broke into as if by compulsion. With a little tightening and clarifying, *Ghost Town* might have remained in the repertory, but it lasted for only one season.

After the fall Metropolitan season, the Ballet Russe spent the winter on a coast-to-coast tour. Meanwhile, American companies and the American Guild of Musical Artists turned up the heat on Universal Art to unionize. When AGMA started unionizing ballet companies at the beginning of 1939, the union was warmly received by such company heads as Lincoln Kirstein (Ballet Caravan), Catherine Littlefield (Littlefield Ballet), and Richard Pleasant (Ballet Theatre). However, they demanded assurances that the Ballet Russe would be lined up too, fearing that they would be driven out of business by this company's lower-priced tickets. Pleasant told reporters that the Ballet Russe was paying a minimum salary of $22.50 while Ballet Theatre was paying the union minimum of $45 per week. He claimed that he could not even begin rehearsals until Ballet Theatre was assured that it would not be bucking unfair competition from the Ballet Russe and stated that his backers planned to withhold their money until the Ballet Russe met the Guild terms.[71]

AGMA gave its promise to get the Ballet Russe on board and contacted Serge Denham before the fall 1939 season, but Denham always managed to find new causes for delay. Pressure from AGMA increased when it was learned that Massine had "hired" several young girls who were willing to work gratis and pay their own traveling expenses. Now, despite furious resentment, the company had left on tour without signing. Lincoln Kirstein and Pleasant led the fight to force the unionization of their Russian rivals. The campaign reached the boiling point with an angry protest in the *New York Herald Tribune* upon the Ballet Russe's return to New York. Kirstein told a reporter that if the Ballet Russe did not sign immediately, he and his dancers would picket the Metropolitan, "in white tights if necessary."[72] The Ballet Russe dancers joined the crusade and voted to strike if the AGMA contract was not signed. Backed up to the wall, Universal Art finally settled with AGMA. The new contract provided princely $45 weekly performance minimums. Denham told the *Tribune* that negotiations for the contract had been "amicable throughout" and that his company had "always been willing to sign, though there were a few technical difficulties."[73]

Cut off from Europe and Russia by the war, the Ballet Russe had a large contingent of American dancers by now, but their names were immediately Russianized. Franklin was spared, because he already had a small following from his Markova-Dolin days. But to maximize the company's exotic mystique, most dancers had to add a suffix or two to their names. "If you were Smith, you became Smithoff," said Seattle native Marc Platt, who became Marc Platoff.[74]

There were two Ballet Russe premieres at the Met in April of 1940. *Nuages* (Clouds) premiered on April 9 with choreography by Nini Theilade. It was set to Debussy's tone poem and showed Night (Lubov Rostova) eternally seeking Day (Frederic Franklin), and meeting for a passionate but fleeting embrace at Twilight (Nini Theilade, George Zoritch). Walter Terry thought this ballet was "pretty wispy."[75]

The second premiere was George Balanchine's *Le Baiser de la fée* (The Fairy's Kiss). There was no love lost between Balanchine and Massine — Massine fairly bristled when he learned that Denham had asked his rival to set a work on the company. Actually, there was no camaraderie between any of the major choreographers of this era. Franklin said, "Nijinska hated Balanchine and Balanchine hated her, and Balanchine hated Massine and Massine hated them both and Fokine you couldn't get near. And we young artists were in the middle of this."[76]

Baiser de la fée was first presented at the Paris Opéra on November 27, 1928, by the company of Ida Rubenstein. Bronislava Nijinska was the choreographer, and Mme Rubenstein appeared in the title role. Sadler's Wells (formerly the Vic-Wells) also presented a version with choreography by Frederick Ashton on November 26, 1935, but the production seen in America is the one that George Balanchine created for the American Ballet in 1937. The occasion was a Stravinsky festival at the Metropolitan Opera House with sets and costumes by Alice Halicka. The Ballet Russe presented *Baiser* at the Met on April 10, 1940, with the Halicka sets and costumes.

Stravinsky composed the score as an homage to Tchaikovsky, whom Stravinsky revered. The score is a suite built from Tchaikovsky melodies that the composer culled from various sources, employing some of their original melodic content, but transmuting them. He selected a tale by Hans Christian Andersen, "The Ice Maiden," as a basis for the libretto. Drawing a parallel to the Ice Maiden's lethal kiss, he wrote on the score's title page, "I dedicate this ballet to the memory of Peter Tchaikovsky.... It was his Muse (like our fairy heroine) whose fatal kiss, imprinted at birth, made itself felt in all the work of that great artist and eventually led him to immortality. Thereby does our ballet (with a similar tale) become an allegory."[77]

Le Baiser de la fée is in four scenes. The first is titled "Prologue — The Snowstorm." A mother, clasping a baby in her arms, is overtaken by a snowstorm. The snow comes down more and more heavily — groups of dancers representing snowflakes block her attempts to escape and separate her from her child. A beautiful fairy, the Ice Maiden (Mia Slavenska) is seen approaching the child. She dances with her attendant shadow, dressed in identical costumes, one glittering white and the other somber black. She kisses the infant tenderly, then disappears. A party of rescuers enters. They look vainly for the infant's mother, and, filled with compassion, adopt the child as their own.

In the second tableau, twenty years have passed. The child, grown into manhood, is to marry the miller's daughter, and the people of the alpine village are celebrating. Soon the musicians, villagers and fiancée go off, leaving the Bridegroom (André Eglevsky, then Frederic Franklin) alone. The Fairy enters, disguised as a gypsy. She approaches the youth and reads his palm. The Bridegroom is both frightened and attracted as she leads him away.

The third tableau takes place in the interior of the mill, where the Bride (Alexandra Danilova) is getting ready for her marriage. There follows a joyous pas de deux for the young couple in anticipation of the approaching wedding. As his fiancée withdraws with her friends to try on her bridal costume, the Bridegroom is left alone. Once more the Fairy appears, this time covered by a long wedding veil. Mistaking the Fairy for his fiancée, he moves toward her as if in a trance. They dance together, and he finally lifts her veil. Forgetting his bride, dominated by her spell, he follows her as the walls of the mill open to allow their passage.

The fourth tableau is an epilogue. The Bride comes into the room searching for her lover. She cannot find him. Suddenly, she sees a vision of her young man struggling to climb a dizzying ascent, at the summit of which lies immortality and the glittering Ice Maiden.

Critical response to *Baiser de la fée* was generally positive. Walter Terry found it "a clear and extremely effective ballet," George Amberg praised its "wonderfully sustained atmosphere of transcendental drama," and Edwin Denby termed it "ballet at its grandest." Grace Robert recalls that Danilova was "an exquisite Bride," and she also praised both André Eglevsky and Franklin for their fine interpretations of a role which is both technically and dramatically demanding. Slavenska she found to be "heavy and overdramatic."[78]

Franklin had to substitute for Eglevsky on short notice when the latter was injured. He learned the principal role in *Baiser* in exactly one day, dancing it that same evening and at subsequent performances, and also taking over other of Eglevsky's roles for the remainder of the season.[79]

Eglevsky was cast both in classic roles and in character parts. He had joined the de Basil company at the age of fourteen, but he left the company in 1934 to study with Nicholas Legat, staying with him for two years at the cost of considerable financial hardship. He then joined Blum's Ballets de Monte Carlo in 1936, where he created the role of the Lover in Fokine's *L'Epreuve d'amour*. Although a large man, he created on stage the illusion of extreme lightness, ease, and elegance. He was particularly renowned for the incredible number of pirouettes he could perform (from twelve to fifteen). Like Franklin, he had a considerable range. His roles for the Ballet Russe included the leads in *Schéhérazade, Petrouchka, Apollo*, and *Giselle*. After his retirement, he taught both at the School of American Ballet and at his own school in Massapequa, Long Island. In 1961 he founded the Eglevsky Ballet Company out of his school.

Baiser de la fée was not performed by the Ballet Russe after 1942. One reason the ballet went out of repertory was that parts of the work posed insuperable staging difficulties. The ending, where the Bridegroom climbed slowly upwards towards the Ice Maiden on a waving net, was a very fitting concept, but it was physically grueling for Franklin and Eglevsky and a bit awkward. Roslyn Krokover thought the Bridegroom looked rather "like a fly caught in a particularly sticky spider web."[80] The net covered the entire stage, starting from the footlights and ascending right up to the top upstage baton. Once the curtain had fallen at the ballet's end, it took Franklin a considerable amount of time to descend safely to the wings. And then the stagehands had to undo the net and put it backstage before it would be possible to take curtain calls. By this time, the applause had all but died.[81] This scene has never been satisfactorily worked out over the years.

When a ramp and suitable pantomime were substituted in 1941, Denby claimed that the last scene had been "mutilated." For him, the slow rope climbing opened up "both in style and emotion, an obscure and terrifying further perspective.... The substitution is an act of vandalism."[82]

Following their spring season in New York, the Ballet Russe embarked on a South American tour in the summer of 1940 and returned to New York in the fall for a season at the Fifty-first Street Theatre. In dizzying succession, five new works were presented in the space of only five days. Two new and unsuccessful Massine works premiered: *The New Yorker* and *Vienna—1814*. Much to the ire of Massine, Balanchine was hired again to stage two works—*Poker Game* and *Serenade*. The other premiere was Alexandra Fedorova's staging of the *Nutcracker*.

Alexandra Fedorova graduated from the Imperial Ballet School in 1902. One of the older boys at the school was Michel Fokine, whose brother, Alexander, she met and married. As a soloist with the Maryinsky Ballet, Fedorova became known for her exceptional technique. She danced briefly with Diaghilev's Ballets Russes in 1909, and in the 1920s she was lead dancer and choreographer with the Riga Opera Ballet in Latvia, staging many ballets, including *Coppelia*, *Swan Lake* and *Firebird*. In 1937 she moved to Manhattan, where she became a popular ballet teacher.

Fedorova was regarded as an invaluable link to Petipa and Ivanov, prompting Denham to ask her to stage a one-act *Nutcracker*. Premiering on October 17, 1940, with designs by Alexandre Benois, this truncated version could conveniently serve as one item on a mixed program. It had a short party scene, one child, no mice and only one soldier. Fedorova's version of the *Nutcracker* introduced this ballet to American audiences all across the country. (The *Nutcracker* was not originally a holiday ballet; it was performed in Russia at all times of the year.)

The *Nutcracker* got generally good reviews. Although Robert Sabin thought it was "something of a bore," he was in the minority. Albertina Vitak found it to be the most successful work of the season. Walter Terry thought that Fedorova's restaging was "splendid" and added, "why it has been absent from a ballet repertory for so long I cannot imagine." Alicia Markova danced the roles of the Snow Queen and the Sugar Plum Fairy, ably partnered by Eglevsky as the Snow King and Cavalier.

However, it was Franklin, "dancing with brilliance, verve and precision in a whirlwind Trepak," according to Vitak, who got the lion's share of good notices in the *Nutcracker*. Sabin wrote, "Frederic Franklin stopped the show with his brilliant performance in the Trepak."[83] Franklin confirms the report of Sabin: "On opening night, I stopped the show. Alicia Markova and André Eglevsky were very upset. She [Markova] was so mean. Bless her heart."[84]

Poker Game (titled at various times as *Jeu de Cartes* and *Card Party*) is a comedy in "three deals." The scenario appended to Stravinsky's original score is quoted below:

The characters in this ballet are the face cards in a game of poker, distributed among several players on the green cloth of a card room. At every deal the situation is complicated by the endless guiles of the perfidious Joker (Frederic Franklin), who believes himself invincible because of his ability to become any desired card. During the first deal, one of the players is beaten, but the other two remain with even "straights," although one of them holds the Joker. In the second deal, the hand that holds the Joker is victorious, thanks to four Aces who easily beat four Queens. Now comes the third deal. The action becomes more and more acute. This time it is a struggle among three "flushes." Although at first victorious over one adversary, the Joker, strutting at the head of a sequence of Spades, is beaten by a "royal flush" in Hearts. This puts an end to his malice and knavery.[85]

Poker Game premiered at the Metropolitan Opera House on April 27, 1937, danced by Balanchine's American Ballet. It was then known as *Card Party*. The Ballet Russe revival, *Poker Game*, debuted on October 14, 1940. There was much enthusiasm for Irene Sharaff's stunning décor, which represented a huge green felt card table with the hand of the croupier at the back. Stravinsky's trenchant score represented the composer neither in his earlier and more vigorous phase, nor in the back-to-Bach incarnation which he assumed later on. It wittily quoted thematic material from the ballet scores of Tchaikovsky and, in the final deal, from Rossini's overture to *The Barber of Seville*.

Balanchine never forgot for one moment that this was a choreographic game of poker, and the deals, shuffling and plays were cleverly drawn. The acrobatic role of the Joker was first danced by William Dollar in 1937. As the inheritor of this role, Franklin was praised for his "superb precision,"[86] as were the four Queens — Alexandra Danilova, Nathalie Krassovska, Alicia Markova and Milada Mladova — who projected the utmost of the spirit and wit of the work.

Balanchine deliberately opted for a narrow range in *Poker Game*. The ballet was content to be simply what it was without false symbolism or hidden meaning. As Edwin Denby noted, "He has the good sense to keep the numbers to their obvious subject: you see the Durante-like Joker egging on the silly Queens against the Aces; you distinguish between Jacks and Kings, you can tell who is winning or losing, and he does not make either too serious for the other. The subject in other words remains real and aboveboard." However, the ballet's very lack of symbolic portent probably prevented it from being a work of wide appeal. When the work was revived again for the New York City Ballet, Doris Hering felt it was merely "a series of long-winded poker deals with a kind of dressed-up literalness. With the exception of charming solos for the four queens, it is a music-hall piece and does not belong in the repertoire of this distinguished company."[87]

Serenade received its first professional performance by the producing company of the School of American Ballet on December 16, 1934. This was Balanchine's first ballet choreographed in America. *Serenade* was an outgrowth of the classes which he had inaugurated at the School of American Ballet. In rapid succession, *Serenade* entered the repertoires of the American Ballet and the Ballet Russe. The latter revival was first seen on October 17, 1940, with guest artist Marie-Jeanne (who had danced the role for the American Ballet).

Set to the music of Tchaikovsky's *Serenade for Strings*, the ballet combines formal design with an intensely lyrical mood. For the sake of building toward a poetic climax, Balanchine took one of his few liberties with the score of a great composer by reversing the order of the third and fourth movements. But this license was slight and justified by his choreographic intent.

A nocturnal atmosphere marks the Sonatina which opens the ballet, as seventeen girls are revealed on a bare stage dressed in blue, romantic-length tutus designed by Jean Lurçat. Arranged in diagonal cross-patterns, the dancers stretch out their right arms, palms forward, as if to ward off unseen danger. Then they turn their heads and touch their wrists to their temples, as if expressing fatigue or despair. Next, led by a solo ballerina (Marie-Jeanne), they begin a flowing, beautifully crafted ensemble section. In the second movement, the Waltz, the ballerina engages a cavalier (Frederic Franklin) in a pas de deux with animated background dancing by the corps de ballet. In the next movement, a Russian theme is sounded. Five girls who have been left onstage from the preceding number move to its measures. The soloists of the Waltz return, and a lively group dance follows. Everyone exits except the ballerina, who has fallen to the floor. To the haunting music of the Larghetto, the principal male soloist (Igor Youskevitch) enters for the first time, accompanied by another ballerina (Milada Mladova). She walks a step behind and blindfolds him with her hand. When they reach the fallen woman, he hovers over her while the standing woman makes swooping arm motions suggestive of a bird or an angel. At the end of the movement, with the pas de trois concluded, the woman who had blindfolded him guides him off as she has led him on. The ballerina melts down to the floor again. Three men enter and pick her up. As they walk slowly offstage, she arches her upper back as if she were preparing for her own sacrifice. The curtain falls.

It's a well-known fact that Balanchine incorporated into the ballet two accidents that happened in rehearsals. At one rehearsal, a dancer dashed into the studio late from her day job and hurriedly took her place among the rows of girls. Balanchine kept her tardy entrance in the ballet. Later, during an exit, a dancer fell down on her on her way off and started crying. This incident formed the basis for the last movement.

Serenade seems to have many undigested scraps of a plot. Like the music, it has hints of tragedy and loss that never quite come to the surface. In his excellent article on *Serenade*, Bruce Fleming sensed that uneasy balance between order and destruction that marks human life: "Individuals fall, or are late, or engage in other all too human actions. The man of the last movement is clearly involved with these two women. But how? ... At the end, it all dissolves into the light and a sense of going somewhere unknown for a reason we cannot fathom."[88]

Critics were very positive. Albertina Vitak wrote, "*Serenade* is one of Balanchine's best works and an excellent example of his ability to inject a dramatic quality into pure ballet movement." Robert Sabin called it "a superb achievement." For him, "finest of all is the adagio, in which Mr. Balanchine dares to indulge in what might be called passionate rhetoric of movement and is brilliantly successful."[89] Today, *Serenade* is performed by numerous regional ballet companies across America and Europe and is the "signature piece" of the New York City Ballet.

It is interesting how ballets and our perception of them change over the years. In the first performances danced by the Ballet Russe, costumer Paul Haikon's dresses were knee-length, short-sleeved and in horrible hues of red and gray. Said Franklin, "They were awful! I was in blue tights with a red heart here [pointing to his left breast]. Igor was in what looked like sackcloth and ashes. I don't know what he was in! And those terrible rolled headbands the girls wore." (Eventually, the Lurçat costumes were restored.) Franklin also recalls that hints of a plot, such as the concluding "Dark Angel" episode, simply didn't exist when he performed the work: "It was originally a piece with students. And now it has become a big story ballet. It never was. When we did it, the last movement didn't mean a thing. All of this happened later."[90]

Nathalie Krassovska and Frederic Franklin in Balanchine's *Serenade* in the original costumes. Ballet Russe de Monte Carlo production, mounted by George Balanchine, 1940. Music: Tchaikovsky. Décor: Longchamp. Costumes: Jean Lurcat. Photograph: Collection of Frederic Franklin.

Franklin was not originally slated to dance in *Serenade*, but took over the male lead in the waltz when George Zoritch sustained an injury. According to Franklin, Balanchine told Denham, "'Well, then, I'd like to use the English boy.' And so my life went on with Mr. Balanchine right from the very beginning."[91]

Massine's *Vienna—1814* first saw the light on October 14, 1940. It was danced to piano pieces by Carl von Weber, orchestrated by Robert Russell Bennett. The scene represented the gala peace ball tendered by Prince Metternich (Marc Platoff) in celebration of the defeat of Napoleon. With the arrival of the ambassadors comes the Princess Lieven (Mia Slavenska), with whom Metternich falls in love. A brilliant polonaise opens the ball, followed by a grand divertissement. The sudden news of Napoleon's escape from the island of Elba causes a panic among the celebrants, though Metternich calms them, prevailing upon the men to exhibit courage, and upon the women to follow their example. Prince Metternich takes tender leave of Princess Lieven.

Both *Vienna — 1814* and the *Nutcracker* were attempts to fill a gap for a classical number in the Petipa tradition. This was once provided by the Petipa divertissement, *Aurora's Wedding*, but that piece was now the property of the de Basil company. As a stock-style suite of ballet variations, *Vienna — 1814* gave the company adequate opportunities to show off the virtuosity of its leading dancers; the plot, however, was no more than a pretext for the divertissement and the display of Stewart Chaney's radiant set and costumes.

The most exciting number in the divertissement was a dazzling dance for the six Legation Secretaries (perhaps because the six were Franklin, Youskevitch, Eglevsky, Zoritch, Roland Guerard and Thomas Armour). The Sicilian Dance for Chris Volkov and a pas de deux for Danilova and Youskevitch were also well received. Massine's duet with Markova as the Chinese Princess and her Unknown Prince failed to make an impression.

Noting its divertissement format, Robert Sabin wrote, "The ballet does not measure up to its predecessors in the same vein." Most critics were puzzled by the ballet's "plot." The title suggested secret pacts and betrayals that were rampant in the Napoleonic Era, but this undercurrent of mystery and political intrigue was seldom in evidence on the stage. Russell Rhodes remarked that *Vienna — 1814* "came to a confused close, as if the choreographer suddenly remembered that he was dealing with an historical episode and recalled himself from a lapse into mere entertainment dancing."[92]

It was writer and caricaturist Rea Irwin of the *New Yorker* staff who suggested a ballet based on the characters who appeared regularly in this magazine. Studying the issues, Massine was quite amused by Irwin's "Eustace Tilley," Helen Hokinson's "Dowager," William Steig's "Small Fry," and Otto Soglow's "Little King." Massine wrote the libretto in collaboration with Irwin.

The score for *The New Yorker* was assembled from a number of George Gershwin's popular songs and concert works. Gershwin selections included "Strike Up the Band," "I Got Rhythm," "Swanee," "Fascinating Rhythm," "Let's Call the Whole Thing Off," and a less familiar Gershwin tune called "Walking the Dog." (Fred Astaire and Ginger Rogers walked their puppies on ship deck to this tune in the 1937 movie *Shall We Dance.*)

Leading roles were danced by Tatiana Chamié as the Hokinson Lady, George Zoritch as Eustace Tilley, Casimir Kokitch as the Maitre d'Hotel, Nathalie Krassovska as the Debutante, André Eglevsky, Roland Guerard and Igor Youskevitch as her Three Boyfriends, Lubov Roudenko and Ian Gibson as the Small Fry, Alexandra Danilova as the Girl, and Frederic Franklin as the Gossip Columnist. In the first scene, the characters were introduced in front of a drop showing the exterior of a nightclub. The second of Carl Kent's drops (both unremarkable) showed the nightclub's interior. Once inside, a divertissement for the leading characters took place.

The New Yorker premiered on October 18, 1940. The choreographic climax occurred in the opening section with the anticipation aroused by the rowdy playing of "Strike Up the Band" and the introduction of the main characters to "Walking the Dog." The opening had some gaiety and a glow of originality, but from there the action took a nosedive. Albertina Vitak reported, "There just wasn't anything for them to do once they were assembled on the stage except many, too many, numbers of a sort of ring-around-the-rosy." Walter Terry put it this way: "Massine doesn't seem to realize that a Hokinson woman and an Arno old man with a white mustache are not funny in themselves, but funny when they get caught up in a predicament foreign to their characters."

The second-scene nightclub divertissement was overlong, and most of its dances fell flat. For Irving Kolodin, "the venom of Steig was absent from the hoydenish pair [Small Fry] who danced 'Let's Call the Whole Thing Off,'" and the burlesque on adagio acts performed by the Debutante and her Three Boyfriends was "not sufficiently pointed to make its intent apparent." In the next number, Vitak was appalled when "Danilova was dragged in and performed a sort of pseudo-tap dance sur les pointes."

Throughout the ballet, the corps de ballet performed theatrical versions of such social dances as the suzy-q, conga and lindy hop. But trained ballet dancers were out of their element compared to bona fide Harlem "rug-cutters." They were not as good as the real thing, nor did they satirize the real thing. Frederic Franklin, though, was an exception because his teenage background as a hoofer gave him a sure sense of style as the Gossip Columnist. Walter Terry remarked, "In the midst of this poor imitation of America at play, the dancing of Frederic Franklin fairly glittered."[93] However, Freddie did not please everyone in the press. Real-life gossip columnist Walter Winchell was incensed and wrote a nasty column after the premiere about that "ballet man" impersonating him.[94]

Constant revision of the ballet continued throughout the New York engagement; Massine even tried to rescue the ballet by changing his merely incidental role as a house painter into a principal role. His new character — the Timid Man — is set loose in the nightclub and coerced into dancing with a steamy siren. It was one of Massine's funniest characterizations, but it was not enough to save the ballet. The New Yorker was defeated almost before it began because it had no real libretto or even a sustained satiric mood. Terry's verdict that it was "one of the worst ballets that it has been my misfortune to see in a long time" and Vitak's that "it really would be best if it were just quietly forgotten" [95] were representative.

In 1940, Massine was the most celebrated choreographer in the world. Referring to the twin failures of The New Yorker and Vienna—1814, Terry wrote, "this seems to be an off year for the great man."[96] Sadly, 1940 would mark the beginning of a long and discouraging slump for Massine, a development which would have surprised Terry when he penned those words.

With the Fifty-first Street Theatre season behind them, the Denham company departed on a long tour of the United States and Canada and did not return to New York until the fall of 1941. Relations between Massine and Serge Denham, always strained, now began to erode at an escalating pace. During the company's first season, Massine was almost invincible — he had no rival in international prestige or in his ability to attract investors on both sides of the Atlantic. But Massine was inevitably weakened by the facts that he was cut off from his main power base in Europe and that America's ballet pioneers were eager to get rid of him. Denham started to chip away at Léonide's power base.

Denham started by giving Massine unsolicited advice on artistic decisions, which prompted angry retorts from Massine. Denham was also trying to prevent him from choreographing any more symphonic ballets, suggesting in a letter to Julius Fleischmann that they were box-office poison. And, of course, he brought in Balanchine to stage three works for the Ballet Russe, beginning in 1939–40. *Dance* magazine reported rumors about the Massine/Denham standoff and alluded to another rumor that Denham had "discussed with George Balanchine the possibility of the latter's replacing Massine as director."[97]

Salvador Dalí was back on the scene, and he took Massine's mind off of the political squabbles for a while. For this second ballet collaboration, he wanted to use Schubert's Symphony No. 7 for a modern rendering of the story of Theseus and Ariadne. He saw a parallel between the uninterrupted continuity of Schubert's melody and the ball of thread which Ariadne gave Theseus to guide him out of the labyrinth.

Once he was drawn into the project, Massine related that he was "both amused and revolted" by some of Dalí's bizarre ideas. For instance, Massine "drew the line" when Dalí suggested that, as a symbol of destruction, the stagehands should drop a Steinway piano onto the stage from the catwalks. Dalí also wanted to use a real calf's head for the episode in which Theseus kills the Minotaur, to be followed by a scene in which the dancers would ceremoniously cut off chunks from the carnage and eat them raw. In his most accommodating mood, Massine accompanied Dalí on a taxi ride to Sixth Avenue where he reported, "we visited one restaurant after another in search of a calf's head. The waiters were stunned, but polite; the best they could do was offer us a veal sandwich!"[98] Thus began the second Dalí-Massine collaboration. It may have been a fiasco, but no one could say it was dull.

The program notes are as follows:

> In Labyrinth one revives the eternal myth of the aesthetic and ideologic confusion which characterizes romanticism, and especially, in the highest degree that of our epoch. The "thread of Ariadne," thanks to which Theseus succeeds in finding the exit from the labyrinth, symbolizes the tradition, the continuity, the thread of classicism, the savior. All romanticism merely searches more or less dramatically for its "thread of Ariadne," of classicism.

In the action of the ballet, the three Fates, who symbolize destiny, attempt to prevent Theseus (André Eglevsky) from entering the labyrinth. But Theseus overpowers his destiny, enters the labyrinth, kills the Minotaur (Frederic Franklin) and thanks to the thread of Ariadne (Tamara Toumonova), finds the exit from that abode of death. Theseus abandons Ariadne on the shore and sets sail for fresh adventures.[99]

Labyrinth's theme — the triumph of classicism over romanticism — reflects the period of Dalí's career when he was moving toward a more traditional style. His vehement distaste for the *dernier cri* in modern art is unmistakable by the time of his 1942 essay "Tradition vs. Modern Times." *Labyrinth* abounded in the same surrealist props that had adorned *Bacchanale*, but there was no levity in *Labyrinth*'s visual imagery.

Dalí designed four tableaux for the four different scenes. The opening scene revealed a tremendous cracked skull and a chest carved out by a tall doorway which gave the effect of archaic grandeur. The second scene, in which Theseus fights the Minotaur, was highlighted by a throne composed of human skulls. The third scene, a corridor of the labyrinth, was memorable mainly for Dalí's ingenious costumes for the Roosters. They were designed to be worn backwards and took advantage of the natural bend of the human knee to lend realism to the posterior flexion of a rooster's knee; this reverse orientation also allowed the arms to function more plausibly as wings. The fourth scene was a seascape. The corps de ballet wore frothy headdresses of white bows: gathered in a clump, they formed a white crest and became a great wave on which Theseus was tossed.

Massine must have sensed from the start that *Labyrinth* would be seen mainly as another Dalí art exhibit. Even the musical choice was Dalí's. Schubert's symphony proved to be insuperably difficult to interpret through dance. It is emphatically unkinetic and was a most unhappy choice for *Labyrinth*.

When the work premiered at the Metropolitan Opera House on October 8, 1941, several reviewers used the word "listless" to describe Massine's choreography for *Labyrinth*. He did not, for instance, take advantage of Toumanova's virtuosic technique. In the second scene, trussed on a narrow overhead platform, she represented what appeared to be a spool of thread, slowly revolving to unwind the thread of deliverance, and that was about the extent of the dancing given to her. As the Minotaur, Franklin's task was to look frightening in a series of threatening poses. He did not succeed in being scary because his costume — a 12-inch unicorn horn and a shaggy, hip-slung miniskirt — provoked more titters than terror from the audience. Yet here and there, Massine rallied and did some imaginative work. The jovial cockfight and the pas de deux for Castor and Pollux (George Zoritch and Chris Volkov), an electrifying blend of ballet and virile athleticism, provided two interludes where the dancing actually upstaged the decor.

In his analysis of *Labyrinth* in *Supplement to the Complete Book of Ballets*, Cyril Beaumont dispensed with his normally comprehensive analysis and said only, "The consensus of opinion of American critics is that the scenery and costumes have been allowed to dominate instead of contribute to the ballet, to the detriment of the production as a whole."[100] Ironically, the music and settings trapped Massine in a labyrinth of his own. And, unlike Ariadne, neither Schubert nor Dalí gave him a thread to guide him out of his artistic maze.

Massine's second ballet, *Saratoga*, had no chance of success from the get-go because exceedingly poor material was foisted on him. To reduce financial risks, Universal Art announced that from the fall of 1941 onward, they would produce only ballets directly sponsored by individual backers. By now, Massine had earned the right to choose his own composers, designers and librettists. Suddenly, he was saddled with a score and libretto that were thrown on his lap as a fait accompli.

The scene for the ballet is turn-of-the-century Saratoga at the height of the racing season. Throngs of elegant patrons parade the streets. A widowed dowager (Tatiana Chamié) enters with her beautiful Daughter (Alexandra Danilova). Although she is somewhat out of her element at this swanky resort, Mama is determined to marry her

Daughter off and has made arrangements for a rendezvous with a Wealthy Suitor (Nicholas Beriozov). When the codger arrives, the daughter's face falls in dismay — he is rotund, crude and ugly.

A Young Jockey (Frederic Franklin) enters and shows off his racing skills with imaginary reins and a riding crop. Eight more jockeys and a group of debutantes join him in the dance. When the Young Jockey invites the Daughter to dance, their amorous duet is too much for the Wealthy Suitor — he snatches the young upstart's jockey cap and stamps on it! Mama pulls the Daughter off by the ear for a private chat, the Wealthy Suitor storms off indignantly, and the crowd disperses. A pair of Dandies (Tamara Toumonova, Léonide Massine) enter and dance a spirited cakewalk.

Bugles sound: the race is about to begin. The crowd gathers excitedly, facing the track at the back of the stage. Whistles sound, and the horses are off. In a successive wave, the jockeys leap high above the guard rails, first one and then another taking the lead. At the home stretch, the Young Jockey and his chief rival are neck-and-neck; the Daughter's heart leaps in her throat as her sweetheart surges ahead to win by a nose.

Now the owner of a handsome purse, the Young Jockey approaches Mama and begs to become her son-in-law. Mama glances down at his bulging nugget pouch and consents at once. Not to be left out, the Wealthy Suitor proposes to Mama — a double wedding! Borne on the shoulders of the cheering throng, the couples and ensemble frolic in blissful anticipation of the nuptial rites, their rapture equaled only by that of the audience.

A great deal of money was lavished on the costumes and scenery of Alvin Colt and Oliver Smith. Colt's colorful turn-of-the-century costumes were the sole features of this ballet to win praise. Both the score and libretto were by Jaromír Weinberger, a Czechoslovakian, naturalized composer. Weinberger is remembered as the composer of the opera *Schwanda the Bagpiper* and of little else. His score for *Saratoga* was written, appropriately enough, as though it was a potpourri of Gay Nineties tunes. However, the similarity of the ditties began to pall after a while. For Robert Sabin, it was "written in the style of a third-rate musical comedy of ten or fifteen years ago, and it succeeds in being singularly bad, even in that cheap and outmoded idiom."[101] The quality of Weinberger's libretto for *Saratoga* speaks for itself.

Saddled with such a sophomoric score and story, Massine again did his work half-heartedly, for the dancing was minimal, and there was a good deal of aimless wandering. For the horse race, though, Massine concocted a clever way to visualize the contest by having the jockeys perform *grand jetés* in canon across the back of the stage. They were hidden from the waist down by the guard rails, so that each was only fully visible at the height of his leap. Massine often designed his character ballets to simmer up to a "potboiler" finale. In most of his ballets, this gimmick worked well: Massine gradually filled the stage with progressive waves of animated dancers and then raised the energy to a fever pitch in a whirlwind climax. But this device could not rescue *Saratoga* because the preceding scenes fell too flat to empower such a climax. To make matters worse, reviews indicate that the dancers were also under-rehearsed, making it hard to judge which was worse — the choreography or its execution. In addition to the premieres, the Ballet Russe had seventeen other ballets in the repertory in the fall of 1941. This put a staggering burden on the corps de ballet, and it showed.

Frederic Franklin and Alexandra Danilova in *Saratoga*. 1941. Ballet Russe de Monte Carlo production. Photograph: Maurice Seymour, courtesy of Ronald Seymour.

Knowing that this ballet was in trouble, Massine decided to insert a cakewalk as a feature spot for Toumanova and himself two weeks after the premiere. They rehearsed this duet on the sly, and no one else in the cast knew a thing about it. One night, Franklin and Danilova were standing in the wings, having finished their polka. Suddenly they saw Toumanova and Massine in their costumes, Toumanova's being twice as elaborate and expensive as the frock that Danilova had been given to wear. "What are they doing?" Danilova asked Freddie. She found out soon enough, for they went onstage, performed a spirited and crowd-pleasing cakewalk and on their exit, headed lickety-split for their dressing rooms. "Choura was beside herself," said Franklin. "She was livid."[102]

Although it was charming, the cakewalk was a contrived interpolation in an already contrived ballet, a brief respite from the ennui that prevailed on both sides of the foot-lights.

Saratoga premiered at the Met on October 19, 1941. Reviews were disastrous. Robert Sabin: "an all-time low"; Walter Terry: "pretty tragic"; Henry Simon: "Saratoga Misses the Spitoon"— and so on. But at least there were good notices for Freddie: Terry wrote, "He literally pulled the miserably flopping *Saratoga* into the realm of entertainment when he was on stage, with the boundless exuberance of his dancing."[103]

It borders on the tragic that this ballet was dumped on Massine at the very time when he most desperately needed a hit. *Saratoga*'s failure was seen as final confirma-tion of a serious artistic slump. He would spend the better part of the next thirty-eight years trying to prove his continuing creative vitality, but without the benefit of his own ballet company. *Saratoga* was Massine's last ballet as artistic director of the Ballet Russe de Monte Carlo.

If anything good came out of this ballet, it at least occasioned a change in Franklin's cool and distant relations with Danilova. At one performance of *Saratoga*, in the mid-dle of the pas de deux, Danilova went blank. Franklin prompted her by whispering the names of the steps in her ear as they danced along. When they reached the wings, Danilova was livid: "How dare you do that! You know you must never speak to me onstage!" A few moments later, when she had calmed down, she apologized and told Franklin, "You may call me Choura," the nickname which only her closest friends were permitted to use when addressing her. "I said 'Yes, Madame Danilova.' 'No, what is my name?' So I said, 'Choura.' And she said, 'you say it beautifully. Now I will take you to supper.'"[104]

The Magic Swan was the third new offering of the 1941–42 Met season. It was a recon-struction of Act III of *Swan Lake*, with choreography by Alexandra Fedorova, patterned after the original by Petipa. *The Magic Swan* was first performed on October 13, 1941. The cast was headed by Tamara Toumanova (Odile) and Igor Youskevitch (Prince Siegfried). This, the divertissement act of the ballet, included a mazurka (led by Eleanora Marra and Marc Platoff), a czardas (led by Lubov Roudenko and Frederic Franklin), a pas de trois (Leila Crabtree, Dorothy Etheridge and Roland Guerard), a Spanish dance (Milada Mladova and Casimir Kokitch), a tarantella (Sonia Woicikowska and Harold Lang) and a waltz (led by Lubov Rostova and George Zoritch). The ballet concluded with the brilliant "Black Swan Grand Pas de Deux" for Toumanova and Youskevitch. The production paused just before the end to throw in a faint semblance of a plot, when Odette fluttered despairingly by the stage-left wing and then flew off, unnoticed by the assemblage. The ending was confusing for audience members because most didn't know the plot of *Swan Lake* in those days. As expressed by Walter Terry, "It is a bit startling to have a storyless one-act ballet wind up with the ballerina laughing maniacally at a stumbling hero who has been stricken by a vision of a white swan."[105] Had Denham asked Fedorova to restage both Acts II and III, the ballet would have had much more cohesion.

While the choreography of the grand pas de deux was authentic Petipa, to what extent the other dances in *The Magic Swan* were staged after Petipa is open to conjecture. Anatole Chujoy thought that the character dances and pas de trois were not very inventive and that the performances were on a higher level than the choreography. Walter Terry thought that the choreography "is not worthy of a dancing school's annual recital."[106] In a mind-boggling programming gaffe, *The Magic Swan* was presented with *Vienna—1814* on its opening night. Both had a ballroom scene, a thread of a (confusing) plot, and were, in essence, divertissements.

After a two-year absence from the United States, de Basil's Original Ballet Russe came to the Big Apple in November of 1941. John Martin believed that the auspices for de Basil's company were quite fortunate "because it comes on the heels of what has been undoubtedly the least distinguished season Massine's company has given." Like Martin, Walter Terry pointed to sloppiness on the part of everyone from the dancers to the stage technicians: "On the debit side, one finds a lighting system which seems to be left entirely in the hands of pixies and a corps de ballet which sends you streaking for the Music Hall Rockettes."[107]

In January of 1942 Massine attempted to prove his continuing artistic vitality by sending Denham a list of twenty ballets he was prepared to undertake over the next few years. But by then, Léonide's unbroken series of ballet failures had put Denham in the driver's seat. In a letter to Fleischmann, Denham spoke of a need to curb Massine's artistic activities and to commission more works from Balanchine.

Sol Hurok called Denham "a mere tyro at ballet and an amateur at that." He wrote, "I had not devoted twenty-eight years of hard, slogging work to the building of good ballet in America to allow it to deteriorate into a shambles because of the arbitrariness of another would-be Diaghileff." Springing to Massine's defense, he noted, "Massine had given of his best to create and maintain a fine organization. He had been a shining example to the others. The company had started on a high plane of accomplishments; but it was impossible for Massine to continue under conditions that daily became less and less bearable."[108]

It was Hurok who actually dominated the ballet world by 1940. In addition to his far-reaching booking apparatus, he alone held the exclusive lease for ballet productions at the Metropolitan Opera House. Thus, he held the fate of any company he sponsored in his powerful hands. In 1941 Hurok dropped his exclusive contract with Denham's company and signed on as impresario for the up-and-coming Ballet Theatre, which had given its first performance on January 11, 1940. Hurok wanted to secure Massine's services for Ballet Theatre. He was shrewdly aware that to the general American public, "ballet" still meant Russian ballet, which, outside the cognoscenti, still meant Massine. His management policy was to embrace "Russianization" to ensure good box-office for Ballet Theatre.

Almost undoubtedly in an effort to further his plans, Hurok selected two dismal failures—*Labyrinth* and *Saratoga*—for the April 6, 1942, Ballet Russe opening night at the Met. This doomsday program was characterized by Walter Terry as "ballet at its nadir." He added, "The current weakness of the Ballet Russe de Monte Carlo is not a sudden occurrence. The process of enervation commenced months, perhaps years ago, and a good share of the blame must be laid to its artistic director.... Every creator needs a rest, and Massine has needed one for two years."[109] The suggestion that he needed a "rest" could only have goaded Massine to follow Hurok's suggestion of obtaining a leave of absence from the Ballet Russe in order to create two new works for Ballet Theatre in the summer of 1942.

Franklin was devoted to Massine. In an interview, he said that that the four "greats" of his life were Dolin, Markova, Balanchine and Massine."[110] He must have been saddened by the downward spiral of Léonide's fortunes at a time when his own career was flourishing. On April 8, Freddie danced the leading roles in all three ballets presented — *Schéhérazade*, the *Polovetsian Dances* and *Seventh Symphony*. Walter Terry was mightily impressed. In an article entitled "Three Times a Star," he noted, "Each role required totally different styles and characterizations of the dancer. Franklin met these demands without hesitation as he proved beyond argument that in him the art of ballet possesses one of its brightest stars." He added that Franklin's performances "helped to wipe out the tragic memory of the Monte Carlo's unfortunate and inept opening program of Monday evening."[111]

In the summer of 1941, while the company was in California appearing at the Hollywood Bowl, motion pictures were made of *Gaîté Parisienne* and *Capriccio Espagnol*. The film titles were *The Gay Parisian* and *Spanish Fiesta*. It was found that Franklin screened well, and in addition to playing his own role as the Baron, a special part was written into *Spanish Fiesta* for him.

Alexandra Danilova did not fare so well. For her film test, she was not asked to dance, but just to pose in practice clothes. In the meantime, the beautiful Milada Mladova was being dressed in the most becoming costume available. Although Danilova was hardly an ugly duckling, she did have a tilt of the nose that made it appear in photographs to be slightly crooked. Jose Negulesco, the director of *The Gay Parisian*, chose Mladova to replace Danilova in her most famous role. He told Mladova, who genuinely hesitated to assume the role so closely associated with this legendary ballerina, that he was not planning to use Danilova because she was neither young enough nor photogenic enough. When he explained his reasons to Danilova, she snapped, "My *nose* doesn't dance,"[112] and she ran out of the room in tears. Feelings in the company ran very high, and resentment was hardly mitigated when Danilova was asked to personally teach her role to Mladova.[113]

The film, wretchedly photographed and edited, was a bitter disappointment to all who were familiar with the ballet. The chance to recapture in Technicolor one of Danilova's most sophisticated interpretations of all time was lost. In his review of *The Gay Parisian*, Terry wrote, that it was "pretentious and far from direct in its approach to ballet ... the dances themselves have lost much of their original flavor due to the nervous camera eye, which refused to light on any one spot for any length of time. Just as a dance was beginning to make its patterns and its moods felt, the camera wandered off to view a staircase, a row of bottles and someone's face." (In one instance, Mladova's extended leg in one of the adagio lifts was lopped off in mid-air.) Terry noted, "Milada Mladova does nothing to make the Glove Seller the worldly, highly romantic and slightly tough figure she should be.... Frederic Franklin's role has been twisted about to the point where the dashing baron emerges as a study in boredom."

Leads in *Spanish Fiesta* were Danilova, Toumanova, Franklin, and Massine. Terry

Scene from the 1941 Warner Brothers film *The Gay Parisian*. Directed by Negulesco, based upon the ballet Gaîté Parisienne (1938). Choreography : Léonide Massine. Pictured are Massine (left) as the Peruvian, Milada Mladova as the Glove Seller and Franklin as the Baron.

found it to be the better of the two films: "The general design of the ballet has been followed, and the camera keeps its focus upon the dances so that the sequences of action are easily understood and permitted to arrive at a logical and dynamically forceful conclusion."[114] So impressed were Warner Brothers executives with Franklin that they offered him a seven-year contract; Freddie was tempted, but feared the move would put an end to his ballet career.

When Massine began preparations for the next fall season, his connections with the company were severed. His contract as artistic director (due to expire in 1948) was annulled in November of 1942. Massine wrote, "After working for them for three years, I was summarily dismissed. It was a bitter blow, which left me feeling bereft and disillusioned."[115] On November 19, Massine officially joined Ballet Theatre.

· 3 ·

A Roper, a Pimp and a Poet:
Agnes, Ruth and Mr. B.

The 1941–42 season had been a miserable one from the standpoint of new productions. The company badly needed a hit for the next season. It got one. Agnes de Mille's *Rodeo, or the Courting at Burnt Ranch* premiered on October 16, 1942, at the Metropolitan Opera House.

Because both the 1938 *Billy the Kid* and the 1942 *Rodeo* had Western settings, cowboys, horses, riding movements and scores by Aaron Copland, comparisons were inevitable, but de Mille denied that she had been influenced by *Billy*'s choreographer, Eugene Loring. *Rodeo* was an outgrowth of dances she had staged in London, when de Mille had worked with a handful of Marie Rambert's dancers who were willing to perform for nothing. She worked on a long piece entitled *American Suite*. Of its four parts, three were enlarged versions of dances she had performed alone: "The Harvesting," "Dust," and "49." The fourth part was called "The Rodeo." This gestational version of *Rodeo* contained all the basic movements Agnes would use in the Ballet Russe incarnation — the riding, the roping, the rhythms of galloping horses, the trotting, the prancing, the pawing, the slides across the floor.[1] The "Rodeo" sketch was first performed publicly on April 25, 1938, in Norwich with de Mille, Hugh Laing and Peggy von Praagh in the solo roles.

When she returned to the States, de Mille became very disheartened. She had spent fourteen years trying to prove her mettle in the dance world, and she didn't have much to show for it. She had only a mixed success with her 1941 *Three Virgins and a Devil* for Ballet Theatre. The work used a crude, naturalistic humor that was far inferior to that devised in *American Suite*. Now, de Mille had no prospects for the future. She intended to throw in the towel, go to Macy's, and get a job at the ribbon counter. In the meanwhile, dance writer Irving Deakin was trying to persuade Serge Denham that it would be a novelty to have an American ballet by a real American and not by Massine. Irving was pushing for de Mille. Agnes had nothing ready, but neither did she have a job. She decided to enlarge on "The Rodeo" sketch and add a scenario: "Drain-

73

ing great pots of tea,"[2] she wrote it out and submitted it to Denham. This is what she cooked up:

Cowboys are loafing around Burnt Ranch, gathered for the weekly rodeo. They ride bucking hoses (imitating the equine movements in stylized choreography). However, their display of riding and roping is continually interrupted by the attention-seeking Cowgirl (Agnes de Mille). The Cowgirl has an enormous crush on the Head Wrangler (Casimir Kokitch), who barely tolerates her.

To the delight of all of the Ranch hands, several glamorous young ladies from Kansas City have arrived for a visit with the Rancher's Daughter (Milada Mladova). In an effort to attract attention, the Cowgirl tries to manage a bucking bronco and gets thrown for her troubles. Everybody, especially the city girls, laugh and jeer at her. The Head Wrangler tells her to leave, which she does, acting nonchalant even though she's broken-hearted. The cowboys pair up with the girls and stroll the grounds in hushed groups. Suddenly, the Champion Roper (Frederic Franklin) shatters their reverie with a tap dance — it's time to get ready for the Saturday-night hoedown. When the Cowgirl returns, she is crushed to see the Head Wrangler going off with the Rancher's Daughter.

In the Interlude before Scene two, the lights come up on a downstage curtain of prancing horses, which shields the setting-up for Scene Two. Four couples move faster and faster as the Caller shouts, "Ladies to the center, form a star. Gentlemen forward and back to the bar." There is no music at this point, only handclaps from the musicians in the orchestra pit and the dancers themselves.

In Scene Two, the inner curtain rises to reveal the ranch house. The Saturday- night party is in full swing. The Cowgirl, not yet recovered from her melancholy of the afternoon, sits alone on a bench at the side. She is still dressed in the dusty man's clothes she had worn in the afternoon. The Champion Roper tries to cheer and tidy her up a bit, brushing off her dusty bottom. He has troubles of his own, for the Champion Roper has a crush on the Rancher's Daughter. But alas, this beauty only has eyes for the Head Wrangler. Now comes the time for the community dance. Boys line up on one side and girls on the other to choose partners. Nobody picks the Cowgirl, and she's mortified that she is the *only* girl not to be chosen. Determined to cheer her up, the Champion Roper consoles her and even dances with her. Suddenly she stops dead in her tracks — she sees the Head Wrangler dancing amorously with the Rancher's Daughter. The Roper is fed up and smacks the ingrate on her behind. Having reached the limits of humiliation, the Cowgirl runs into the house.

As the party builds to a peak of excitement, the Champion Roper steps forward to clap the rhythms of a hoedown. During the dance that follows, he chases the Rancher's Daughter — without success. Suddenly the Cowgirl reappears, and her entrance causes a sensation. She has put on a pretty dress and decorated her hair with a bow. The men fall all over themselves: she is beautiful! The Wrangler and the Roper vie for the privilege of dancing with her. She is tugged to and fro between them, until the Champion Roper, who has always liked her and is now really in love with her, gives her a kiss on the lips. In a sudden epiphany, the Cowgirl realizes that it is actually the Roper, not the Wrangler, whom she has loved all along. The ballet ends with a vigorous dance for the full cast.

To de Mille's great relief, Denham was interested in her tale, and he summoned her to an interview. At their first meeting, de Mille noted, "He tiptoes through large circumventions and maneuverings with pussy-cat elegance." He spoke "with the caressing rubato of enthusiasm as he talked of grandiose monetary involvements, or Michelangelo, or the advisability of accepting an insupportable salary." After five months of wrangling with her lawyer, Denham finally offered de Mille five hundred dollars for her scenario and choreography. De Mille noted, "this guaranteed me twenty-five dollars a week, just about the ribbon saleswoman's salary I'd hankered after."[3] One condition of the contract was that de Mille herself would dance the Cowgirl for the first New York performances. Once contracts were drawn with composer Aaron Copland, designer Oliver Smith and costumer Kermit Love, the project was up and running.

De Mille accompanied the Ballet Russe on its tour in the spring of 1942. In her autobiography, she describes what she was up against: "Rehearsal time was limited and the dancers were exhausted. They carried in their heads a repertory of thirty or forty ballets ... performing until 11:30 nearly every night, sleeping more often in Pullman cars than in hotels. Understandably, they were not eager to learn a new ballet at 10:30 the next morning, especially from a woman."[4] What de Mille does not mention is that some dancers also looked down on her because of her limited ballet technique.

When de Mille had belatedly started ballet training at the Koslov School in Los Angeles, she tackled it with typically expressionist *Sturm und Drang*. Her mother allowed her only two lessons a week, and de Mille tried to compensate for this by practicing on her own, working with the most violent effort. Her private practice, while her technique was still unformed, gave her many faults which she never succeeded in completely eradicating. For George Amberg, even more serious was the "wrong attitude which she developed towards the classical technique. Instead of it becoming for her a natural means of expression, it remained a distant and almost unattainable goal which could only be approached by superhuman efforts; one might almost say that it was for her an enemy to be conquered by brute force."[5]

De Mille started rehearsals for *Rodeo* while the company was performing at the Hollywood Bowl. She recalled, "I asked for the men first. If I could break them, I would have the whole company in my hand." De Mille was terrified when the time came for this dreaded first rehearsal: "I turned deliberately and faced them. There they were — nineteen of them. Male. Great muscled brutes leaning against the barre and staring with watchful smoldering eyes. Behind them were Paris, Covent Garden, Monte Carlo and, in three cases, the Maryinsky. And behind me? A wall." She continued, "I took a deep breath. 'We are going to begin,' I said in a scarcely audible treble, 'with men riding horses in a rodeo. For instance, if you were riding a bucking horse and were thrown, it would look like this.'" She then hurled herself across the studio, crashing to the floor on her head. Franklin (cast as the Champion Roper) rushed over to her and admonished, "Darling, you'll hurt yourself!" "Did it look good, Freddie?" she asked. "It looked wonderful! But you'll kill yourself!" he replied. "Not me," she said. "It's you who are to do it." Franklin then turned to the nonplussed men in the studio and said, "Well, no help for it. Come on boys, let's have a try."[6]

De Mille had sound logic for her movement, and she knew exactly what she wanted. She wanted to express the exhilaration of riding, but the movements were very difficult

because the dancer "had always to look as though he were propelled by an unseen animal.... He did not jump, he was thrown or wrenched upwards. His feet never touched
earth, it was the horses' feet that clattered in the pebbles. The very essence of the movement was shock, spasm and effort." "Don't plié!" she shouted at the men. "Sit your
horses. There's a difference."[7]

For the next two hours, de Mille "rolled on the floor with them, lurched, con-
torted, jack-knifed, hung suspended and ground my teeth." She claims that she bested
the boys in resilience and endurance: "I broke them to my handling. I broke them technically, which was where they lived and worshipped." But, actually, her triumph was
far from complete at first. Some of the Russians were still lolling at the barre, taking a
very dim view of the proceedings: "'It is not dancing,' they said. But I had never said
it was, and I was delighted to excuse them. They picked up their towels and left in
haughty silence." From eighteen cowboys, de Mille settled for ten. When he heard from
the disapproving male dancers, Denham lost no time in contacting de Mille's lawyer,
insisting on a clause guaranteeing him the right of veto. De Mille said no: "This was
my last job, and I intended to have fun and do exactly what I pleased."[8]

Although much of her seeming assurance was bravado, de Mille did look down
her nose at the Ballet Russe as a "down-at-heel, shabby company who had got by with
hokum for far too long."[9] If she communicated this sentiment to her dancers, even sub-
liminally, it may explain why her rapport with them wasn't always what it should have
been. Add to this the fact that her choreography was not only alien to the men, but
also so strenuous that they had sore muscles all over their bodies. One day, Casimir
Kokitch, the Head Wrangler, reached the end of his rope. Dancer George Zoritch has
graced us with this account:

> He got more cocky and arrogant by the minute, while Agnes de Mille tried to convince Kokitch
> to do her zippity-doo-dah movements. After a hangover from the previous night, he became less
> cooperative and told her, "I am classical dancer. I do *entrechat six, glissade, grand jeté, grand pirou-
> ette* ... but what is this?" He then proceeded to imitate her choreography, hopping on an imagi-
> nary horse, slapping himself on the rump, turning his back, making the sound of a horse breaking
> wind, and trotting away offstage. Miss de Mille could not take the humiliation, bursting into tears
> in complete frustration.[10]

Even the more docile females gave de Mille a hard time. Agnes spent two hours
with them working strictly on characterization rather than dance steps, which the ladies
found unreasonable. According to de Mille, they told her, "Oh Madame, we will be
funny when we have costumes. Please do not concern yourself. We will assuredly be
funny." "You be funny right now on count *eight*!" snapped de Mille.[11]

Lubov (Luba) Roudenko was slated to take over the role of the Cowgirl after de
Mille's departure. De Mille relates, "Luba Roudenko came to me. She was very happy
with the role, but her friends had told her she had a great technique and might she
please, Miss de Mille, might she please do some *fouettés* in the hoedown? I said no." A
few days after this chat, "Luba Roudenko came to me. She was very happy with the
leading role, but her friends had told her she was not showing off her strong technique.
Perhaps if she did some *batterie* and brilliant *chainé* turns in the hoedown? I said no."
Of the third encounter, de Mille wrote "Luba Roudenko came to me. I said no."[12]

Even Freddie had his differences with Miss de Mille. After the Hollywood Bowl

Frederic Franklin as the Champion Roper in *Rodeo*. 1942. Ballet Russe de Monte Carlo production. Photograph: Maurice Seymour, courtesy of Ronald Seymour.

performances, when the company went on the road again, de Mille told Franklin on the train that she planned to end the ballet with the loving union of the Cowgirl and the Head Wrangler. Franklin said, "What! Well, in that case, Agnes, I won't be in your ballet. It's not right. I go through all of this fuss, and then you go off with somebody else." For the next three days, Freddie didn't go near de Mille's rehearsals. Then he got a telephone call from Agnes. She said, "You know I just realized how right you are. I have a crush on the Head Wrangler, but I spend all of my time with you in the ballet. Suddenly it dawned on me — that's the right ending! Fred, come back! How could I have been so stupid?[13] The surprise twist at the end of *Rodeo* is one of the best conclusions a ballet has ever had because it is so inevitably right. But had Freddie not threatened to quit, we might well have been left with an ending of a very different sort — predictable and banal.

Once he returned to the fold, Frederic became Agnes's right-hand man throughout her time of tribulation. She drew strength from his boundless energy: "There was always Freddie, barking the counts and snapping at their feet. And dancing, dancing until the sweat poured from his back and head."[14] "'Oh, darling,' he would say gasping, 'this is impossible. Well, there's no help for it. Come on boys, let's try.'"[15] Looking back, she wrote, "He [Franklin] was as strong as a mustang, as sudden, as direct, and as inexhaustible. There was no slacking off at the end of a long effort, no marking. He came into the room briskly, dressed and ready at the first minute of rehearsal. And he worked full out without a second's deviation of attention until the rehearsal finished, and the very last lift was as precise and as vigorous as the first."[16]

In September, the company returned to New York. By then, some of the Russians were starting to understand and to like *Rodeo*, and it began to look like a hit. On opening night, the cast waited nervously backstage in their cowboy pants. Franklin spat over de Mille's shoulder and bumped his knee against her rump. For the quaking de Mille, "This was a terrible moment, but I had company. I was no longer alone." She stated, "if it is possible for a life to change at one given moment, if it is possible for all movement, growth and accumulated power to become apparent at one single point, then my own struck at 9:40, October 16, 1942."[17]

Chewing gum, squinting her eyes under a Texas hat, Agnes strode onstage. There was applause on her first exit, which she hadn't expected. In fact there was applause or laughter on almost every phrase as the ballet proceeded. And — yes — they laughed at the girls on count eight, just as de Mille had told them they would. The dancers were elated:

"Great exchanges of excitement and force and gaiety were taking place all around.... And throughout the pace which was too quick for me, beyond my understanding, faster than could be savored or appreciated, was Freddie's hand, Freddie's arm, Freddie's strong back propelling, pushing, carrying, and Freddie's feet like bullets on the wood."[18]

When the ballet reached the exhausting closing hoedown, de Mille nearly collapsed. At the back of the stage she gasped to Franklin, "I'm fainting. Loosen my collar." "No time duckie," he said. "Here we go." He then propelled her to the footlights. When the curtain fell, de Mille could think only of what had gone wrong. Panting hard, she said, "Oh Freddie, what a lousy stinking performance. We must rehearse like demons tomorrow."[19] On the eighth curtain call, de Mille looked down into the orchestra pit and saw that the fiddlers were beating their bows on their instruments, while the others were standing up yelling. Even so, she thought that Denham must have hired a claque. Franklin assured her that the ovation was the real thing. *Rodeo* received twenty-two curtain calls.

John Martin rightly predicted that *Rodeo* "bids fair to be the company meal ticket this season."[20] America was ripe for a ballet like *Rodeo* in 1942. It was wartime, and

Casimir Kokitch (left) as the Head Wrangler, Agnes de Mille as the Cowgirl and Frederic Franklin as the Champion Roper in *Rodeo*. 1942. Photograph by Fred Fehl, copyright Gabriel Pinski.

nationalist sentiments were running high. *Rodeo* offered an American theme. It was true to the social mores of its time (although it was not exactly a ballet for feminists). It was highly entertaining, it did not tax the mind, and it was an instantaneous success. The settings by Oliver Smith formed a perfect background for the action of the ballet, suggesting the infinite space and flat horizon of the ranch country. Copland made skillful use of Western melodies, and his "Hoedown" is familiar to all of us, if only from beef commercials. This ballet gave Franklin one of the greatest roles of his long career. Robert Lawrence wrote, "Frederic Franklin danced brilliantly, bringing to 'Rodeo' all of the vitality, technical skill and joy in his work that distinguish every one of his roles."[21]

Unfortunately, this wonderful ballet suffered some attrition over the years. Few people recognize the importance of timing in comic ballet. Without split-second timing, *Rodeo* degenerates into slapstick. In 1948, Nina Novak was deplorably miscast as the Cowgirl. In her contract, de Mille had the right to approve casting. In the 1950–51 season, de Mille categorically withheld approval of casting, which meant, in effect, that the Ballet Russe could no longer present *Rodeo*. In 1950 it entered the repertory of Ballet Theatre.

Nijinska had choreographed two works for this 1942–43 season at the Met: *Chopin Concerto* and *The Snow Maiden*. Both premiered on October 12, 1942. *The Snow Maiden* was based on a Russian fairy tale about a winter sprite who remains on earth until she is liquefied by the warmth of spring. The theme was a bit childish. As one critic explained to his readers, "'Snow Maiden' is a ballet about a guy who falls in love with a snow flake, only she melts!"[22]

Nijinska's plotless *Chopin Concerto*, however, was a work of considerable distinction. Edwin Denby wrote, "*Chopin Concerto* is one of her best ballets — her stylization is strangely poignant." John Martin compared it favorably with Nijinska's 1923 masterpiece, *Les Noces*, and added, "'Chopin Concerto' is one of the most beautiful examples of the absolute ballet that has yet been made."[23]

Both of these ballets featured Igor Youskevitch, rather than Franklin, in the leading roles. While Franklin had enormous versatility, it was Youskevitch who was considered the first male dancer in the strictly classical roles. Youskevitch grew up in Belgrade. Although he had been an Olympic athlete, he did not begin the serious study of ballet until the age of twenty-one. He realized that he would have to overcome the handicap of his age and work very hard on his technique.

His career began when dancer Xenia Grunt, who needed a partner, began to give ballet instruction to Youskevitch. All the while, Grunt made ready for the concerts that would see her and her young protégé performing in various cities. Youskevitch had received only two months of ballet training when he made his formal debut as a dancer. In general, the critics said that he was good material, but needed work. Xenia was not so lucky: the critics disliked both her choreography and her dancing. Ultimately, she went back to Belgrade, and Youskevitch studied in Paris. He danced briefly with Les Ballet de Paris and Les Ballets Léon Woizikowski and then joined de Basil's company in 1936. When the 1937 split occurred, Youskevitch went to the Massine camp.

A young girl named Betty (later Maria) Tallchief had joined the Ballet Russe for the first time in the 1942–43 season. One night Krassovska, who was dancing the second lead in *Chopin Concerto*, sustained an injury. Fred walked up to Denham and said, "Oh, but that new girl [Betty Tallchief] knows it. She just told me. She rehearsed it with Nijinska."[24] On went this soon-to-be star to dance her first important role. She quickly captured John Martin's attention: "With careful handling this young Midwesterner (her father is an Osage Indian) may very well develop into ballerina material."[25] Within a year, she would be discovered by George Balanchine.

Like the previous spring season, Hurok's fall "Season of Ballet" at the Met was shared by Ballet Russe and Ballet Theatre. (Agnes de Mille wrote that the members of the rival companies used to shoot daggers at one another as they passed in the hallways of the Met.[26] Unbeknownst to Denham, Sol Hurok was preparing to kiss the Monte Carlo and Universal Art good-bye, in favor of the up-and-coming Ballet Theatre.

After the premieres of *Rodeo*, *Chopin Concerto* and *Snow Maiden* in the fall, the company toured cross-country until May. The next New York season began on May 19, 1943, at the Broadway Theatre. There were no premieres for this spring season, and the company had been unable to secure a New York theatre for the following fall. For the first time, they would have to open out of town, in Cleveland. Denham was uncertain whether he even had sufficient funds to get the company to Cleveland. While the dancers sat on their suitcases in a New York dance studio, Denham went walking the streets to rustle up some cash. Franklin recalls that he turned up a short time later shouting, "Go to the station immediately. I've got the money. We're going to Cleveland!"[27] Houses in Cleveland were sold out, so now the company was able to move on to Chicago. Houses in the "Windy City" were also packed, which enabled the troupe to move on to the next city. And that was how the company managed to tour the country that season.

The Red Poppy opened in Cleveland on October 9, 1943. It was originally a ballet in three acts and six scenes, first produced in St. Petersburg in 1926 and then at the Bolshoi in Moscow the following year. At three hours, it was one of the longest ballets on record. The Ballet Russe premiere was a condensed version, with an entirely new story and choreography, both by Igor Schwezoff. The score, arranged by Arthur Cohn, retained the best features of the original music by Reinhold Glière. Settings and costumes were by Boris Aronson.

To make the ballet timely and topical, Schwezoff cast sailors of the allied nations as the "good guys" and the Japanese as the villains. The theme is of a swiftly budding romance between Taia-Hoa (Alexandra Danilova), a dancer in a Chinese waterfront café, and a Russian Sailor (Frederic Franklin). Before he leaves, the sailor gives her a red poppy for remembrance. The Japanese proprietor of the café (Grant Mouradoff) is mad with jealousy and threatens the girl, who is rescued for the time being by an American Sailor (James Starbuck) and an English Sailor (Igor Youskevitch). The scene changes to an opium-induced dream in Taia-Hoa's home, and the ballet closes with a dock episode which begins with revelry by the sailors and ends with the dramatic death of the Japanese proprietor after he has attempted to kill Taia-Hoa.

It goes without saying that the plot was silly, but it was still a crowd-pleaser by virtue of the spectacular sailor dances given to the male leads and the male ensemble. John Martin noted, "It is certainly corn and frequently gets right down to the shucks, but it allows for some first-rate dancing." Robert Sabin reported, "Frederic Franklin, James Starbuck and the other sailors practically gave themselves hernias to put the work over." Martin thought that the specialty dances were "extremely effective" and that "the boys dance them like a million dollars." (However, more than one critic accused Freddie of overplaying his role a bit.) Although this was essentially a ballet for males, Alexandra Danilova was not entirely overlooked. Edwin Denby remarked, "No matter how foolish her part (and this one is plenty foolish) she always lends it a wonderful charm."[28]

Few would argue with Sabin that *The Red Poppy* was "hopelessly outdated in style and completely undistinguished in substance." However, the *New York Journal-American* critic thought that this ballet was just swell: "in spite of a practically worthless score, it's a mighty good show."[29]

The Cuckold's Fair premiered on the same evening — October 9, 1943. Choreographer Pilar Lopez had thus far composed no works for a large cast, though she had provided some excellent smaller pieces in her programs with her sister, Argentinita. Music was by Gustavo Pittaluga, the libretto was by Garcia Lorca and Rivas Cherif, and setting and costumes were by Joan Junyer.

The Cockold's Fair tells the story of a barren wife named Sierra (Alexandra Danilova) who wants a child. It is a Spanish custom for barren women to make a pilgrimage to a shrine at fair time and disappear into the forest with a young man, ostensibly to look for verbena. She who finds verbena will bear a child — or so goes the legend. Sierra's husband Chivato (Frederic Franklin) accompanies Sierra on her journey. When they arrive at the shrine, Sierra goes off into the woods with the Village Sacristan (James

Franklin as the Russian Sailor in *The Red Poppy*. 1943. Photograph: Gerda Peterich, New York, in the collection of Frederic Franklin.

Starbuck) while Chivato drinks and dances. Presently, Sierra returns with her dearest wish granted.

The Cuckold's Fair was not a success. John Martin wrote that it was "one of those ballets in which all the action takes place off-stage, and in this case, that is perhaps just as well." Most critics felt that Lopez caught nothing of the saltiness of her theme. Robert

Sabin marveled that "'The Cuckold's Fair' accomplished the well-nigh incredible feat of making adultery seem boring."[30] This ballet was a Spanish piece danced by an ensemble of non–Spanish ballet dancers who could not imbue their roles with the requisite style. Franklin, though, was an exception. Trained in a variety of regional Spanish dances by Massine, Argentinita, and José Greco, he gave a fine demonstration of legitimate Spanish dancing, with its arrested rhythms, its sudden and startling variations of tempo, and its volatile emotionality. Franklin recalls, "I had a lovely farruca. I had all the Spanish people screaming on opening night."[31] Denby wrote, "He keeps his dignity like a Spaniard and so saves the story." Martin disagreed: "Not even the energy of Alexandra Danilova, Frederic Franklin and James Starbuck can save it from dullness and ineptitude."[32]

Bronislava Nijinska's *Etude* also premiered in Cleveland on October 9, 1943. It was set to excerpts from Bach's Brandenburg concertos and orchestral suites. The work was a highly-stylized, neo-classical interpretation of the religious spirit in Bach's music. Nijinska first composed *Etude* in 1924, and it went through at least four versions before it entered the repertoire of the Ballet Russe. Designer Boris Belinsky costumed the dancers in halo-like headpieces and unisex tunics, perhaps to suggest that angels are sexless. However, the unfortunate result was that it was hard to tell the boys from the girls, and the men looked a tad effeminate. Franklin maintains, "The only way you could tell the boys from the girls was that the boys had hair on their legs."[33]

The chief criticism of *Etude* was that it was hopelessly dated, too rigidly stylized. Ann Barzel reported, "When the curtain rose on *Etude*, Ballet Russe well-wishers groaned. Here was one of those abstractions, a stale breath from the 20's complete with dancers posed on various stair levels." Robert Sabin noted, "Nijinska, fine artist that she is, has left this style far behind in her later works. Why dig up *Etude*?" Edwin Denby quipped that *Etude* "looks like evolutions by a recently demilitarized heavenly host." Nathalie Krassovska, Maria Tallchief and Franklin danced the leads in *Etude*. Although it is difficult to imagine Freddie prancing around in an angel tunic, Ann Barzel gave him credit for being "too good a dancer not to do a creditable job in this role."[34]

The last of the premieres was Nijinska's *Ancient Russia*, danced to Tchaikovsky's Concerto for Piano and Orchestra in B-flat Minor. It used Gontcharova's sets and costumes from the 1938 *Bogatyri* and dealt with the rescue of a Russian Princess (Alexandra Danilova) from a Tartar Prince (James Starbuck) by a Russian Prince (Frederic Franklin). It was no more successful than *Bogatyri* had been. For Franklin and his colleagues, Nijinska's narrative intent was utterly obscure: "The story, as far as we could tell, [was this]: There's a nice Russian and an evil Russian. The evil Russian has some princess slaves [led by Alexandra Danilova], which the nice Russian frees."[35] In a subsequent interview, he recalled, "There was one moment when the princesses were all bound up together with rope, and we [Franklin and Igor Youskevitch] had to lead them, but we didn't know where we were supposed to be taking them. We never did know. She never told us. Neither Igor nor I could begin to fathom the plot of this work. We just did it."[36] Denby wrote, "Alexandra Danilova and Frederic Franklin have nothing of interest to do, but they remain agreeable and serious."[37] Franklin was relieved that Nijinska left after this season, because she was a sworn enemy of Balanchine, who was soon to arrive as resident choreographer. "It [her departure] spared us a great deal [of angst]. It was bad enough when Balanchine and Massine were there together, in the early forties."[38]

Meanwhile, World War II raged on. Youskevitch had become an American citizen, and he was inducted into the United States Navy as a seaman second class on January 5, 1944. The *Dance News* correspondent wrote, "In Igor Youskevitch ballet has given to the cause of victory the best it had. We wish him happy landing and a safe and speedy return."[39]

In the spring season of 1944, the Ballet Russe became the first ballet company to dance at City Center, a building acquired by the City of New York through a tax default by a Masonic lodge. Finding themselves in possession of a large building with a number of offices and a large auditorium, the New York authorities decided to operate the building as a center for popular-priced entertainment. City Center was hardly an ideal facility for dance. The stage was very shallow and sightlines were abominable. (According to Edwin Denby, the fence of footlights cut off the dancers' feet for orchestra patrons as far back as Row R.)[40]

The Ballet Russe season coincided exactly with the Ballet Theatre season at the Metropolitan, both opening on April 9. *The Red Poppy*, *Cuckold's Fair*, *Ancient Russia* and *Etudes* were seen in New York for the first time. Both companies had sold-out houses, but the weakness of the Ballet Russe's new offerings was duly noted by critics. There were also charges of unfair competition.

Robert Garland wrote, "At the Metropolitan, Sol Hurok presents the Ballet Theatre at prices ranging from 85 cents to $4.20 each. At the 'City Center of Cut-Rates and Culture,' La Guardia presents the Ballet Russe de Monte Carlo at prices ranging from 85 cents to $2.20.... I'm both disappointed and surprised not to have heard a great big squawk out of Impresario Hurok of the Ballet Theatre." *Dance News* went into a tirade over the situation:

> On April 9 two ballet companies will open their spring seasons in New York. Not since the famous London ballet war of 1938 has there existed a more deplorable situation in the ballet business. We want to go on record as condemning this state of affairs vigorously and unequivocally. There is no excuse for it. Only spite, only a desire to hurt someone else could have created this condition.... The management of the Ballet Russe has never been accused of having strong business ethics, but the government of the city of New York, representing the greatest city in the world, must adhere to a code of ethics beyond any reproach.[41]

John Martin's concerns were more for the development of an educated ballet audience than for unfair competition: "There are indeed several reasons for feeling pretty unhappy about it. The City Center has taken a certain pride in reaching a new audience; it seems likely, in fact, that more than half of the people who attended these performances had never before seen a ballet performance. That is deeply regrettable, for the new taste should be formed by exposure to the highest standards only, and this particular season was far from that level."[42]

It was George Balanchine who noticed that Franklin had a good memory for steps and could teach them accurately. He was also favorably impressed with Franklin's part-time teaching at the School of American Ballet in 1940 and again in 1942–43. Franklin's first experience with the duties of a ballet master came with *Poker Game*. After setting

Stravinsky's ballet for the company, Balanchine asked Freddie to rehearse the dancers and keep the ballet in shape on tour. In June of 1944, he was officially appointed *maître de ballet* on the recommendation of Balanchine. It was a very logical choice, as for some years past, Franklin had been indefatigable in assisting with rehearsals, helping younger dancers with new roles, and so forth.

The announcement of Franklin's new position was made by Serge Denham after a performance in San Francisco. It also happened to be Freddie's birthday, so there were two things to celebrate during the onstage party given in his honor. While the party was in full swing, Danilova came up to Frederic and said, "Ooh, Fredka! You mean you going to be my boss?"[43]

At first Franklin was a bit frightened by the magnitude of his responsibilities, but he had the confidence of the dancers, and from the beginning, his authority was recognized. Having come up from the ranks of a company that had suffered a great deal from temperamental leadership and unfair practices, he knew what things to do and what to avoid. One of his first acts was to clean up ballets that had become ragged. For instance, he had every corps de ballet dancer go through the movements of *Les Sylphides*, all alone. He discovered that the sloppiness of the corps was due to the fact that many girls actually did not know the correct steps of the ballet; they merely followed and imitated their neighbors and had never once been coached. When everyone learned the correct movements, they all felt more comfortable.[44]

Franklin was now responsible for reviving old ballets as well as rehearsing the new ones. He proved to be sensible, efficient, and organized. Until his appointment, principals did not normally have understudies for their roles. If a dancer was ill or injured, someone would be almost literally thrown onto the stage as a replacement. While such incidents still occurred throughout the entire history of the company, Franklin tried to ensure that they would happen as seldom as possible by establishing a roster of understudies for every solo part. This in itself was an incentive to ambitious dancers in the corps de ballet.[45]

He also became famous for his speed in setting a ballet. "He taught quickly and always very clearly," Rochelle Zide remembers, and Franklin to this day has not lost his ability to mount big productions in a short time. When André Eglevsky died unexpectedly in 1977, Franklin was hurriedly called in to stage the production of *Giselle* that the Eglevsky Ballet had announced as its next attraction, and he set the entire work in only three days.[46]

Franklin's most amazing asset as ballet master was his phenomenal, nearly superhuman, kinetic memory. He had only to hear the music and the steps came flooding back. Ballet Russe dancer Leon Danielian recalled, "After some ten years, Freddie revived *Ballet Imperial*. What he did looked as perfect as the day Balanchine had finished it. If a company does a revival that Frederic Frankin stages, it will be as close to the original as anyone remembers it, even the choreographers." Wendy Toye stated:

Fred always was a wonderful leader and organizer and always had that terrific gift of making everyone love working for him and making the work so interesting and such fun.... He has the most fantastic memory for choreography of anyone I have ever met. This isn't entirely something he's worked on, although I'm sure he's improved it over the years, and with necessity.... I have known him after years hear a piece of music that perhaps he and I might have danced to, and remember every step, not only of his, but of anyone else who was in it.[47]

Franklin said modestly, "It's a gift, this ability to remember ballets. We must take care of the gifts we are given."[48]

Not the least of Freddie's attributes as *maître de ballet* was his affability. Freddie could get along with just about anyone. He did not indulge in emotional outbursts and in casting decisions, he had a strong sense of fair play. In appraising Franklin's handling of this position, Martin wrote, "Frederic Franklin, the new ballet master, has established an atmosphere of back-stage fairness which is said to have reduced the customary intrigues and politics of ballet tradition to the vanishing point." Ann Barzel observed, "A wonderful choice, since Franklin is a first-rate dancer, a good comrade entirely without 'sides,' who fires all with his own tireless enthusiasm and who maintains discipline by leadership, not tyranny."[49]

By now, Franklin had become something of a matinee idol. Ann Barzel described some of the manifestations of worship:

> Adolescents get crushes and crowd around outside the stage doors. More common is the mother instinct he arouses. Nice ladies are always plying him with foot-warmers and giving him mufflers and begging him not to get his feet wet. The quality that inspires people to adore Franklin offstage is the same quality that makes his dancing attractive to audiences, and that makes him a good ballet master. That is the genuine liking for people.[50]

De Mille wrote, "Franklin was the 'inner motor' of the Ballet Russe, the reason why they get through the sheer amount of labor involved in each tour."[51]

At a 1944 ballet performance in Columbus, Ohio, the opening page of the program read, "Mlle Danilova, Frederic Franklin and Company." It was only by reading the small print on page three that the audience was informed that the real name of the group was Ballet Russe de Monte Carlo.[52] Of course, it was only a printing error, but it spoke volumes about the duo's star quality. Danilova and Franklin ruled the company. On the road, local managers insisted upon them, and they always danced. But the reign of Danilova and Franklin in the 1940s forwarded a tendency of the management to neglect their duty to groom other talented dancers to the point where they could share stellar burdens with the two stars. Consequently, the company was always at a disadvantage when either one of them was out with an injury.

During the summer of 1944, Franklin received an offer to appear in a summer musical. His friends Robert Wright and George Forrest were adapting the music of Edvard Grieg for a show based upon Grieg's life to be called *Song of Norway*. The musical was to have been choreographed by David Lichine, but he abdicated in favor of a Hollywood film contract. The honors fell to George Balanchine, who was completely without prospects at the time. This gig led to Balanchine's two-year residency with the Ballet Russe. Much to the delight of Wright and Forrest, Denham offered eighteen Ballet Russe dancers to be in the show as well, including Danilova, Krassovska and Leon Danielian. Since this meant extra money during the vacation period, the dancers accepted the engagement with alacrity.

Balanchine contributed Norwegian folk dances, including "Freddie and his Fiddle," a peasant dance for Franklin, a satire on ballet mannerisms to the *Peer Gynt* music, and, as a finale, an ambitious and serious classical ballet to an abridgement of Grieg's piano concerto. *Song of Norway* was first presented in Los Angeles by Edwin Lester as part of his annual Civic Light Opera series on June 12, 1944. The production moved

Franklin starring in the Broadway musical *Song of Norway* in 1944. Franklin as "Freddie" in "Freddie and His Fiddle," the number especially written for him by Wright and Forest. Choreography: George Balanchine. Photograph by Fred Fehl, copyright Gabriel Pinski.

to San Francisco on July 3 and settled down for a Broadway run at the Imperial Theatre on August 21.

Song of Norway's plot mixed fact and fiction. Of course, the libretto has never been
considered to be the strong point in operettas. Books for operettas usually consist of a
few bare announcements concerning who the people are and what they are about to
sing, and Song of Norway was no exception. The operetta had lavish settings by Lemuel
Ayers, and the Metropolitan Opera's Ira Petina led a cast of singer-actors. The musical
was such a success in New York that in order to prepare for its own fall season, Franklin
had to superintend the formation of a new dance ensemble to appear in the show while
the Ballet Russe returned to City Center. The New York public supported the show for
an 860-performance run, and Hollywood made a movie of Song of Norway in 1970.

The plot of Song of Norway deals in summary with Grieg's dawning realization of his
mission as a Norwegian, whose art should embody the spirit of his land. He is brought
back to Norway by the death of his mentor Nordraak and then comes to a resolute and
clear-sighted commitment to his destiny as Norway's composer. Before the finale, Grieg
sits at the piano in the living room with his bride in the house given him by his faithful
countrymen. He plays the romantic "Song of Norway" and, lo, a transformation: the back
walls of the house disappear and the mountains of Norway are revealed.

Next, as described by music critic Olin Downes, "there is inescapably a ballet ...
that, believe it or not, is just what happens and a more far-fetched and incongruous
'dance interpretation' of Grieg's music, one more ludicrously at odds with the whole
story would be impossible to achieve." Downes believed that the operetta would have
been better-served with Norwegian folk dances in native costumes for the finale. Denby
disagreed: "The finale ballet offers you, modestly and touchingly, a sentiment not at all
commonplace. 'Song of Norway' does not falsify ballet as most musicals do on the
ground that adulteration is the first principle of showmanship."[53] Audiences didn't seem
to care one way or the other, for they flocked in droves to see it.

There were many reasons to look forward to the fall season of 1944. The previous
one had yielded three out-and-out bombs and The Red Poppy, a crowd-pleaser of scant
artistic merit. The company had been at its lowest ebb thus far in the fall of 1943. Now
the Ballet Russe was on the verge of a renaissance. George Balanchine had agreed to
serve as choreographer-in-residence. He was attracted to this position, not only because
his career on Broadway and in Hollywood was going nowhere, but also because the stability of the Ballet Russe as an organization made it possible for him to revive older
works originally choreographed for short-lived groups and to present them in repertoire season after season.

Balanchine immediately improved standards in the company. He insisted that
dancers attend daily company class and also allowed them to study free-of-charge at
the School of American Ballet. He replaced many of the old Russian dancers with eager
young Americans, most of them SAB graduates. He let the company know, in his quiet
but authoritative way, that he would not tolerate any more of the shoddy, slack dancing some of the performers had been trying to skate by with. In addition to supervis-
ing the staging of a number of his older works, he choreographed four new ballets:
Danses Concertantes, Raymonda, a pas de deux for Danilova and Franklin, and Night
Shadow. For the next two years he would work enthusiastically with the Ballet Russe.

The Ballet Russe had its second season at City Center on September 10–24, 1944. *Danses Concertantes* premiered on opening night. Although Stravinsky composed *Danses Concertantes* in 1942 in ballet form, this was the first time the score was used for its original purpose. *Danses Concertantes* is a ballet in five sections: *Marche-Introduction*, *Pas d'Action*, *Thème Varié*, *Pas de Deux* and *Marche-Conclusion*.

A brief orchestral march is heard and then the group makes its entrances by threes — two girls and one boy — in front of an inner curtain, followed by the two leads (Alexandra Danilova, Frederic Franklin). They all parade and introduce themselves in the manner of traveling players, or circus folk. Now the inner curtain rises and the concert dances are about to begin. The corps de ballet has taken its place on stage with the ballerina presiding. Next come a series of four pas de trois, varied by the shifting patterns of the groups, solo variations and a climactic pas de deux for the principals. The finale which follows the pas de deux has the same choreography and music as the prologue, save that it is presented on a full stage instead of before the footlights. At its conclusion, the dancers run forward to bow, the inner curtain of the prologue falls behind them, and the ballet ends with the performers facing the audience in formal greeting.

For Balanchine, the Stravinsky piece suggested the Italian spirit of commedia dell'arte, and in designer Eugène Berman he found an artist to match the wit and tongue-in-cheek humor of the music. Setting the tone was Berman's colorful front curtain, which rose to reveal the fourteen dancers. Berman designed the tights and tutus in rhinestone-studded, jewel-like tones of topaz, sapphire, purple and rose. Glittering sharply in front of a charcoal backdrop the dancers looked, in Denby's words, "as brilliant as scarabs."[54]

Franklin had a say in the designs for these exquisite costumes. Rehearsals for *Danses Concertantes* began in California, during the run of *Song of Norway*. Apparently, Balanchine, Berman and Stravinsky were fighting like cats and dogs over the designs. A meeting had been arranged at Stravinsky's house, and Balanchine brought Frederic along to make a party of four:

> Balanchine says, "Freddie, you will decide." I said, "I'll decide what, Mr. B?" So what happened was that Stravinsky threw a piece of black velvet on the table and took from his pocket colored stones and threw them onto the black velvet. Mr. B. said, "Choose the colors." And I chose all the colors.[55]

Danses Concertantes is a work of irony and exuberance as Balanchine makes sly fun of the classicism on which his work is so firmly based. The ballet contains several moments of slight exaggeration, restrained before it becomes burlesque. The score is one of extreme rhythmic complexity, and Balanchine gave it a visual grace and logic that illuminated Stravinsky's intentions. Denby heralded *Danses Concertantes* as a "singular masterpiece," "the boldest ballet of the season." Lillian Moore was also struck by the work: "Balanchine's choreographic invention seems to be limitless and the constantly changing patterns are infinitely varied and always stimulating."[56]

But the piece was not an unqualified success. Abstract ballets were rare in 1944, and some important critics voiced objections to what was rapidly taking form as Balanchine's definitive style. John Martin accused him of a "soul-destroying dullness" and continued as follows:

Igor Stravinsky, Frederic Franklin and Alexandra Danilova after a performance of *Danses Concertantes*. 1944. Choreography: George Balanchine. Music: Igor Stravinsky. Décor: Eugene Berman. Ballet Russe de Monte Carlo production. Photograph: Collection of Frederic Franklin.

According to the program notes the work is "abstract," which it undeniably is and "of great depth and beauty," which it just as certainly is not. Stravinsky's music is gravely *demodé,* belonging to that *avant-gardisme* of about 1925 which is now as quaint as grandmother's antimacassar.... One has not time when watching a spectacle to follow and figure out perversities of musical form and phrase.... Mr. Balanchine has done a clever, somewhat mathematical job of choreography, almost totally devoid of dancing.

Although Anatole Chujoy praised Balanchine's musicianship and technical inventiveness, he was hardly won over either: "It is trite to repeat that ballet is or should be theatre first and always. When it ceases to be theatre, it ceases to be ballet, no matter how brilliant the choreography devised for it."[57]

In a revue of *Danses Concertantes* a year later, Martin observed that it was a very technically demanding ballet and that "its difficulties for the dancers must be considerable."[58] While Franklin created this role, he only danced it twice. At the second performance, he suffered a severe injury to the cartilage of the right knee that kept him out for the rest of the fall season and well into the subsequent tour. *Danses Concertantes* remained in the repertory until the1947–48 season, but its score was so difficult that pick-up musicians on the road often had difficulty playing it. The work was performed less and less as time went by. Although a film was made of *Danses Concertantes*, it was lost and has never been located since. Nobody remembered the original choreography, and so, in Franklin's words, it has sadly "evaporated."[59] In June of 1972, Balanchine did a less-than-successful revival with new choreography for the Stravinsky Festival.

Le Bourgeois Gentilhomme opened at City Center on September 23, 1944. It was danced to Richard Strauss's incidental music for the Molière play of the same name. Balanchine had staged it earlier for the René Blum Ballets de Monte Carlo in 1932.

As the curtain rises, Monsieur Jourdain (Michel Katcharoff), a conceited member of the nouveau riche, is preening himself in his new mansion under the solicitous eyes of his tailor, servants and instructors in music, fencing, dancing and philosophy. He is determined that his daughter, Lucile (Nathalie Krassovska), will marry a member of the nobility. However, he is opposed by the bourgeois youth Cléonte (Frederic Franklin), who is equally determined to wed the girl himself. Lucile's sympathies go out wholly to Cléonte.

Without Lucile's knowledge, Cléonte resolves to defeat and humiliate Monsieur Jourdain. Dressed as a Muslim prince, with several slaves in his retinue, he arrives at Jourdain's house with great pomp and ceremony and asks for Lucile's hand. Jourdain consents and in return, the potentate presents the vain old man with a patent of nobility.

Anxious to impress the Muslim, Jourdain stages an elaborate divertissement in his ballroom. In the midst of the festivities, Lucile appears. On seeing the Turkish suitor, she is horrified and tries to escape. Having been accepted by Joudain as his new son-in-law, Cléonte removes his disguise and claims Lucile in marriage. Jourdain resigns himself to the inevitable. The ballet ends with a finale to celebrate the engagement.

Le Bourgeois Gentilhomme was in a ragged and half-baked state on the evening of the premiere. It didn't open until the next-to-the-last day of the New York season, but even so, Serge Denham denied Balanchine's urgent request to postpone the ballet until the spring season. Edwin Denby accused Denham of "malpractice"[60] for this decision.

There was no dress rehearsal before the opening. As a matter of fact, the costumes were delivered after the September 23 performance was well under way, while the second ballet of the evening was in progress. Some of the dancers had to be pinned and sewn into their costumes before going onstage, and several costumes ripped open while the ballet was in progress! Denby perceived that "the company was valiant, inaccurate and frightened." The sole feature of this ballet to win praise were the splendid sets and (tardy) costumes of Eugène Berman. Otherwise, in the words of Anatole Chujoy, "it was a mess."[61]

Franklin had only danced the role of Cléonte twice before he sustained his knee injury. After the accident, Nicholas Magallanes took over the part of Cléonte, but he was inadequately prepared and unsuited for the role. Magallanes was a very competent dancer, but he lacked the sparkle and zest required for Cléonte. *Le Bourgeois Gentil-homme* needed someone with Franklin's charisma to pull it together and provide a focus. As if things weren't bad enough, Magallanes turned his ankle, and at a performance that Denby saw, "when the crucial love duet got going, he could barely hobble through it."[62] On a bigger stage, with more rehearsals, and the proper dancers in their proper roles, *Le Bourgeois Gentilhomme* could have been a nice enough closing piece, but the ballet appeared to be jinxed.

When the company went back on the road, Balanchine began rehearsing three new productions: *Ballet Imperial, Mozartiana,* and *Concerto Barocco. Ballet Imperial* entered the rep in Chicago on October 4, 1944. When Lincoln Kirstein organized a new American Ballet in 1941 to tour South America, Balanchine had arranged two ballets for the repertoire — *Concerto Barocco* and *Ballet Imperial.* The latter is performed to the music of Tchaikovsky's G-major Piano Concerto No. 2. It has no plot but is a choreographic impression of the concerto's architectural plan, and, like its source, is divided into three separate movements.

The "Imperial" part of the title suggests the Imperial Ballet of pre–World War I Russia, and Balanchine designed the ballet as a tribute to Petipa and Tchaikovsky. Having grown up in the Imperial Ballet School, Balanchine was eminently qualified to pay such a tribute. The theme of this ballet in three movements is grandeur. This sense was conveyed not only by the dancers, but also by the regal and sumptuous new sets and costumes of Mstislav Dobujinsky.

The prima ballerina in *Ballet Imperial* has an almost brutally demanding role, perhaps the most difficult in Balanchine's repertory. In the original version of 1941, the role was danced by Marie-Jeanne, who is still remembered for the brilliance and speed of her jumps and beats and her clarity of line. In the Ballet Russe version, this role was danced by Mary Ellen Moylan with Maria Tallchief, Nicolas Magallanes, Herbert Bliss and Nikita Talin as secondary soloists.

When New York first saw *Ballet Imperial* in March of 1945, reactions were quite positive. Anatole Chujoy wrote, "'Ballet Imperial' was the height of the opening. Artistically, Balanchine is the direct descendent of Petipa, and if classicism in ballet is to continue, Balanchine is the man to take care of it.... The fact is the ballet is grand."[63]

Denby was struck with Balanchine's positive influence on the company: "It has been astonishing to see how such thoroughly experienced dancers as the great Danilova, Franklin, Krassovska and Lazowsky have all revealed their best qualities under his influence. As for the younger soloists, they have seemed to be bursting into bloom like forsythia all over the stage." He singled out Moylan, Maria Tallchief, Ruthanna Boris, Leon Danielian and Nicholas Magallanes as the main benefactors of Balanchine.[64]

Because of his knee injury, Franklin didn't dance in *Ballet Imperial*. By the end of 1944, Franklin's knee was on the mend, and he was back in commission. His next project was the taking over of one of the title roles in Ruth Page's *Frankie and Johnny*.

This work premiered in Kansas City on January 7, 1945, but it was the New York opening that caused the big ruckus. The New York City Center season ran from February 20 to March 25, and *Frankie* was first shown to New Yorkers on February 28.

Ruth Page's long career as dancer, choreographer, and company director was marked by adventurousness. From her beginnings, Page was highly creative, choreographing scores of solos which she performed in concerts given during the first decades of her career in Chicago. There was an awareness of contemporary American life, such as the sports scene and the "roaring twenties" in her earliest works such as *The Flapper and the Quarterback*, *St. Louis Blues* and *Gershwiniana*. More than a nod to the Spanish Civil War, then raging, was her full-cast ballet, *Guns and Castanets*, a 1939 version of *Carmen* in a new time frame. Page created a number of solo dances inspired by poetry — the works of García Lorca, E. E. Cummings, Edna St. Vincent Millay, Baudelaire, Langston Hughes and Dorothy Parker were all sources of inspiration. In some of her solos, she spoke verses while dancing.

In the 1920s, she was premiere danseuse of Adolph Bolm's Ballet Intime and was frequently partnered by Bolm himself. When she launched her avant-garde concert career, she invited a succession of well-known dancers to partner her. Although most of her works were created entirely by herself, she sometimes created in tandem with her male leads. For two decades beginning in 1935, she worked with Bentley Stone both as partner and choreographic collaborator.

In 1938 Page, with the contribution of Stone, composed *Frankie and Johnny* in connection with the WPA Federal Theatre Project. *Frankie and Johnny* was based on the famous American folk ballad of the same name. It was destined to be the ballet that spread the name of Ruth Page far and wide.

The libretto by Michael Blandford and Jerome Moross followed fairly closely the actions depicted in the ballad. Moross composed the score and, for the Ballet Russe production, the set was by Clive Rickabaugh with costumes by Paul du Pont.

The ballet is set in a Chicago slum area in the late nineteenth century. The set reveals a low-life saloon adjoined by a brothel. A flight of wooden stairs gives entrance to the house of ill repute, the apartment on the ground floor being reached by a doorway under the stairs. When the curtain rises, Nellie Bly (Vida Brown) is seen at the first-floor window, while Frankie (Ruth Page and then Ruthanna Boris) and Johnny (Bentley Stone and then Frederic Franklin) are seated on the wooden stairs. Frankie retires to her room on the ground floor, and Johnny directs occasional passers-by to her abode. Other customers call on Nellie. (The frequent rolling up and down of window shades signifies that certain transactions are in progress.) The scene ends with Johnny sitting alone on the steps.

Frankie returns, and she and Johnny dance a music hall routine. When she retires to her room, Johnny gives vent to his youthful animalism in a solo. The front of the

Ruthanna Boris and Frederic Franklin in *Frankie and Johnny*. 1945. Choreography: Ruth Page and Bentley Stone. Music: Jerome Moross. Décor: Rickabaugh. Photograph: Collection of Frederic Franklin.

Franklin as Johnny in Ruth Page's *Frankie and Johnny*. 1945. Ballet Russe de Monte Carlo production. Photograph: Collection of Frederic Franklin.

saloon rolls up to disclose the interior: behind the counter stands the Bartender (Nikita Talin). Some of the prostitutes, accompanied by their tricks, patronize the bar.

Nelly Bly enters the saloon, and Johnny whirls her into a dance. The Bartender and the crowd take a malicious delight in his flagrant betrayal of Frankie. When Frankie herself enters the bar, the patrons hide Nellie and Johnny as the two escape to Nellie's room. Everyone leaves except for Frankie and the Bartender, who comes from behind his counter and, in a dance of innuendo, reveals to Frankie the infidelity of her lover. Frankie dances out her jealous rage.

The "Saving Susies," Salvation Army girls, sing the verses which describe Frankie's purchase of a revolver and her murder of her lover. The shooting is re-enacted at the head of the stairs. A coffin is brought on, and Johnny is placed inside it. Frankie and the Salvation Army sisters express their grief by drinking beer and performing a melancholy tap dance.

Musically, the piece was divided into seven dances: "Bawdy House Stomp," "Frankie and Johnny Blues," "Beer Parlor Rag," "Bartender's Rag," "Frankie Tune," "Fox-Trot Murder" and "Funeral Party One-Step." It was composer Moross who suggested the use of three Salvation Army lassies who, in the manner of a Greek chorus, sang an appropriate line or two of the ribald ballad at the beginning or ending of each scene, as required.

Rachel Chapman, the Ballet Russe's Polish rehearsal pianist, was very disdainful when she was asked to play the "revolting" score of *Frankie*. At one rehearsal, she actually refused to play it one more time, and Balanchine stepped in to play it for her.[65] Chapman, a brilliant pianist, was one of the legends of the Ballet Russe. During performances, she seemed to lead the entire orchestra with the tempo from her piano. When Massine started to work on his first symphonic ballet, *Les Présages*, she taught him how to read music and got him through all four movements. Rachel had a loud and explosive personality, and she was the first person a dancer was likely to encounter when joining the Ballet Russe. According to George Zoritch, "One easily thought Ballet Russe de Monte Carlo belonged to her from the way she bossed and ordered everyone without regard." Rachel called herself "The Queen of Uprights." She never permitted anyone to touch her "instrument," even when it was a broken down, rinky-dink, out-of-tune clunker. Said Zoritch, "No one, but absolutely no one, could approach or use the piano as a barre during our classes, nor were we permitted to leave any of our belongings or valuables on or around the piano at any time."[66] Newcomers who transgressed the Piano Law were told in no uncertain terms, "This is not a garbage dump and it is not a clothes closet and it is not a bookcase."[67] According to Franklin, the Piano Law stemmed from an unfortunate rehearsal incident:

> Mr. Massine took off a beautiful watch that Diaghilev had given him, and he put it on top of the piano. And when rehearsal was finished, the watch was gone. And it was a phenomenal watch, and it was a gift from Diaghilev. And he searched and searched, and he couldn't find it. And Rachel said, "There will be nothing on this piano ever again after this tragedy."[68]

Rehearsals for *Frankie and Johnny* began on the West Coast and continued on tour. There was one rehearsal that Franklin will never forget:

> Riding by train, we have a long layover in Kansas City. There's Ruth [Page], Ruthanna [Boris] and me. Ruth says, "Look, we've got four hours. We're not going to waste them. We're going to find a hotel." I brought the camera, and we put a sheet up on the hotel wall. It was very hot, there was no air conditioning. Ruth is in a bra and panties, so is Ruthanna, and I'm in very little. We're all wearing next to *nothing*, and we're watching, we're learning *Frankie and Johnny* on a hotel sheet! That is how it used to be in those days.[69]

Frankie and Johnny's sexually explicit subject matter caused a good deal of controversy when first performed in 1938, especially since it was produced with public funding from the WPA. In commissioning *Frankie* for the Ballet Russe, Denham assumed that the dust had settled by 1945. He was wrong. The fracas began with the altogether unrelated presentation in Philadelphia of a play called *Trio*, which dealt with lesbianism. Before long, private pressures from religious groups were being brought to bear upon City Hall officials to prohibit *Trio*'s importation into New York. They didn't succeed at first: *Trio* opened at New York's Belasco Theatre shortly after Christmas of 1944 and ran for some five weeks. But in February of 1945, Commissioner Paul Moss, the city's commissioner of licenses, revoked the license of the Belasco Theatre, and *Trio* closed perforce. *Frankie and Johnny* was scheduled to open four days later.

As commissioner of licenses, Moss was assistant to the president of City Center. On February 26, the noted playwright Elmer Rice resigned from the board of directors of the City Center, declining to work in any capacity under Commissioner Moss, whose exercise of official censorship he condemned. On February 27, Margaret Webster, a renowned director of Shakespeare, also resigned for the same reason. Both of them made their actions known to the press in strong statements.[70]

The February 28 presentation of *Frankie and Johnny* at the beset City Center itself put Commissioner Moss in a real bind. While *Trio* had been closed for alleged immorality, *Frankie* went *Trio* one better in that it not only featured two lesbians, but a band of whores and, to boot, a pimp as the hero of this ballet. It is almost certain that Moss called on Denham to make alterations in an effort to escape "people who live in glass houses" charges.

In the account of John Martin, on February 25, Denham discussed the *Trio* scandal with Ruth Page and asked that certain changes be made. Ruth agreed to make some of them, provided that she be given sufficient rehearsal time to smooth out the alterations. But this wasn't possible, because the rehearsal schedule was already crammed to capacity. On February 28, just before the rise of the curtain, Denham made a second plea to Ruth to do some last-minute ablutions. According to John Martin, she agreed, but the unrehearsed modifications caused considerable confusion among the cast members, while the ballet itself lost much of its logic because of the dramatic nonsequiteurs that kept popping up.[71]

Ruth Page and Bentley Stone danced the title roles on February 28 and were scheduled to dance the ballet's second performance two days later, after which they would be replaced by Ruthanna Boris and Franklin. John Martin relates that at the last minute, Page and Stone refused to go on for the second performance, and Boris and Franklin had to put on their costumes in frantic haste.[72] According to the tabloid *P.M.*, Denham and Moss, prior to the second performance, "came on bended knees and asked for still further changes, whereupon Ruth Page and Bentley Stone withdrew from the company." The tabloid also reported that Commissioner Moss had refused permission to *Life* magazine to take pictures of the ballet and that orders were also issued to the Ballet Russe to send no pictures of the ballet to the press.[73]

The above account of the censorship of *Frankie and Johnny* is based substantively on John Martin's book, *Ruth Page: An Intimate Biography*. Interestingly, Franklin's memories of this episode are different on several key points. He said, "There were no changes in the original choreography. When we got to Boston, Oh! The publicity was outrageous. So all we left out was that we didn't lower the window shades up and down.

Otherwise, we just danced it like it was. That was the only change that was ever made in it."[74]

Franklin has a slightly different account of the casting changes as well. He stated, "In the second performance, out goes Bentley, and I go in with Ruth [Page]. And the critics [who wrote that the ballet was lewd] said, 'that's a little better.' So the next performance, out goes Ruth and in goes Ruthanna [Boris]. They said, 'Finally, it's acceptable.'"[75]

While it is quite to be expected that some critics would find *Frankie and Johnny* sleazy and sordid, others loved its humor and novelty. Stating that *Frankie and Johnny* was "no bawdier than Nedick's orange drink," Denby added that it was "good, clean fun, and nobody meant anything they did." While he rightfully pointed out that "choreography was its weakest element," John Martin nevertheless felt that *Frankie* was "a fresh and original piece of theatre." He also noted wryly, "This story ain't got no moral.... Commissioner Moss may be called upon to revoke the license of his own theatre for presenting it."[76]

The *Frankie and Johnny* scandal tended to overshadow the other works that had their New York premiere—*Mozartiana* and *Pas de Deux*—but these ballets actually did raise their heads in the midst of all this hoopla. *Mozartiana* was first performed by Balanchine's Les Ballets 1933 during their season at the Théâtre des Champs-Elysées. Its American premiere was offered by the American Ballet at the Avery Memorial Theatre, Hartford, Connecticut, in December of 1934. *Mozartiana* was first performed by the Ballet Russe on March 7, 1945, with the original set and costume designs of Christian Bérard.

The choreography for *Mozartiana* was inspired by Tchaikovsky's orchestral work of the same name. In 1887 the Russian composer, who revered the music of Mozart, finished a suite for small orchestra based on lesser-known melodies by that master. The first two movements, "Gigue" and "Menuet," came from a set of twelve piano pieces. The "Preghiera" which follows was derived from Mozart's motet "Ave Verum Corpus." The finale of the suite was based on a set of variations written by Mozart to a melody from Gluck's opera *The Pilgrim from Mecca*.

In this work for four principals and eight girls, the curtain rises on a sunlit Italian piazza. Three dancers perform a gigue, led by Yurek Lazowski, in costumes that suggest an eighteenth century version of the commedia dell'arte. Now eight girls in red enter to the music of a court minuet. After an elaborate ensemble number, a white-robed figure (Dorothy Etheridge) is borne onto the stage on a litter topped by black plumes. This is the "Preghiera," or "Prayer." An Italian funeral procession is suggested by the two fully-draped litter bearers and the somber dancing of the soloist. There follows a series of lively dances by the corps de ballet and by the first young man and the sad lady, now very gay in a tarantella costume. The climax of the ballet arrives with a closing adagio, containing a pas de deux for the two principals (Alexandra Danilova, Frederic Franklin). This leads into a final set of variations on a folk theme, during which gypsies in green and lavender — their skirts sewn with coins —flash across the stage. The work ends with the three performers of the opening gigue, posed as they were at the beginning.

Edwin Denby, ever the ardent Balanchine fan, loved this ballet: "'Mozartiana' is another of his unassuming pocket masterpieces which restore to ballet its classic clarity and joyousness." For him the performances of the four principals were "wonderfully effective." [77] Although he later changed his mind, John Martin took a very dim view of Balanchine's works in the 1940s:

It [*Mozartiana*] follows essentially the — oh, so familiar — Balanchine formula. It is cool, clean, difficult and devised. It has its ensemble movement in which everybody plays "London Bridge" like mad, its slow movement devoted to chicly lugubrious sentimentality.... To Miss Etheridge falls the unhappy "Preghiera," in which she is supported by two figures suggesting (no doubt intentionally) animated pilasters from an ornate hearse. If this movement is serious, it is slightly foolish; if it is supposed to be funny, it is in bad taste. In either case, last night's audience laughed at it.

Martin did, at least, have praise for the principals: "Alexandra Danilova and Frederic Franklin dance brilliantly the brittle adagio."[78]

Franklin saw the original *Mozartiana* when performed by Balanchine's Les Ballets 1933 at London's Savoy Theatre. Tamara Toumanova and Roman Jasinski then danced the roles taken later by Danilova and Franklin in 1945. According to Franklin, few changes were made in the 1945 version, except in the costuming: "Toumanova was heavy, so she was in a black tutu all the way through. Here, Choura had a white tutu with white plumes and then a black one... No! Dark mauve! She would never, but never, have worn black for a pas de deux."[79]

Pas de Deux (also billed as *Grand Adagio*) premiered on March 14, 1945. It was set to the entr'acte music from Tchaikovsky's *Sleeping Beauty*. The music was composed to carry a mood of suspense through an interval required for a scenic transformation, but it was omitted in the original production by the order of Tsar Alexander III, who thought it would be more entertaining to speed up the machinists. Balanchine had always loved this violin solo and wanted to do something with it, so he choreographed an adagio, without solo variations or a coda, for Danilova and Franklin.

Although *Pas de Deux* was brief, the piece was not fragmentary in feeling or in form. Edwin Denby described the piece as follows: "A prince appears with a lovely princess, he holds her gently and as she flutters and turns and bends, he lets her free, and she returns to him, and they exit together. Their intimacy is that of young people in love and engaged, and their dance figures express the dewiness, the sense of trepidation in the girl and the generous strength of the man."[80] This lovely *pièce d'occasion* only remained in the repertory for one season.

With its new, controversial, cutting-edge repertory, the company seemed to be recovering from its all-time low of 1943. John Martin may have had misgivings about Balanchine's creative output, but he could not deny his invaluable effect on company standards:

The Ballet Russe de Monte Carlo today closes what is certainly one of its best seasons, in spite of a miserable theatre.... What is more, it achieved this excellent result after having touched, in its preceding two engagements at the City Center, quite the lowest level of its existence.... George Balanchine, with five new ballets in the repertoire this year, has spent a great deal of time rehearsing the company and has given it both an artistic and a technical fillip of enormous value.

Franklin also had much to do with the company renaissance. Denby praised Franklin for having done "a remarkable job in getting a large repertory with a dozen new dances and several productions successfully launched in the very first week."[81]

After their national tour, the Ballet Russe re-opened in New York on September 9, 1945, at City Center. The opening night of this season featured the premiere of *Concerto Barocco*, which had been created for the American Ballet in 1941 with décor by Eugène Berman. It was danced to Bach's D-minor Concerto for two violins. Marie-Jeanne returned as guest artist in her original role with Patricia Wilde as the second ballerina and Nicholas Magallanes as her cavalier. Marie-Jeanne was considered an ideal interpreter of Balanchine's work — her style was cold, sharp, precise, and technically unequalled.

Eugène Berman had been unhappy with his 1941 designs for *Concerto Barocco*, and he refused permission to the Ballet Russe to use them. As a result, the girls appeared in black tunics and pink tights; the boys sported black tights and white t-shirts. There was no backdrop. Some critics objected to the starkness of this production. Anatole Chujoy wrote, "Lest the success of *Concerto Barocco* lead to a trend of doing ballets without scenery and costumes, let it be strongly emphasized that *Concerto Barocco* is artistically successful in spite of the absence of décor, not because of it."[82]

Franklin told an interviewer that *Concerto Barocco* was not a success at all outside New York:

> They thought it was terrible. It was not until the mid–1950s that people started to turn around and like what he did. He had a terrible press. The public wasn't ready for it. The Ballet Russe was known for its décor, known for its costumes, known for its story ballets. We were suddenly presenting what they [the audience] called "Underneath the Arches" or "London's Bridge Is Falling Down." [Franklin is referring to the second movement, where the corps link hands and form intricate daisy chain figures, as in children's games.][83]

The long series of scathing reviews during the 1945–46 tour prompted Balanchine to say to Freddie, "I wonder when they'll write something nice about me!"[84]

A seventy-nine city tour followed this fall season, and then the Ballet Russe returned to City Center for its 1946 spring engagement. Rehearsals had been ongoing for two ambitious new productions — *Night Shadow* and *Raymonda*.

Night Shadow (*La Sonnambula*) premiered on February 27, 1946. Franklin was to have danced the leading role of the Poet, but a back injury prevented him from performing, and he had to be temporarily replaced. It was danced to an arrangement by Vittorio Rieti of the music of Vincenzo Bellini, principally from the opera *La Sonnambula*. The décor by Dorothea Tanning set the action at a nineteenth century masked ball in the garden of a great mansion.

The Coquette (Maria Tallchief) has the Host (Michel Katcharoff) in the palm of her hand. The Poet (Nicholas Magallanes, then Frederick Franklin) enters, and the Host reluctantly introduces him to his mistress. There follows a divertissement for the entertainment of the guests: a Shepherds' Dance (Constance Garfield, Nora White, Herbert Bliss, Nikita Talin), a Blackamoor Dance (Ruthanna Boris, Leon Danielian), a Harlequin Dance (Marie-Jeanne) and a Hoop Dance (Yvonne Chouteau, Pauline Goddard, Gertrude Tyven, Patricia Wilde). All of the guests except the Poet and Coquette leave the garden. The Poet and Coquette dance a passionate pas de deux. When the masked revelers return, the Host is angry to discover his mistress with the Poet, but she reassures him, and all excepting the Poet go indoors again. The Poet sees a beautiful Sleepwalker (Alexandra Danilova) walking in her trance with a candle. He fails in his attempts to wake her up. The Coquette returns and is furious to see her new love following the woman in white offstage. When the Host and guests return, the Coquette whispers to the Host. He leaves the garden, dagger in hand. In a moment, the Poet staggers on with a stab wound and falls to the ground, mortally wounded. The guests stare at the beautiful woman in white, who moves, still in her sleep, across the garden. She is the wife of the Host. Still in her trance, the Sleepwalker receives the lifeless body of the Poet and bears him away.

Tanning's backdrop, painted with a palette of greens and yellows, showed a moor occupied by a fantastical building of columns, archways and, at stage left, a tower. Headdresses for the guests suggested the heads of animals, fans, and other odd fantasies. Some critics tried to read surrealism into her designs; however, since the scene is a masked ball, there was a straightforward logic for dressing up as a ship or a bird cage, etc.

For those who identified George Balanchine with astringent abstractions, the ultra-romantic scenario and score came as quite a surprise. Critics were divided on the merits of *Night Shadow*. Walter Terry found it absurd: "Take a portion of left-over hash, garnish with bits of surrealism, add one poet and serve: the resulting dish will be called 'The Night Shadow.'" John Martin dismissed it as "a rather foolish little piece of pseudo-surrealism." Edwin Denby, however, was taken by its sense of mystery and even of horror: "It is disconcerting, absurd and disproportionate, but its effect when it is over is powerful and exact. It gives you a sense — as Poe does — of losing your bearings, the feeling of an elastic sort of time and a heaving floor."[85]

For all its virtues, the ballet did suffer from a lack of cohesion and sustained mood. The major break in continuity occurs right after the pas de deux for the Poet and the Coquette. As Walter Terry noted, "the air of romance which is supposed to be stated with the meeting of the coquette and the poet is suddenly dropped to make way for the divertissement; the dances of the divertissement, as I have indicated, are not of the caliber to warrant the dropping of any plot, no matter how feeble."[86]

But even the most negative critics agreed that the extended pas de deux for the Sleepwalker and Poet was hauntingly beautiful. With a soft, emotionless face, barely lit by the glow of the candle she carries in her hand, the Sleepwalker wafts to and fro around the stage as though urged on by gentle eddies of air. The Poet tries in vain to stop her. He embraces her, but she slips through his arms. He stretches on the floor, hoping that his body will stop his beloved, but she steps over him. She is like a toy on wheels as he causes her to run or to turn. And yet, in her detachment, there is a sense that she is aware of his presence and in his death this is realized, as she carries his body, alone and unaided, back to the bedroom from which she has come.

Danilova never once came off pointe for the entire pas de deux, and Balanchine gave her yet another challenge at the ballet's end. This ending, with its reversal of the usual pas de deux roles, caused audiences to gasp. It requires careful positioning of the Poet, who is lowered onto the Sleepwalker's outstretched arms. She must not falter when she receives his weight and must appear to float as she exits with his body. In an interview, Franklin explained the strategy for this lift: "She has to take his weight on her chest." He added that Danilova would always hiss at him, "Freddy, hook!"[87] as a reminder that he should immediately clamp his arm around her shoulder for better leverage.

Frederic Franklin as the Poet and Alexandra Danilova as the Sleepwalker in *Night Shadow* (later renamed *La Sonnambula*). 1946. Ballet Russe de Monte Carlo production. Photograph: Maurice Seymour, courtesy of Ronald Seymour.

Franklin noted, "If ever there was a ballet that rested on one person's shoulders, this [*Night Shadow*] was the one." Interestingly, John Martin complained that *Night Shadow* lacked focus when he saw the work on opening night. When Franklin took over the role on the second night, Martin believed that the focus had been found. Nicholas Magallanes was a good dancer, but, as in *Le Bourgeois Gentilhomme*, he could not deliver the magnetism and charisma of a Frederic Franklin. According to Franklin, "Nothing happened on his [Nicky's] face, ever, never. It was just blank."[88] A year after the premiere, Martin wrote, "'Night Shadow' was quite the feature of the program. From a dubious beginning a season or so ago, it has developed into an interesting theatre piece, overweighed with divertissements, but touching effectively on the macabre and unusual."[89]

On March 12, 1946, Balanchine and Alexandra Danilova presented their staging of *Raymonda*. As in *Night Shadow*, Franklin had to be replaced, resuming the role of Jean de Brienne when he recovered from his injury. First presented at the Maryinsky on January 19, 1898, *Raymonda* had been Marius Petipa's last major ballet. This work never became a repertoire staple as had Petipa's earlier masterpieces — *Sleeping Beauty, Nutcracker, Swan Lake.* There is a reason for this. Although *Raymonda* boasts a glorious score by Alexandre Glazunov, a picturesque medieval setting and masterful choreography, the ballet has a thin and unconvincing plot.

Raymonda takes place in Provence, France, from which Jean de Brienne (Nicholas Magallanes, then Frederic Franklin) is departing for the Crusades. During his absence, the castle is invaded by a Saracen Knight (Nikita Talin), who is on the point of abducting the noblewoman Raymonda (Alexandra Danilova). Jean returns unexpectedly and kills his adversary in a duel. Each of the few incidents in *Raymonda* offers an excuse for a divertissement. In the first act, Jean's departure is celebrated with dancing; in the second, the Saracen's slaves provide the entertainment; in the third, the betrothal of Raymonda and Jean is the cause of the festivities.

The Maryinsky *Raymonda* was three-and-one-half hours long. Balanchine and Danilova wisely cut the ballet down to one hour and forty-five minutes, but its length was still problematic. New Yorkers, accustomed to a mixed bill of short ballets, were unused to the leisurely, panoramic pace of Petipa. They were simply bewildered by such an approach and form. Add to this the problem of style. Martin wrote, "The work is a hodgepodge of styles.... Danilova captures the feeling of the period, but in the main, Balanchine's hand and his marked personal style are plainly in evidence. Without a more successful recapturing of the spirit of the original, the restoration seems to lack point." In the same vein, Lillian Moore pointed out, "The current revival has been mounted on a rather small scale, with none of the luxurious pageantry which is so necessary to the success of ballets of this type. The corps de ballet, which is quite at ease when confronted by the breath-taking technical feats demanded by modern choreographers, revealed a sorry lack of style in the simplest court dances."[90]

Eventually, *Raymonda* was reduced to a divertissement in one act and as such remained in the touring repertoire for many years. Later, for the New York City Ballet, Balanchine threw out any vestige of a story and culled three wonderful ballets from the score: *Pas de Dix, Cortege Hongrois* and *Raymonda Variations.*

Balanchine never considered allying himself permanently with the Ballet Russe. For one thing it eeked out its living with long one-night-stand tours of the country. Touring was Balanchine's idea of hell. But many dancers seemed to enjoy life on the road. While constant touring imposed a great deal of hardship, it also gave them a wealth of adventures and memories to savor.

"You cannot buy with all the money in the world the fabulous tours,"[91] said Miguel

Souvenir photo from Casino Russe, New York. Left to right: Tatiana Grantzeva, Frederic Franklin, Alexandra Danilova, Valentine Denham, George Balanchine, Irina Denham, Serge Denham. 1945. Photograph: Collection of Frederic Franklin.

Terekhov, a Uruguayan who joined the company as an impressionable youth. Asked if the tours were exhausting, Franklin replied, "Well you know, they weren't. We were young, we were kids, it was a new country. We really were having a wonderful time. I think back now — it was America, it was something. We'd only seen it in the movies."[92]

De Mille has left us with some vivid accounts of what it was like on tour:

> Riddled with sexual insecurity, financial instability, ambition, jealousy, and terror, they are herded from one engagement to another, locked within the frenzied confines of their group for ten months at a stretch. They never stop anywhere en route long enough to make outside contacts. Intrigue assumes Renaissance proportions. Romance is a kind of round-robin tournament and psychoses the hallmark of every experience.[93]

The company traveled like a circus, covering more than 20,000 miles in a season. At the beginning of the company's life, the Ballet Russe had its own private train. Those were the posh days of train travel for the company. But with America's entrance into World War II, the necessity of transporting military personnel by rail made private trains unavailable. From World War II onward, the Ballet Russe would usually travel in special cars attached to regularly scheduled trains, which limited travel flexibility and made the tours more onerous.

During a long string of one-night stands, the dancers would often emerge from the theatre at 11:30, grab dinner in a hash house or drug store and then board the train. They laundered their tights in the Pullman washrooms. Nylon being unavailable in the wartime years, the dancers had to wear woolen tights. Franklin remembers that it was exhausting to scrub all the glue off the heels. Moreover, the woolen tights shrank badly after washings: "Pulling them on and getting them off took away half of the energy you had reserved to dance."[94]

The dancers also slept on the train — when there was room, that is. Sometimes there were no special cars to be had or the cars would be claimed by servicemen, so the dancers had to stand in the aisles all night. De Mille wrote that when there were no Pullman sleepers to be had, the boys tore the seats apart to make beds for the girls. Agnes bedded down among them in the aisles, "three in a row." [95]

This troupe did not make the lives of the train porters any easier. Franklin remembers, "You get on the train and the porters would go through. Two coaches. Sleeping bodies blanketing the aisles. We never put our stuff back up in our valises. We just left it strewn about, and that upset them very much."[96]

De Mille described the scene at journey's end for a longer engagement with a train switch:

> On arrival everyone frantically stuffs belongings into bags and boxes. Down come Slavenska's furs from the case on the rack. Slavenska's cat is put in a basket by Slavenska's mama. Danilova unpins last night's orchids from the back of her seat. The poker players settle their debts rather loudly. Wet wash is stuffed into hatboxes, knitting into the cosmetics. All, girls and boys, load up and stagger out. There are not arms enough for gallantry, and no one can afford a porter; the girls lug their own suitcases. The car looks like an abandoned picnic ground.[97]

During short train stops, it was not unusual to have outdoor classes and rehearsals. Irina Baronova recalls, "We wrapped towels around barbed wire fences in the farm land and did barre. Gradually the cows would come over and get interested. And the traffic! I'll just leave that to your imagination."[98] When the train stop was over, workaholic Léonide Massine would even pull dancers into the train corridors to rehearse.

Many of the dancers traveled with pets. Not just dogs and cats, but also rabbits, tortoises, and parrots. Colonel Wassily de Basil toured with two monkeys. According to George Zoritch, Massine's dog Smokey partook in a performance of *The Polovetsian Dances* one night in Kansas City. He strolled out quietly from the wings, just behind the footlights. When the audience started to roar with laughter, he barked out at them indignantly and then proceeded to sniff his way across the stage before making his leisurely exit. During one of the tours, Lubov Rostova picked up a stray fox terrier. She brought the dog to the theatre and, without time to purchase a dog collar and leash, she improvised and tied him up in her dressing room with a long red ribbon from an admirer's bouquet of roses. In the middle of *Les Sylphides*, at that famous moment when the soloist and corps assemble to form three human fountains, the terrier chose to make his appearance, dragging the twelve-foot red ribbon behind him. He then proceeded to sniff each of the three formations of dancers in turn, anxious to find his new mistress.[99]

In 1942, Ballet Russe corps de ballet members earned forty-five dollars a week as opposed to weekly salaries of $121 for company stagehands and $140 for pit musicians.[100] On longer engagements, the dancers stayed in hotels, but few people in the company could afford the luxury of a private hotel room. Instead, dancers often slept eight to a room in a practice known as "ghosting." One dancer would officially check in while the other seven schemed up strategies for sneaking up to the room unobserved. The "ghosts" would then pull the bed apart, some sleeping on the box springs, some on the mattresses. During the war, even the principals sometimes had to ghost. Once, passing through a hotel lobby, Franklin discovered Danilova lurking behind a potted plant. "Whatever are you doing, Choura?" he inquired. "Ssh," she whispered, "tonight I am the spook!"[101]

Thanks to their worldly reputation, dancers were sometimes invited to the homes of wealthy benefactors and well-heeled fans after the show, though as Marc Platt off maintained, the dancers typically exited the theaters in the one suit or black dress they owned, even if they weren't going anywhere, just to maintain the company aura of glamour.[102]

Given her privileged upbringing, it's not surprising that de Mille was struck by their meager existence: "What does the Russian Ballet look like on tour? Different from what you've been led to believe. Most of the girls and boys are simply, even poorly, dressed. They have no money. In fact they have borrowed months ahead on next season's contract in order to get through their two-month's vacation. They live like indentured servants."[103] Nor were the paychecks, small as they were, always on time. Moscelyne Larkin remembers a South American tour when payday was mysteriously postponed to a new day in each country they entered.[104]

Besides "ghosting," another way for the dancers to economize was to avoid eating in restaurants. However, all hotels in those days had a strict policy against taking meals in the rooms. Hot plates, at the time, were extremely dangerous fire hazards in the confined space of a hotel room. Even so, the hallways of the local hotel usually reeked of cooking when the Ballet Russe was in town. Sometimes the management would send up detectives and evict the dancers without a refund.

George Zoritch had hot-plate cuisine down to a fine art. He always tested the air circulation before cooking. If the air was going out the window, he would cook there. If there was a strong vent in the bathroom, he would cook his steak there. Here was his recipe: "After cooking fresh vegetables, I drained the vegetable juice, placing the steak over the vegetables. Turning the hotplate *upside down* [author's italics], I grilled the steak, letting the juices drip down onto the vegetables I had already cooked in a small pot.... Many hungry dancers lining up for the dining car would pass my seat and ask what I was having for lunch that day. The idea spread."

Zoritch found clever places to hide his food from the management, but sometimes he just settled for the window ledge. After a performance in Portland, he returned to his room to discover that sea gulls had stolen his provender. "[They] made a party out of my dinner and left no thank-you except for their lime calling cards on the ledge."[105]

While Zoritch may have been the most resourceful of the food bandits, he was not the only one. Katie Geleznova joined the Ballet Russe in 1957, and her mother traveled with the company. One Christmas, when the company was staying at the Sherman Hotel in Chicago, she decided to smuggle a turkey into her room. She hid it under her coat, but there was one contingency she hadn't thought of. Franklin recalls, "there was steam coming out; she had the bird, but there was steam coming out of the top of the coat. I thought, 'What *is* this?' We got in the elevator and she looked at me and the people were staring at her and there's steam's coming out of her coat!"[106]

Road Manager Maury Winters had tried to nip these goings-on in the bud in 1940. He had noticed that several of the "ballet mothers" carried mysterious shoe bags with them wherever they went, and he finally discovered what was in them. When the company arrived in Chicago, he confiscated all the shoe bags and dumped their contents onto the stage floor of the theatre: "There were pots and pans all over the stage! Because we had five mothers. The young girls could never eat otherwise. And somebody went to Mr. Winters and said, 'Look, you can't do this. They're earning forty-five dollars a week. That feeds two people — a mother and a daughter.' And they managed. Oh, dear me."[107]

"Ballet mothers" were simply a company fact of life. Most of them were Russian émigrés, and since many no longer had any place they could call home, it might just as well be the Ballet Russe. When the company had trouble getting supernumaries at one of their tour stops, the moms would volunteer. Massine's *Union Pacific* was a railroad ballet in which rigid dancers in brown sacks were carried on to the stage to be laid as rails on the tracks. It often happened that the mothers were unceremoniously stuffed into the bags, thus making themselves useful for a different reason.

In larger towns, it was easier to recruit the requisite supers. Usually they came from the local dance schools, but it often happened that the volunteers knew absolutely nothing about ballet. Jack Anderson describes a hysterical incident where supers were asked to portray the warriors of the Persian Shah in *Schéhérazade*. Hasty instructions were given to the teenage boys in broken English: "When zere is great excitement on ze stage, zou must rush in and stab zem all." The boys stood backstage in their exotic Persian costumes. After a while, they noticed that the action on stage had built up to a frenzied pitch of excitement. Anxious not to miss their cue, the boys dashed onstage and proceeded to slay with their scimitars all the cowboys in the "Hoedown" of *Rodeo*.[108]

Interaction with the locals could take a variety of forms. Franklin recalls an incident in 1939, when he was to perform with the Ballet Russe in Phoenix or Tucson (he's not sure which):

> The local promoter thought the best way to drum up publicity was to send four dancers through town in a horse-drawn cart firing off guns. I told the man, "You're crazy." He said, "We have to let the town know you're here." They put a Ballet Russe billboard on the side of the cart. I'd never held a gun in my hand in my life, but we went around shooting to get the audience in that night. That's how it was.[109]

Two years of touring was just about all that George Balanchine could take. He was also disturbed by commercial pressures, which decreed that the repertory be geared to the box office. This meant big-name stars and plenty of flashy onstage fireworks out in the boondocks. Money matters also meant that the Ballet Russe could afford only a small orchestra on the road, which limited the range of ballets the company could present. The standards of pickup musicians were often low and prevented Balanchine's Stravinsky works, in particular, from being performed properly.

Balanchine left to create works for Lincoln Kirstein's new Ballet Society. He also did a brief stint as artistic director of the Paris Opéra, Serge Lifar having been accused of collaborating with the Nazis and dismissed. But the clever Lifar had always made it a policy to secure the loyal adoration of his dancers, and they successfully petitioned to have him reinstated. The experience left Balanchine with a bitter taste in his mouth, as he had probably hoped that his Paris Opéra post would be permanent.

When Balanchine returned to Ballet Society, this small subscription troupe was offered a permanent residency at City Center and was re-christened the New York City Ballet in 1948. There was great mutual admiration and respect between Balanchine and Franklin — they had even been roommates on the Ballet Russe tours. Balanchine asked Franklin to join the new venture as both ballet master and choreographer. Freddie declined because he still wanted to perform. For Franklin, Balanchine was one of the great influences in his life, and his respect for the choreographer was immense. But he was not above a delicious imitation of Balanchine's habitual nose sniffing, which resembled an animal trailing an interesting scent.[110]

· 4 ·

Ballet Russe de Monte Carlo:
The Twilight Years

The 1946–47 season returned the Ballet Russe to the situation in which it had found itself after Massine's departure in 1942. It was a company without a resident choreographer, and it never acquired one again. The Balanchine boom was over.

The company had a City Center season from September 4 to 16, 1946. On September 6, New York saw *The Bells*, which the Ballet Russe had first presented on August 30 at Jacob's Pillow. This was Ruth Page's second work for the Ballet Russe. Page's own company in Chicago had premiered the ballet on April 26, 1946.

The Bells was based on an 1849 poem by Edgar Allan Poe. In the popular estimation, "The Bells" is rated above all other poems by Poe, excepting "The Raven." Poe had no specific literary theme in his poetic progression from "the jingling and the tinkling of the bells" to "the moaning and the groaning of the bells," but Page attempted to parallel its psychological development with a libretto about the breakup of a marriage. *The Bells* is divided into five sections: "Silver Bells," representing the carefree gaiety of youth; "Golden Bells," symbolic of marriage, happiness and fulfillment; "Bronze Bells," which give warning of tragedy to come; "Iron Bells," symbolizing the approach of the forces of evil; and "The Ghouls," representing final futility, death and destruction. Franklin starred as the Bridegroom with various dancers as the Bride and Nikita Talin as the King of the Ghouls.

The simple and effective décor by Isamu Noguchi consisted of the skeleton of a church, which rose gradually in the background until at the climax of "Golden Bells," it dominated the scene, only to collapse into ruins at the end of the ballet. For the dance of the "Iron Bells," Noguchi designed bell-shaped costumes which made the dancers appear as six pairs of detached, bodiless black legs. Unfortunately, the costumes were unintentionally humorous because they were so literal.

The music of Darius Milhaud proved to be a major problem. When originally performed for the Composers' Concert Series in Chicago, the symphony orchestra was able to conquer the difficulties of the score. However, the Ballet Russe orchestra had never had the luxury of adequate rehearsals, and its musicians were not of the same caliber as those in a symphony orchestra. Denham decided that there was not enough money for a complete dress rehearsal with orchestra, lighting and full company for *The Bells*. To make matters worse, Alexandra Danilova pulled a tendon, and Ruth Page had to step in for her as the Bride at the last minute.

The New York premiere of *The Bells* was a disaster. Edwin Denby grumbled, "'The Bells' is a piece that goes on for half an hour being puerile in public.... Everybody suffers more and more and works hard at it." George Amberg found it "a choreographic experiment eminently worth doing," although he added that *The Bells* was "unlikely to become popular."[1] Page was bitterly disappointed, but she didn't give up. There was no way to solve the discrepancy between the magnitude of Poe's poetic vision and the scope of its realization on a stage. However, changes and improvements were made on the road, and when the company returned to New York for its spring season, Page had pulled *The Bells* into better focus by sharpening the characterizations of the leads. Franklin and Ruthanna Boris, the new Bride, were praised for their excellent perform-

Alexandra Danilova, Frederic Franklin, and Nikita Talin in a publicity still for *The Bells*. 1946. Jacob's Pillow Dance Festival, Becket, MA. Décor and costumes: Isamu Noguchi. (Danilova, shown as the Bride, was injured and did not perform; Ruthanna Boris did the role.) Photograph: Larry Cowell, in the collection of Frederic Franklin.

ances. *The Bells* gave Franklin an outstanding dramatic role in his thus far generally lyric career.

Although the work improved considerably, Milhaud's difficult score remained an insuperable problem, even after he rewrote the finale to make it easier for the orchestra to play. Later on, Milhaud is reported to have said that if he ever composed another ballet, it would consist entirely of whole notes for one finger on the piano.[2]

Following yet another lengthy tour, the Ballet Russe had a season at City Center from February 16 to March 30, 1947. *Le Baiser de la fée* was revived, with Franklin and Tallchief in the leading roles. Walter Terry praised their performances: "Mr. Franklin's characterization was strongly drawn, disclosing the bewilderment, the vain defiance and ultimate subjection of a marked youth. One of the most sinister and compelling portrayals in ballet is that of Maria Tallchief as the Fairy, for she dances it with arrogant intensity and cruel beauty as if she were presiding over an evil incantation."[3]

Virginia Sampler premiered on March 4, 1947, with choreography by modern dancer Valerie Bettis. The title of Miss Bettis's work can be said to have a double application. It is not only a figurative version of an old-fashioned piece of needlework devoted to early Virginia, but it is also a sampler of an experimental choreographic approach. *Virginia Sampler* had a sketchy story about the disruption of the conventional pattern of a Virginia town, in the period after the American Revolution, by the arrival of strangers. It does not tell a dramatic story nearly so much as it develops dramatic themes and weaves them together formally. The General (Casimir Kokitch) and his dapper couriers form one set of figures passing through the town, and the Frontiersman (Leon Danielian) and his bearded comrades are another set. There is the Young Girl (Marie-Jeanne) with a choice to make between the eminently eligible but fairly stuffy Young Bachelor (Frederic Franklin) whom her mother urges upon her, and her strong romantic attraction to the Frontiersman. There is also an Unidentified Lady (Valerie Bettis) on horseback who serves in some manner not altogether clear to resolve the romantic situation in favor of the Frontiersman. For most critics, the tensions in the narrative were not fully developed, and the dramatic impact was slight. But the most substantive criticism related to Bettis's lack of experience in the ballet idiom.

Virginia Sampler was the first work by a modern dancer to be produced by any American ballet company. George Amberg wrote:

> Because of her particular background, she was used to a different kind of dance impulse and dynamic response, another kinesthetic pattern and a more directly intuitive projection of emotional states. The result was altogether unsatisfactory, since the dancers went quasi-mechanically through the motions prescribed in the choreography, but evidently, through no fault of theirs, did not fully grasp the essential meaning they were called upon to convey.[4]

John Martin stated categorically, "Modern dance deals in expressive movement evolved from inner emotional impulse while the ballet dancer on the contrary is trained to execute expertly an established vocabulary of objective movements designed for brilliance and spectacle." In a later review he wrote, "These are antithetical approaches and when put together must necessarily cancel each other out." In his review of *Virginia Sampler*, Anatole Chujoy concurred, declaring ballet "objective and impersonal" and modern dance "subjective and personal."[5] The merger of the disciplines — the most sweeping phenomenon of twentieth century ballet — was still a few decades away, and critics at this time took a dim view of mixing what was then regarded as "apples and oranges." *Virginia Sampler* was an interesting, but unsuccessful, experiment. Although few would have predicted it in 1947, Bettis's second foray into the ballet world — her 1952 *A Streetcar Named Desire*— would be resoundingly successful.

Madroños premiered in New York on March 22, 1947. It was choreographed by an American concert dancer named Phyllis Nahl who adopted the stage name of Antonio Cobos. She was extremely talented, but she was reputed to be an agonizingly slow worker. Jack Anderson wrote that her rehearsals resembled "sessions at Penelope's loom because of her tendency to undo each day what she had accomplished the day before."[6]

Taking its title from the Spanish word for the pompons on some of the exquisite costumes by Castillo, a designer for Elizabeth Arden, *Madroños* was credited with music by "Moszkowski, Yradler and others," the term "and others" referring to tunes by Cobos herself. The premiere was scheduled for March 20, 1947, but it had to be postponed until March 22 because of an injury to Cobos, who danced the leading female role of La Niño del Oro as a guest artist. Critics were refused admittance to that performance, company management considering the ballet still unready for appraisal by the press. The first critics' performance was on March 25.

Just as Cobos kept changing her mind in rehearsal, so *Madroños* kept changing its shape, which it could easily, since it was a suite of dances related only by their Spanish character. Highlights of the first version consisted of a solo for Franklin as Meneteroso in a battered beggar's costume and a pas de deux for him and Cobos; a dance with castanets for Ruthanna Boris (introduced after the first performance); and a scene starring Leon Danielian as the vain and foppish toreador, El Bonito, flocked by adoring females. In a later version, Franklin acquired a rich velvet costume and ceased to be a beggar.

Although he found Cobos's choreographic intent somewhat hazy, John Martin essentially liked the work: "Whatever the reservations, it is a richly talented and generally rewarding work. Miss Cobos is a young woman of rare gifts."[7]

Danielian walked off with the laurels in *Madroños*. He was one of two American-born premier danseurs in the United States in his generation. (The other was John Kriza.) Danielian was well-known for his exceptional speed, purity of line, theatricality and lyricism. Martin wrote, "The boy can dance like a house afire."[8] Danielian had danced with the Mordkin Ballet since 1937 and had been with the Ballet Theatre as a soloist since its inception in 1939. He remained in Ballet Theatre through the end of 1941, danced briefly with de Basil's ballet and joined the Ballet Russe de Monte Carlo in 1943.

The most important personnel changes of the 1947–48 season were the departures of Marie-Jeanne, Maria Tallchief and Nicolas Magallanes after the City Center season. In the late spring, Roman Jasinski joined the organization. The company opened in Mexico City on May 19, 1947, then returned to the United States for summer bookings, including an engagement at the Hollywood Bowl. This is where Ruthanna Boris's *Cirque de Deux* premiered on August 1, 1947. Earlier, John Martin had written, "It is rumored that Miss Boris is turning her thought toward choreography these days, and it is a hopeful rumor. If she can match her musicianship, her dramatic instinct, and her gift for seeing the total form of a work with an equal flair of invention, she should make an admirable choreographer indeed."[9] His prediction was correct.

It was not easy for a young, untested ballerina to get a choreographic commission from Serge Denham. According to Franklin, Boris went over and over again to Denham, saying that she wanted to do a ballet, but he kept putting her off. He gave her the chance only when she agreed to pay all the expenses herself.[10]

Cirque de Deux was a triumph for Ruthanna Boris, an emphatic hit with both audiences and critics. It is an intimate and ingratiating comedy-ballet with scenery and costumes by Robert Davison and music drawn from the "Walpurgis Night" sequence of Gounod's opera *Faust*. *Cirque de Deux* was a parody on the rock-ribbed tradition of classical ballet, and it followed the format of a Petipa grand pas de deux. The whole ballet was couched in brassy, glittering circus terms. Not two, but four, performers graced the cast. Both the ballerina (Ruthanna Boris) and her partner (Leon Danielian) had pages (Patricia Wilde, Frank Hobi) who had their own definite functions within the form of the performance, but who made their own personal observations *about* the performance when and where they had the opportunity.

The curtain rises on a stage festooned with streamers, flags and balloons. In the center is an ingenious circular platform, which can be turned on its own base and also wheeled about the stage. At the end of an opening procession, which constitutes the *entrée* of the classical pas de deux, the principals remove their capes, hand them to the pages, and make ready for the exploits that lie ahead. These begin with the adagio. First, the ballerina sustains difficult poses atop the revolving platform, while her partner wheels her around the stage to extend the movement into space and at the same time to emphasize the static quality of its ostentation. There follow two variations, the male's danced with a baton and the female's danced with a riding whip. The closing section, corresponding to the Coda, employs most of the technical tricks known to standard ballet. The ballerina whirls in the inevitable series of *fouettés*. Every time her partner soars in a series of *entrechat six*, the two pages sag so that the spectator has the impression of a human seesaw. When the fireworks have ended, the pages retrieve the capes and drape them augustly about the principals. A deep bow to the audience concludes this tongue-in-cheek performance.

Boris managed to express the circus throughout, not so much by an imitation of circus acts as by her translation of them into pure dance terms. As in a circus arena, Boris displayed her dancers at all angles, flattering and otherwise. The boy's solo touched upon the problem of balance and of *ballon*, as it might occur in tightrope-walking maneuvers; the ballerina pranced through her variation like an equestrienne and her horse. *Cirque de Deux* did not depend on inept execution for its humor as did many "humorous" ballets of this era. Walter Terry's remarks typified the critical response to *Cirque de Deux*: "Ruthanna Boris's first choreographic effort delighted me not only because of the theme but because of her expert handling of it." John Martin wrote, "It actually gets under the surface of the whole Petipa era and tells us something about it with an eloquence that words could not approximate."[11]

According to Franklin, Ruthanna remains quite the individualist to this very day: "She is wild. She goes to prisons."[12] It is true that in her later years, Ms. Boris has been active in undertaking on-site visits and letter correspondences with inmates in various state prison systems, devoting much of her time in the effort to bring them hope, comfort and spiritual strength.

After the Hollywood Bowl performances, the company had a season at City Center from September 7 to 21. *Cirque de Deux* had its New York premiere. The other premiere was *Lola Montez*, first seen on September 12, 1947. Based on a book by Dr. N. Wolf, *Lola Montez* had music by Fred Witt, orchestration by Ivan Boutnikoff, and costumes by Raoul Péne du Bois and Paolo d'Anna. To minimize financial outlay, *Lola Montez* was fitted out with the discarded sets of *Ghost Town*, designed by du Bois.

Lola Montez may well have been the worst ballet ever produced by the Ballet Russe, with the possible exception of *Saratoga*. Choreographed by Edward Caton, it was first performed in 1946 for a small company called Ballet for America. According to the program notes, *Lola Montez* depicted a "romantic escapade" of the notorious courtesan-dancer Lola (Ruthanna Boris), in a California mining community in the period of the Gold Rush and her subsequent adventures with a Hero (Frederic Franklin). Early in rehearsals Caton realized that his ballet was going to be an embarrassing flop and requested that it be withdrawn, but the management, having promised it, felt it had to be presented, and it hit the boards against Caton's wishes.[13]

George Amberg called *Lola Montez* a "stillborn piece of Americana." John Martin said that it was "formless, pointless and a general waste of time and effort on both sides of the footlights." But he did add that the piece was "mercifully brief."[14]

At the end of September, the company embarked on its annual tour. When the company returned to City Center for a four-week season beginning February 15, a new Ruth Page ballet was shown. *Billy Sunday* was originally presented in a 1946 lecture-demonstration in a series at the University of Chicago. It had its Ballet Russe debut in York, Pennsylvania, on January 29, 1948, with set designs by Alexander Calder and a score by Remi Gassman. New York first saw it on March 2.

Billy Sunday was inspired by a colorful early twentieth century evangelist who preached in the vernacular of the baseball diamond and street corner. Nicknamed "The Baseball Evangelist," Billy Sunday was a former Chicago White Sox player–turned–preacher. In his peak years from 1900 to 1925, he spoke to over one hundred million people in the days before radios and loudspeakers and was regarded by many as the savior of the national heritage.

The simple terms to which he reduced all issues and the colorful way in which he presented them were the keys to his appeal. His tie to sports afforded Sunday a useful evangelistic tool — a body of baseball metaphors by which to convey his understanding of the gospel. For example, God was the "Great Umpire of the Universe" who called people out at the end of their lives. According to Billy, Satan "could pitch with the best of them," and possessed "a spit ball that spits fire."

It was estimated that he walked a mile back and forth across the platform during every sermon. But it was not merely walking: it was also running, sliding, jumping, falling, staggering, whirling, catching, throwing and other baseball antics. When he was not pounding the lectern or the kitchen chair on which he sat before he began to speak, he was as often as not standing on one or the other, sometimes with one foot on the chair and one on the pulpit. Frequently he picked up the chair and swung it around his head, and he was known to crash the chair down upon the pulpit, smashing it to bits in order to express his wrath.

Page said in her memoirs that when she was being "finished off" in Miss Williams's and Miss McClellan's French School for Girls in New York, the schoolgirls were taken en masse to a Billy Sunday revival meeting. She never forgot that experience. Still, it is odd that she should choose Billy Sunday as the subject for a ballet if for no other reason than that Sunday preached that dancing was the first step down the road to a life of immorality and charged that three-fourths of all fallen women fell as the result of the dance![15]

The ballet's sermon on temptation consisted of four stories: David and Bathsheba, Joseph and Mrs. Potiphar, the Wise and Foolish Virgins, and Samson and Delilah. All four were based upon sermons in Billy's volume, *Love Stories of the Bible*. Ray Hunt, Sunday editor of the *Chicago Times*, wrote sermon texts that paralleled the style of the original ones, which Page couldn't use because of copyright restrictions. The stories present a strange combination of fierce sincerity, *naïveté* and American corn.

For the past five years, Page had been giving solo performances in which she danced and recited poetry at the same time. While Page had used onstage singers in *Frankie and Johnny*, *Billy Sunday* was her first full-scale ballet where spoken words were employed. Most of the lines were delivered with a broad, nasal Midwestern accent by Franklin (a Liverpudlian of all people) in the role of Billy. Franklin recalls people reeling in their seats the first time he boomed the opening lines of Hunt's text: "Temptation is the Devil looking through the keyhole.... Yielding is opening the door and letting him in!" The ballet ended with Franklin exhorting the audience to "Swing the bat of righteousness!—Swing the Bat of Faith! Hit a home run and knock the Devil out of the box!"[16] Some of the lines were delivered by Danilova as Mrs. Potiphar, sporting a marcelled blonde wig, feather boa and lorgnette as she emoted over the sanctimonious Joseph. The audience reportedly shrieked with delight at her hilarious lines in Russianized English.

In his revival meetings, Billy often enacted the various characters in the Bible himself. In the ballet, Franklin stepped into the roles of the men he was preaching about and stepped out of them again to make comments to the "congregation." In each instance, he remained in his preaching clothes, but put on something to suggest the character he was portraying—a crown for David, a wig for Samson. For dramatic purposes, Page put some of the female characters en pointe. The Wise Virgins did an American trucking step on their toes, in contrast to the Foolish Virgins, who did the same step *terre-a-terre* in a jazzy style. The role of Mrs. Potiphar was also en pointe in order to enhance her snootiness. The Samson and Delilah episode caused quite a stir, for Page made Ku Klux Klanners of the Philistines.

Anatole Chujoy told Danilova that she was belittling herself as a great classical ballerina by playing such a low comedy role, but, according to Page, "the audience found her spicy and really laughed." During rehearsals, Page bragged to Danilova that she could speak loudly and clearly even while turning multiple pirouettes. Choura looked at her quizzically and asked, "And Ruth, about what do you speak when you do pirouettes?"[17]

Page wrote that "the real Mrs. Billy Sunday was horrified that I made a ballet out of her husband's life work. I tried to assure her that I was not making fun of him, that I was simply trying to make a ballet in the vernacular, just as Billy had done with bible stories. She was never convinced."[18]

One gathers from accounts that *Billy Sunday* had insufficient rehearsal time, a problem exacerbated by the fact that composer Remi Gassman did not finish the orchestration until just before the opening. The music was also very reedy and introspective, when the subject matter called for something brash and brazen. Franklin believes that "all the weaknesses were due to the strange music," noting that "it had dissonant overtones of Stravinsky and Hindemith and nothing of the spirit of the piece."[19]

Even with post-premiere revisions, *Billy Sunday* was only a mixed success. With a suitably animated score and more time for Page to work out her ideas, there might still have been hope for this piece. It did not help matters when New York's Roman Catholic diocese struck again (as they had for *Frankie and Johnny*). Among other demands, church officials insisted that the Wise and Foolish Virgins be renamed "The Wise and Foolish Maidens" in order to remove the sexual connotations from the parable and also that in the scene in which Delilah betrays Samson to the Ku Klux Klan, the crosses be removed from the Klansmen's costumes.[20] When Danilova announced in the fall of 1948 that she would no longer dance Mrs. Potiphar because of so much shocked criticism from balletomanes, the ballet died a quiet death.

The other Page ballet to premiere this season was *Love Song*. It opened in Rochester, New York, on April 5, 1948, but did not get a New York premiere until 1949. *Love Song* concerned a Sad One (Ruthanna Boris) who sinks into melancholy when her lover, the Romantic One (Leon Danielian), leaves her for the Flirtatious One (Yvonne Chouteau). This lyrical, classical ballet was way off the beaten path for Ruth Page, and it was not successful. Walter Terry observed, "Its sentimental, romantic theme provided the noted choreographer with little opportunity to display those gifts of wit, ingenuity and adventurousness which distinguish many of her compositions."[21]

Page had great affection for Franklin. Freddie said, "Ruth used to call me the choreographer's delight because I could push anything over the footlights."[22] When asked if he really was as ebullient as he always seems, Page responded:

> Yes! He was apparently born that way. When any choreographer starts a new ballet with Freddie, he gives his all. He is always with you or even a step ahead, and sometimes a quite mediocre ballet will be a success on account of his immediate rapport with the audience.... Some people say that such boundless enthusiasm must be superficial, but knowing Freddie as long as I have, I totally disagree.[23]

Until the mid–1950s, Ruth Page danced the principal roles in her own works and others in the repertoire presented by the Page-Stone Ballet. From 1954 to 1969, she limited her roles to that of ballet director and choreographer for Chicago's Lyric Opera. At the opera, she developed a company with excellent principal dancers and expanded it into a ballet troupe, Ruth Page's Chicago Opera Ballet, which had a repertoire of Page ballets and long, independent touring seasons. Ruth continued to take a daily ballet class until she was well into her eighties. She died on April 7, 1991, at the age of ninety-two.

Franklin restaged *Giselle* in this 1947–48 season. When Serge Lifar returned to the Paris Opéra after his Ballet Russe appearances in 1938, Massine had no interest in overseeing the work. The ballet went right out of the repertory after 1940. Franklin's staging drew on the very similar versions of the Markova-Dolin company and the Vic-Wells. The revival gave Freddie his first opportunity to dance the role of Albrecht and a chance to prove yet again his amazing versatility. Danilova danced the title role, with Mary

Ellen Moylan as Myrtha. When *Giselle* was performed in Montreal that year, one critic wrote, "This ballet should have been called 'Albrecht.'" According to Freddie, Danilova (who danced the title role that night) was furious.[24]

In the season that saw the premieres of *Billy Sunday, Lola Montez* and *Love Song*, a Polish dancer named Nina Novak joined the Ballet Russe. She began her career as a member of the Polish Ballet, but during the war, she and her brother were sent to labor camps. She emigrated to America in 1947 and began studying with Tatiana Chamié. It was Chamié who introduced Novak to Serge Denham, and Denham fell madly in love with her. Soon after she joined the Ballet Russe, Denham began to insist on casting her in classical roles, when she was far better-suited to character and *demi-caractère* parts. As time went on, Novak would play an increasingly powerful role in company operations, with a resulting plunge in company morale.

Sol Hurok had recently announced that he was through with ballet. He relinquished his rights to the ballet seasons at the Metropolitan Opera House, making the Met available to companies not under his auspices. Since the spring of 1944, the Ballet Russe had been associated with the cramped and uncomfortable City Center. The company was now able to move to the more prestigious Met for a gala season from September 18 through October 10, 1948. It was a fateful decision to leave City Center since, in the same year, New York City Ballet was offered a permanent residence there.

By 1948, Massine and Denham had buried the hatchet, and Denham asked Massine to restage *Seventh Symphony* and *Rouge et Noir*. He also invited Markova, Slavenska, and Dolin to appear as guest artists. Three new ballets had their premieres. Anton Dolin staged *Pas de Quatre*, José Torres performed a suite of solos in *Spanish Dances* (which Walter Terry described as "the nadir of the season"[25]) and Ruthanna Boris presented her second ballet, *Quelques Fleurs*. Franklin did not create any new roles this season, but he alternated with Dolin as Albrecht in *Giselle*. Agnes de Mille returned to give a nostalgic performance as the Cowgirl.

Pas de Quatre was danced by Danilova, Markova, Slavenska and Krassovska, with Markova as the great romantic ballerina, Marie Taglioni. The audience read intense rivalry into the ballet. Freddie remembers, "the audience hooted. They laughed their heads off, and the ballerinas did things like you've never known.... They were eyeing each other, taking away the hands — oh, you'd have to see it to believe it."[26] Of the Dolin revival, Martin wrote, "it was as heavy, farcical and styleless a presentation as the little piece has had within memory."[27]

Franklin believes that the acid interpretations of the ballerinas were due to something more than the unrestrained impulse to mug and overact — the ladies squabbled during rehearsals. For example, at one point in *Pas de Quatre*, there occurred a crossing from one side of the stage to another. Dolin rehearsed it so that Mia Slavenska was to pass in front of Alicia Markova. Markova stopped the rehearsal and said, "No, No, No!" To Slavenska she said, "Darling, after all, Taglioni would *never* go behind people. I must go in front, always." Said Franklin, "This was going on, and there'd be snide remarks to each other, and looks. This went right on the stage. Dolin had absolutely no control over any of it."[28]

Quelques Fleurs premiered on September 30, 1948. The ballet was actually a publicity stunt. Planning to reintroduce *Quelques Fleurs*, a scent unavailable in America during the war, the Houbigant perfume company decided it would sponsor a new ballet as part of its promotional campaign. The ballet could be on any subject — the only stipulation was that its title must be *Quelques Fleurs*. Although Ruthanna Boris had been promised total freedom, she played it safe by creating a scenario that had at least something to do with perfume. The haughty Contessa Illaria (Mary Ellen Moylan) is unsuccessful in her attempts to snare Zenobio Bonaventuri (Leon Danielian). An alchemist presents her with three Fragrant Ladies (Yvonne Chouteau, Gertrude Tyven, Patricia Wilde). But the perfumes are of no avail, because the youth prefers the perfumes to the Contessa. The work had a modest success.

All in all, this fall season was successful. Evidently, Denham was more willing this time to pull out his pocketbook, for Martin reported that the company's season represented "a new lease not only on the opera house but also on life. A spate of glamorous guest stars, an augmented and generally overhauled company, décors and costumes all spruced up, and a good deal of restudying of the repertoire conspired to make the old outfit look once again like a first-rate company, which it has not done for quite a while." Walter Terry concurred: "The organization girded up its loins, spruced up its dress and submitted to a few transfusions in the forms of guest ballerinas and additional personnel." He added, "Monte Carlo has its financial problems, but cruelly enough, the public is not interested in such details and expects its ballet to glitter and gleam as if its treasury were full."[29]

After its tour, the Ballet Russe returned to New York for a February12–March 20 season at City Center. The repertory was virtually the same as it had been for the previous successful season at the Met. However, they did not fare as well as they had in the fall: critics reported that the company looked tired and that the dancing was substandard. Markova and Dolin appeared for much of the season, but the company's regular stars were missing, as Danilova and Franklin had gone to London to dance as guests with the Sadler's Wells (formerly Vic-Wells). Robert Lindgren inherited most of Franklin's roles while he was in England.

In the spring of 1948, Franklin had made his first visit to London since the war. While there, Ninette de Valois approached him on the subject of guest appearances for Mme Danilova and himself with her company in March of 1949. Freddie believes, "She wanted to know just how we were and how her company stacked up."[30] Denham agreed to furnish a leave of absence for the duo, and in the early spring of 1949, they sailed for England and appeared for a month at Covent Garden with the Sadler's Wells.

On the night of his arrival, de Valois stationed Freddie in a stage box of the Royal Opera House to watch a performance of *Swan Lake*, with Margot Fonteyn and Michael Somes in the leading roles. Fonteyn's Odette was exquisite, but she rarely made it to the full thirty-two in her Act III *fouettés*. As Act III was concluding, the door to Franklin's box opened and Ninette barked, "'Well, how many did she do?' I said it was twenty-seven. She exclaimed, 'Oh! Two more than the last time!'"[31]

Halfway through the season, Danilova ruptured a calf muscle during the second act of *Giselle* and had to miss eleven of the scheduled performances. This occasioned Franklin's first run-in with the formidable Ninette de Valois:

> I went down to Miss de Valois and asked, "Could I dance with one of your ballerinas?" "No," she said. "We don't mix the guest artists with the regular." It was the management at Covent Garden

Alexandra Danilova as Mrs. Potiphar seducing Frederic Franklin as Jacob. Ballet Russe de Monte Carlo production of *Billy Sunday*. 1948. Photograph: Collection of Frederic Franklin.

who said, "look, that's not right. We paid these people to come here." And then the following day, she called me at the hotel and said, "Come down tonight. You will dance *Coppelia* with Moira Shearer."[32]

There was scant time to rehearse, and the Sadler's Wells version of the ballet was slightly different from that of the Ballet Russe. So Moira said, "Freddie, I'll do half of yours if you do half of mine."[33] Franklin and Shearer had a chemistry together that delighted the press and public. He was promptly paired to dance with her again in *La Boutique Fantasque*, and the response was even more enthusiastic. There was a flurry of publicity about the new Shearer/Franklin partnership.

At the time, the gorgeous, redheaded Moira Shearer was the most famous ballerina in the world. She had just danced and acted the leading role in the motion picture classic *The Red Shoes*. Emeric Pressburger's screenplay revolves around a ballet impresario who demands nothing less than utter devotion from his artists. When his prima ballerina, Victoria Page, falls in love with the company's musical director, the impresario forces Victoria to choose between her career and her lover and inadvertently causes her death.

Aware that most people in highbrow artistic circles considered a film contract to be an arrangement of the utmost vulgarity, Moira at first turned down the offer to star in *The Red Shoes*. She held out for nine months against the pleading of director Michael Powell. Moira thought that her steadfast and dedicated stance would earn her respect and support from de Valois, but this was far from the case. De Valois finally urged her to do the film: "Why don't you just do it, get it over with, get if off your chest, get if off ours?" Shearer was aghast.[34]

The Red Shoes took ballet out into a new mass market. When Michael Powell screened the film for Eagle Lion Classics, Inc., he said that the executives were "scared shitless. This was an art film with a vengeance! And everyone knew art and money were two different things." Most Eagle Lion executives believed that the film would simply have to be written off, but board member Benjamin Heineman finally persuaded the other executives to give it a chance. The film was booked at New York's Bijou Theatre, but only after Heineman had guaranteed its managers a run of six months. After it had run a year, Heineman was crowing, "I told you so!"[35] *The Red Shoes* ran for 108 weeks at the Bijou, setting a new record in Broadway movie history. The film also had record-breaking runs in Los Angeles, Chicago, Miami Beach, San Francisco, Boston, Philadelphia and major British cities as well.

At the time of Franklin's visit, reporters were still sniffing about the Sadler's Wells, knowing that any scoop on Moira would make great copy. Ninette de Valois was upset about the publicity because her "chosen one," Margot Fonteyn, wasn't featured in any of it. According to Franklin, "Ninette was furious! All the publicity was going to Moira and me. It created a sensation in the company. And Ninette did not like it."[36] The flurry over Moira and Freddie only increased her desire to push Moira to the side in favor of Margot.

When Danilova recovered, Franklin appeared with her in *Coppelia*, *Swan Lake*, *Giselle* and *La Boutique Fantasque,* but Shearer and Franklin were still the talk of the town. Freddie admits, "I had a small affair with Moira. Hullo! It was well-known in the country that I was going around with her. I adored her.... But the upshot of it was really rather terrible, because Ninette got worse. They treated me even more nastily, and I had a very unhappy season at Covent Garden."[37]

The Sadler's Wells was due to make its New York premiere at the Metropolitan Opera in October of 1949. Shortly before the company's departure, Margot Fonteyn held a farewell party for Franklin and Danilova. While Fonteyn was chatting with Miss de Valois, Freddie came over with some frosty words of farewell: "I said, 'Margot, I'm awfully sorry, but I can't stay.' She said, 'uh-oh.' And then I said, 'Oh, by the way, Miss de Valois, I am sure that when you get to America that you will be treated so beautifully. Unfortunately, that's not the way I was treated, returning to my own native country.'"[38]

The rep for this critically important American debut was to center around the company's lavish production of *Sleeping Beauty*. Hurok wanted Shearer to dance Aurora on opening night because of her fame in the U.S. De Valois retorted, "In that case, we're going home."[39] She was adamant that Fonteyn should have the premiere. Margot was the dancer whose success de Valois was betting would carry the company in New York, and she would not budge. Hurok lost the battle, but he at least got a promise from de Valois that Shearer would appear in some important role on opening night.

Shearer believes that de Valois did everything she could to sabotage her in her efforts to promote Margot:

> Ninette did something bad to me at the beginning of the season so that I would go down the drain, and I was just too confused not to do what she asked. Everyone had to be on the first night of *Sleeping Beauty*. I at once thought that I'd do my old roles of Fairy of the Crystal Fountain and one of Florestan's sisters, which I'd done in 1946. But no: "I want you to do Bluebird with Alexis Rassine," Ninette told me. She promised me plenty of rehearsal; in fact, I got two run-throughs in the basement of the Kingsway Hall. I'd never even had the costume on. She knew I'd go to pieces with nerves.[40]

As Nadia Nerina explains, Shearer's "confusion" cost her dearly:

> Moira just gave in. I could never understand it. Bluebird wasn't her role. It isn't a role for a ballerina — it's the man's part. Moira had never danced it. But obviously Ninette had promised Hurok that she'd be on the first night. Moira only had to say, "No, I'm not doing it, I'll wait until I appear as Princess Aurora." But Ninette got her on.... one can only speculate on what effect a Shearer first night would have had on Margot's career, and whether Moira herself realizes, to this day, the enormity of the error she made.[41]

Sleeping Beauty opened on October 9, 1949, at the Metropolitan. Curtain calls went on for at least half an hour. Fonteyn received unprecedented adulation and became an internationally famous star overnight. Shortly after the debut, Fonteyn appeared on the covers of both *Time* and *Newsweek*. For Margot, the New York experience was the public accolade of a lifetime. As for Shearer, she danced in Fonteyn's shadow for the rest of her career. For a time, this exquisite and underutilized ballerina refuted *The Red Shoes* myth that one must choose between a stage career and romantic bliss when she married Ludovic Kennedy shortly after the American tour of 1949–50. Soon after the birth of her first child, she retired from the ballet stage completely.

It was with great sadness that Shearer and Franklin parted ways in the summer prior to the American tour, but there were no good opportunities for Freddie in England, especially since de Valois had made it clear she didn't want him in the Sadler's Wells. Before returning to America, Franklin and Danilova appeared as guest artists with the short-lived Metropolitan Ballet Company at the Empress Hall at Earl's Court, Massine also being a guest. *Le Beau Danube* was given with Massine, Danilova and Franklin in the famous roles they had first danced together in 1938. The two stars of the company were Svetlana Beriosova and Erik Bruhn. They hoped to keep the Metropolitan running on their names, but their lesser-ranked dancers trailed far behind them in artistry and technique.

The Ballet Russe had a fall season at the Metropolitan from September 16 to October 3, 1949. Ballets that had their premiere were *The Mute Wife*, *Paquita*, *Graduation Ball* and *Birthday*. Franklin's late return from England precluded his creating any new roles. Antonia Cobos originally choreographed *The Mute Wife* for the Marquis de Cuevas

Ballet International in 1944. The Ballet Russe staging premiered on September 16, 1949. The libretto concerns a Husband (Leon Danielian) seeking a cure for his mute Wife (Nina Novak). But when the Doctor (Robert Lindgren) heals her, she becomes such a "talkaholic" that the husband finds relief only by piercing his own eardrums to drown her out. In the Ballet International version, the recovery of speech was wittily indicated through the wife's use of clattering castanets.

The Mute Wife was to have been done as a vehicle for Ruthanna Boris, but she apparently had "a little row" with Cobos, and the role was given to Nina Novak. According to Franklin, "It was Denham who put her in." Unlike Boris, Novak couldn't play the castanets, so they were used offstage instead of in the hands of the Wife. The point, therefore, was mostly lost. For the next year, Novak worked like a dog to master the castanets, and they were restored to the stage for the 1950–51 season. By then, Freddie reports, "She was really marvelous doing it."[42]

Paquita premiered on September 20. This was Danilova's staging of the Maryinsky classic by Petipa. She went back to the third act of *Paquita*, which she had seen as a schoolgirl at the Imperial Ballet. Originally made for Carlotta Grisi in 1847, *Paquita*, like many romantic ballets, found its way to the Imperial Russian Ballet, where it was mixed with Léon Minkus's music and Marius Petipa's choreography. Remembering what she could of the style and steps and checking with Lubov Egorova, Danilova arranged a suite of variations, pas de trois, pas de deux and group numbers. The ballet had costumes by Castillo, and it used one of the backdrops that Eugène Berman had designed for *Devil's Holiday*. While *Paquita* charms us today, a string of variations à la Petipa was considered passé in the 1940s, and critical response was lukewarm.

Graduation Ball was the novelty for the next performance on September 21, with choreography by David Lichine, reconstructed by Vladimir Dokoudovsky. This ballet depicts a ball for cadets and young girls at a military academy, and the leading roles were danced by Leon Danielian, Yvonne Chouteau and Nina Novak. First staged for de Basil's Original Ballet Russe in February of 1940, this work has always been a crowd-pleaser, and most critics responded positively. John Martin, however, groused that "youth is rampant to the point of becoming positively repellent."[43]

The last new premiere of this season was *Birthday*. It opened on September 27 with choreography by Tatiana Chamié. The ballet concerns a sophisticated Lady (Nana Gollner) on her fiftieth birthday, who, seated before her birthday cake, receives a nosegay. It sends her back to her fifteenth birthday, when there was a smaller cake and a similar nosegay. In particular, she remembers the Beloved (Oleg Tupine), who was among the guests. *Birthday* was a slight work, although critics did appreciate the technical performances Chamié pulled out of the dancers. Overall, despite all the new productions, the critics felt that the fall season was a disappointing one.

Following its tour, the company returned to the Metropolitan Opera from April 9 to 30, 1950. Though no one knew it, this was to be the company's last New York season for seven years. The season was distinguished by the remarkable dancing of the Paris Opéra Ballet's Yvette Chauviré, who performed as guest artist.

Chauviré brought three productions from France. *Mort du Cygne* was presented on April 11, 1950. It was a short pas de deux to Chopin choreographed by (whisper the name softly) Serge Lifar. Lifar had choreographed this work for a French film of that name starring Yvette Chauviré, Mia Slavenska and Janine Charrat. The film was released in America as *Ballerina*. *Mort du Cygne* was staged for the Ballet Russe by Chauviré's husband, Constantin Nepo, and starred Franklin and Chauviré.

Mort du Cygne was yet another one of those hunter vs. swan contraptions. Walter Terry reported, "the swan dies gracefully (after many a summer, one might add), and the hunter is belatedly regretful for his impetuous act." Terry praised Franklin for his "dignity and commendable patience" in witnessing the swan's demise.[44] Franklin was out-and-out chagrined to be dancing this role in public. He wailed, "I had to come on and hide behind a bush that wasn't there.... And then [after Yvette's solo], I had to *shoot* her!! How embarrassing!"[45]

Roméo et Juliette, with Franklin and Chauviré in the title roles, premiered on April 18. It was a digest version of Shakespeare's tragedy set to Tchaikovsky's tone poem and followed the tradition of Robert Helpmann's ballet adaptation of *Hamlet*. Just who choreographed this production is by no means clear. Basically, it was a version of the *Roméo et Juliette* created by Lifar in 1942 for the debut of Ludmilla Tcherina, but Ballet Russe programs said only that it had been staged by Nepo, and some programs on tour attributed the choreography to Chauviré herself. Anatole Chujoy termed it "a naively obvious pantomime mounted in a homemade high school dramatic-group fashion with the *enchaînements* never leaving the limits of an advanced adagio class." Doris Hering wrote, "It will remain forever a mystery to us how a choreographer (and this work smacked of Lifar, too) can presume to base a ballet upon a play without considering the structural continuity or the subcutaneous continuity of the original work."[46] *Roméo et Juliette* had somber monks among its characters who came onstage and proceeded to perform *entre-chats*. When asked about this piece, Franklin said, "Oh, it was really pathetic."[47] Nonetheless, *Roméo et Juliette* was the one work imported by Chauviré that remained in the repertoire after her departure, when it was danced by Yvonne Chouteau and Oleg Tupine.

The third Chauviré work premiered on April 25. *Grand Pas Classique* had choreography by Victor Gsovsky and was a well-danced exhibition piece for Chauviré and Oleg Tupine. For this season, there was also a revival of *Les Elfes*, which Fokine had arranged for René Blum's company. Franklin and Mary Ellen Moylen danced the leads for the Ballet Russe revival of this rather bland, abstract ballet.

The eclecticism in the commissioning of new work that the company had adopted as policy since Balanchine's departure had at first seemed exciting and experimental. But critics were increasingly disturbed by the company's lack of a clear artistic point of view. By 1950, the company seemed to be drifting without long-range goals. Ominously, there was no New York engagement during the 1950–51 season. The Ballet Russe began its fall season in Chicago instead.

The company opened in Chicago on October 16, 1950. The first new offering occurred on October 25, when Tatiana Chamié's *Prima Ballerina*, danced to the music of Charles Lecoq and arranged by Lucien Cailliet, had its world premiere. The set by Mstislav Doboujinsky showed the arched ballet rehearsal room of a continental opera house. Karinska made the Degas-style tutus, and the men wore the gray knickers and soft white shirts of a ballet company at work.

Prima Ballerina was a comic account of backstage intrigue, replete with male dancers in drag in the guise of "Stage Mothers." The ballet started with a class in which ten boys danced the gamut from barre work and adagio to some intricate allegro and proved the company had excellent male personnel. The rehearsal that followed brought in a temperamental prima ballerina (Alexandra Danilova). When she walks out on the company after slapping the face of the Premier Danseur (Frederic Franklin), her Understudy (Nina Novak) is given a shot at stardom. The cognoscenti may well have thought that Chamié was indulging in an insider's joke by casting Danilova as the leading ballerina and Novak as her scheming young replacement. The ballet was an entertaining trifle, but no more.

After *The Mute Wife*, *Prima Ballerina* was Nina Novak's second major role. She would play an increasingly dominant role in the affairs of the Ballet Russe de Monte Carlo with each year that passed. When asked if he could see anything coming vis-à-vis Novak, Franklin replied, "No, the writing was on the wall, but none of us saw it."[48]

Tatiana Chamié danced with Diaghilev's Ballets Russes and was a charter member of de Basil's Ballet Russe de Monte Carlo. During the 1938 split, she went with the Massine contingent. In 1943, she resigned from the company to start her own studio in New York. Both at the time of her active connection with the Ballet Russe and after her resignation, her role in that organization was far greater than it seemed to the casual observer. Neither Chamié's *Birthday* nor her *Prima Ballerina* were works of much significance. *Prima Ballerina* lasted only one season. Franklin believes that the opportunity to choreograph two works was a gift from Denham to Chamié.[49] It was through her that Denham became an aficionado of the ballet because of meeting her in 1936 on a boat when the de Basil company was returning to Europe. It was Chamié who introduced Serge Denham to millionaire Julius Fleischmann and who helped talk Fleischmann into donating the funds that got the company up and running. For many years, Chamié maintained an open house in her studio on evenings known as "The Wednesdays," to which Russian dancers, ballet masters, and directors of companies came to exchange news and opinions and at which many a new enterprise found its origin. Chamié died of spinal meningitis in November of 1953, at the age of only forty-eight.

As had been the case in 1950–51, there were no New York performances in 1951–52. Instead, there was constant touring, and it was a season of rumors, quarrels, reunions and farewells. Increasingly, the repertory was restricted to three staple ballets—*Nutcracker*, *The Magic Swan* and *Schéhérazade*. This menu of surefire crowd pleasers was jokingly referred to by the Ballet Russe dancers as "ham and eggs." Franklin joked, "whenever we needed money, we did ham and eggs."[50]

Chauviré and Slavenska returned for guest appearances in the 1951–52 season, as did Massine. In *Giselle*, Franklin partnered Chauviré as Albrecht, giving the role "a distinction it often lacks."[51] There was a good deal of attrition this season: by the time it ended, Franklin announced that he and Slavenska would leave and form their own company. Danielian went off to Les Ballets des Champs Elysées and at the end of the season, Danilova resigned, giving her last performance in Houston on December 30, 1951. There were rumors that she was angry over Denham's determination to grant ballerina status to Nina Novak. This was certainly Franklin's impression:

> We could see the way things were going. We could see what was happening. That it was Nina Novak who was creeping around and doing everything. Denham was so completely obsessed with

this young lady that there was, I believe, a terrific row. I was not there, so I don't know whether it's true or not. But there was a great unpleasantness between Mr. Denham and Danilova…. Choura had lost her footing in the company completely through this girl [Novak]. She'd gotten rid of Mary Moylan and Ruthanna Boris as well. They were in her way. Next there was Danilova. Because she got rid of them all. It's all there, and it can all be laid at Nina's door. And the company was gradually going down. And it closed.[52]

There were no new productions in 1951–52. The Ballet Russe dancers were demoralized by the end of this season, for much of their old prestige and glamour had vanished. Denham realized that it was time to call a halt to company activities. He created the Ballet Russe Concert Company, which toured during the seasons of 1952–53 and 1953–54 under the auspices of Columbia Artists Management. This chamber troupe of fifteen dancers, plus technical staff, did one-night stands by bus and truck with a single program consisting of *Swan Lake*, *Cirque de Deux*, the "Bluebird Pas de Deux" and *Gaîté Parisienne*.

In the meanwhile, Franklin and Slavenska were working feverishly on their new enterprise. Starting in 1948, Franklin and Mia Slavenska had been organizing small tours with a pick-up company, mostly from the Ballet Russe, during Ballet Russe vacation periods. They had high hopes that their new company would be for keeps.

Born in 1916, Slavenska began her studies at the Zagreb Opera School, where she became prima ballerina at age seventeen. She first won international fame for her role in the 1937 prize-winning film *La Mort du Cygne*. Slavenska played a leading ballerina of the Paris Opéra in rivalry with Yvette Chauviré for the devotion of a student. She joined the Ballet Russe in 1938, but left after the 1942–43 season and danced with Ruth Page's Chicago Opera Ballet, the Metropolitan Opera Ballet, Ballet Theatre and London Festival Ballet. Next, she organized a short-lived touring group, *Ballet Variante*, in 1947, touring with six dancers and two pianists. She returned to the Ballet Russe as a guest artist for three seasons, beginning in 1948.

Slavenska was an extremely beautiful woman with wonderful red hair. Franklin said that her beauty was "a mixture of Dietrich and Garbo." She had a womanly body, and always had to watch her weight, which "went up and down like a yo-yo."[53] She was nicknamed "The Businessman's Ballerina," a reference to that large sprinkling of tired businessmen who regarded ballet as an amusing opportunity to ogle the bodies of pretty dancers. Slavenska had exceptionally strong technique. According to P. W. Manchester, she could do thirty-two *fouettés* in either direction. When she hurt her left knee one year, she simply started spinning to the left.[54]

The Slavenska-Franklin company began its offerings with stadium performances. Ballet in summer theatre was beginning to click, and the local box office hit a new high when the company debuted at the amphitheatre in Olney, Maryland, the week of July 1, 1952.[55]

Franklin and Slavenska scored a coup when Danilova agreed to join the company as guest artist, following her performances with the London Festival Ballet. After some preliminary road engagements, the company took on the Big Apple with an outdoor performance at the Lewisohn Stadium on July 19, 1952. Some 15,000 people packed the stadium for this event, part of the Lewisohn's annual "Night of Ballet" series.

For this occasion, the Slavenska-Franklin company was augmented by dancers selected from New York's High School of the Performing Arts. For Walter Terry, "the result was surprisingly good. Not every one danced accurately and not all of the choreographic lines were neat, but the corps seemed to capture Mr. Franklin's own effervescent spirit." In the same review, Terry complained about the less-than-ideal dance conditions at the Lewisohn. In this huge outdoor theatre, one had the choice of sitting at a great distance from the stage and seeing whole bodies but missing details or sitting close and not seeing anything below the knee. Terry reported that it was a pleasant performance, "from the knees up."[56]

The performance, conducted by Franz Allers, opened with the company's shortened version of the *Nutcracker*. Franklin did double duty, partnering Danilova in the "Snow Pas de Deux" and returning in the second act as the Cavalier with Mia Slavenska, the Sugar Plum Fairy. Later in the show, Danilova and Franklin performed the Waltz from *Gaîté Parisienne* in matchless fashion. As Terry noted, "This duet and their dancing of it is now almost historical, and many of us will unashamedly shed a tear or two when the time comes that they will dance it together no longer."

The performance closed with a dish of spinach called *Settler's Sunday*. The ballet was choreographed by Slavenska and set to folk music arranged by Harold Byrns. *Settler's Sunday* was designated in the program as "a choreographic adaptation of American folk dances for the ballet stage." This ballet was a folksy disaster. Hints of action reminiscent of *Rodeo*, *Billy the Kid*, *Ghost Town*, *Union Pacific* and other Americana ballets were present, but the sum total was a hodgepodge. Walter Terry described it as "a pretty dreadful number. It has no discernible plot—although a good deal of inexplicable mugging goes on—and what it has to do with either a settler or a Sunday I fail to see." Miles Kastendieck called it "rhythmic, horsey and corny. A bit of courtin', of flirtin', and sparkin' and the like."[57] Fortunately for Franklin, he was not cast in this piece.

The remainder of the summer was spent rehearsing the company's four major new productions: *A Streetcar Named Desire*, *Mlle Fifi*, *Symphonic Variations*, and *Portrait of a Ballerina*. In the fall, the company toured the Midwest and Canada, where the new works had their first tryouts. *A Streetcar Named Desire* and *Mlle Fifi* began to look like hits.

The touring schedule was pretty gruesome. A November 1952 calendar in *Dance* reveals that they were in Reading on the first, Buffalo on the second, Rochester on the third, Erie on the fourth, Jamestown on the fifth, Oil City on the sixth, Cleveland on the seventh, and Zanesville on the eighth. They stayed for two days each in Columbus and Cincinnati—a relative luxury—and then it was on to Louisville. They actually had a day off on the fourteenth. There was no slackening of pace for the rest of the month.[58]

The Slavenska-Franklin Ballet opened at New York's Century Theatre on December 8, 1952. On the bill were the local premieres of *A Streetcar Named Desire*, *Symphonic Variations* and the shortened *Nutcracker*. John Martin reported that this modest ballet company "succeeded in surprising us all.... by its talent, its taste and its sense of adventure, it managed without difficulty to outclass more than one company with more insistent claims to eminence."[59] The troupe was scheduled for only one week at the Century, but sold-out houses prompted the management to extend their stay until January 3.

It was Valerie Bettis's *A Streetcar Named Desire* which marched off with the laurels at the Century. The work was to have been choreographed by Antony Tudor, but he backed out at the last moment. According to Franklin, "He got nervous. He thought about it and said, 'No, I can't do it.'" Franklin then thought of Bettis: "I called up Valerie and asked if she wanted to choreograph *Streetcar*. She said, "'What, *Streetcar Named Desire*? Oh, I don't think so. When do we start rehearsals?'"[60]

Valerie was a strikingly beautiful, tall, blonde Texan. She studied with Hanya Holm, danced with Holm's company for two years, and then began choreographing and dancing solo concerts in 1941 in New York. Her most famous work was a solo dance, "The Desperate Heart," accompanied by Bernard Segall's music and a recited poem by John Malcolm Brinin. She first performed this angst-ridden, yearning solo at the Humphrey-Weidman Studio in New York on March 24, 1943. Louis Horst called it "the finest modern dance solo of this decade."[61] Bettis was a pioneer in television dance and also had a considerable stage career as an actress and singer. After her 1947 *Virginia Sampler*, *A Streetcar Named Desire* marked her return to the ballet world.

Streetcar, which had its world premiere in Montreal on October 9, 1952, took New York by storm. As Freddie remembers, "In fear and trembling we opened, but it worked."[62] It was based, of course, on the Tennessee Williams play. Some viewers loved the ballet, some abhorred it — but it was certainly talked about. The action takes place in the flat of Stanley Kowalski in the French Quarter of New Orleans and also in the inner mind of Blanche DuBois.

Blanche (Mia Slavenska) is the last of a long line of Southern gentry who has come to visit her sister Stella (Lois Ellyn). Blanche is down and out: her husband has committed suicide, there has been a succession of family deaths, and the old plantation has been lost. Blanche is to blame for some of this. She is unable to face reality and seeks escape in promiscuity. She has been unable to hold a job. She has just been exiled from her own town. She is a fading Southern belle with dreams of former ladyhood, and her sister is her last refuge.

Stanley (Frederic Franklin), Stella's husband, takes an instant dislike to Blanche. The feeling is mutual. Stanley is too uncouth and bestial for Blanche and her decayed gentility. Blanche is much too pretentious for Stanley. He is also very curious as to why Stella received no share of the proceeds when the plantation was sold. His curiosity and suspicion lead him to rifle Blanche's suitcase, where he finds love letters from her dead husband. This invasion of her privacy throws Blanche into a state of fear and anxiety.

One night, Stanley's friends stop by for a poker game. Blanche meets Mitch (Marvin Krauter) and tries to seduce him, disrupting the game and throwing Stanley into a rage. When Stella tries to calm him down, he slaps her. Both women flee the house. Finally, Stella returns to Stanley, while Blanche is afraid to go inside.

In the days which follow, Blanche becomes mentally unhinged. She places all her hopes on Mitch. Aware of this, Stanley cruelly tells Mitch about Blanche's checkered sexual history, and Mitch jilts her. Blanche now escapes into a world of fantasy. She dresses herself in one of the few nice gowns she still has left. Stanley comes home, exuberant from the news that Stella is expecting a child. Blanche backs away from him, trying to flee through a series of doors that represent her past. Stanley can no longer bear her haughtiness and alibis, and he attacks her. Now Blanche becomes completely insane. She is taken away to the asylum, still living in her private fantasy world.

Designer Peter Larkin created a flexible setting of a winding staircase and four shuttered doors that pinpointed mood and atmosphere and seemed to open and close on inner secrets. The costumes by Saul Bolanski provided the ballet with its final touches of the real and the dreamed. Alex North's jazzy score, orchestrated and adapted by Rayburn Wright, was the same score used in the film version of the Williams play, and it enhanced the ballet's contemporary feel.

Streetcar was by no means a literal translation of the Williams play into dance and mime. Bettis took the characters, the situation and certain key incidents and telescoped them into forty minutes, creating an independent theatre piece of enormous dramatic power and emotional urgency. Every moment of the ballet is an illumination of Blanche's descent into madness. Walter Terry remarked that Bettis "has let a gesture of nervousness grow into wild actions which bare a shattered spirit, and from there she has borne Blanche into that dream-world of gaiety and terror where, in her heart, she hopes to find escape."[63]

One of the most fascinating aspects of *Streetcar*— alluded to by Terry — was the mingling of fantasy and reality as Bettis revealed the cumulative tension which beset the deluded Blanche, the rough and arrogant Stanley, the sweet and loving Stella. She exposed the raw emotions of her key characters as they face each other in a world of reality, and as one of them sees herself in dreams. Larkin's set carried out the ballet's corelation of reality and fantasy to perfection. John Martin wrote, "When the angry Stanley chases the hapless Blanche through a series of shuttered doors, rather like the set for one of those surrealist ballets in every MGM musical, it delivers a wallop that you are not likely to forget."[64]

The success of this production was in no small part due to a magnificent performance by Franklin. He startled the ballet world in the role of Stanley. A sensitive and endearing personality, long noted for his boyish charm, Franklin left behind his engaging ways to create a brutal, loutish character, bursting through the doors as a "pajamaed" Marlon Brando. This was a difficult role for Freddie:

> It was Mia's idea to do this. I said, "Mia, it's fine for you, but what about me and Stanley?" I worked with Valerie. We started with me. And she said, "Freddie, if you'll just let me go right in and bring it out, we can make this work." I said, "Valerie, I'm wide open." And I worked so closely with her. She was living in a lovely studio in the Village and one night, I got a phone call at four o'clock in the morning. "Freddie, come down immediately. I've got the Stella theme all worked out." And I got a taxi, and we worked and worked. And I was on the floor, and I was all over the place and at the end she said, very wisely, "Now Freddie, can you do this eight times a week?" And I said, "Well, I'll break my neck, but I'll do it, because what you've done here is so wonderful."[65]

Many critics believed that Stanley was Franklin's greatest role, and most could scarcely believe that it was actually Freddie on the stage in this ballet. John Martin wrote, "As Stanley, Mr. Franklin offers the finest performance of his life." Echoing this opinion, Walter Terry wrote that Franklin's Stanley was "the most telling characterization in his illustrious career.... He dominated the ballet throughout. Never was there a false gesture, never a moment when conviction seemed lacking."

Slavenska got good notices for her portrayal of Blanche, but the praise was not unqualified. Walter Terry said that she "performed her difficult role expertly," but noted

Frederic Franklin as Stanley in *A Streetcar Named Desire*. 1950. Slavenska-Franklin Ballet production. Choreography: Valerie Bettis. Music: Alex North. Décor: Peter Larkin. Photograph: Marcus Blechman. Museum of the City of New York. The Marcus Blechman Collection.

a tendency "to lean on wild-eyed glances a trifle too much." For Claudia Cassidy of the *Chicago Tribune*, Slavenska was "never Blanche. She is sometimes beautiful, vivid, even brilliant, but she is never vulnerable."[66]

   While *Streetcar* created a sensation back in 1952, the work has unfortunately not held up well over the years. Bettis quite obviously designed her ballet to be a shocker. As Rosalyn Krokover noted, "It is heavily burdened with garish symbolism, deals with

Mia Slavenska as Blanche. *A Streetcar Named Desire*. 1950. Photograph: Marcus Blechman. Museum of the City of New York. The Marcus Blechman Collection.

sex in capital letters, and concentrates more on sex and the story than on dance interest." Martin agreed: "It is certainly not a ballet, and whatever its particular theatrical classification may be, one can only hope that it will not set any precedents."[67]

In his enthusiasm for *Streetcar*, Robert Coleman went out on a limb: "We think it will rank with Antony Tudor's magnificent 'Pillar of Fire' among the top-drawer modern works."[68] The two pieces were similar in that both dealt with raw emotions, unbearable tension and desperation. However, Bettis just didn't have the same degree of Tudor's psychological astuteness or his instinct for the telling move. *Pillar of Fire* also had memorable, extended choreographic sequences uninterrupted by mime, while *Streetcar* rarely boasted a completed choreographic phrase. Bettis choreographed *Streetcar* in abrupt, short, harsh dance sentences, and this dates the work today.

The Slavenska-Franklin Ballet sold its production of *Streetcar* to Ballet Theatre, and it went into the latter company's rep at the McCarter Theater in Princeton, New Jersey, on October 26, 1954. At this performance, Valerie Bettis herself danced the role of Blanche and a dreadfully miscast Igor Youskevitch appeared as Stanley. Dance Theatre of Harlem restaged the work in 1982 and then again in 1994, but revivals have been few and far between.

Symphonic Variations, like *Streetcar*, had its Broadway premiere on December 8, 1952. It was a plotless ballet choreographed by Slavenska to the music of César Franck. Although it was apparently danced superbly by Lois Ellyn, Robert Morrow and Ronald Colton, the ballet as a whole did not fare well with the critics. *Symphonic Variations* was essentially an old-fashioned music visualization and Terry dismissed it as "a dreary little bit of uninspired choreography." Rounding off the opening-night offerings was a performance of the "Don Quixote Grand Pas de Deux" by Slavenska and Franklin. Terry found that it was "hammed up for all it was worth, especially by the ballerina."[69]

Mlle Fifi was first shown to New York on December 9. It was danced to the frisky music of Theodore Edouard Lajarte, arranged by Samuel Grossman. *Mlle Fifi* dealt with a scheming tightrope walker who attracts the attentions of an ardent young lover and his rich, elderly father. Papa seeks to rescue "sonny boy" from the siren and falls in love with her himself. *Mlle Fifi* was pure fluff, and the only reason for its existence was to serve as a vehicle for Danilova. It was expertly tailored for her by Zachary Solov, choreographer for the Metropolitan Opera, and *Mlle Fifi* showed off to perfection Danilova's genius for effervescent comedy in her depiction of the amorous antics of a soubrette. Bewitching in blonde wig and pink satin and black-tasseled circus gear designed by Helen Pons, Danilova showed off the most celebrated legs in ballet as she pranced, preened and capered her way through this French farce. Walter Terry marveled, "What a performer she is!" and remarked that Danilova "knows how to make danced love to her audience."[70]

Portrait of a Ballerina premiered on December 10. It was choreographed by Slavenska to the Dohnanyi "Nursery Rhyme Variations." *Portrait of a Ballerina* was the only piece in the repertoire that boasted the presence of all three of the company's stars. The ballet was suggested by the Degas sculpture *La petite danseuse à quatorze ans*. A rebellious and inattentive Ballet Student (Mia Slavenska) causes the Ballet Master (Frederic Franklin) no end of irritation. She is finally persuaded by a great Ballerina of the past (Alexandra Danilova) to give herself fully to her art. The ballet closes in modern times with another Young Student (Lois Ellyn), going through the same doubts and pangs, being inspired by another great ballerina of the past — our first young girl, now among the dance immortals.

The theme of *Portrait of a Ballerina*, of course, is the conflict that some young dancers experience between the harsh demands of the profession and the desire for a freer, less regimented life. "Its idea," wrote John Martin, "which is a sound enough one for a nostalgic ballet, is a good deal better than its realization in choreographic terms." Walter Terry was of the same opinion, writing that the ballet's theme "is not treated with any great profundity nor, as a matter of fact, especially imaginatively."[71] Rounding off the Century offerings was the "Black Swan Grand Pas de Deux," performed by Danilova and Franklin.

The repertory of the Slavenska-Franklin troupe was assembled and designed for the primary purpose of touring. At its peak, the company traveled with eighteen dancers and its own small orchestra. With eighteen dancers, the company couldn't fit on some of the stages that Mia's company of six, *Ballet Variante,* had been able to do. As Franklin said, "We were really a cumbersome company. We were too big for one thing and too small for the other."[72] This was an impediment to getting bookings, but they still managed to garner enough to embark on another grueling, cross-country tour in the winter and spring of 1953.

Early in 1953, a modern dancer named Yechi Nimura, who had seen the company, asked Franklin if they would like to perform in Japan. Franklin said, "Oh my God, we'd love to go to Japan."[73] So Nimura wrote to the *Mainichi* newspaper (the Tokyo equivalent of the *New York Times*), and suddenly the company principals got an invitation to perform in Tokyo. They departed for Japan in mid–May. The flight from New York to San Francisco took eleven hours. From there, it was nine hours to Hawaii and five to Guam. By then, Franklin's feet were so swollen he couldn't get his shoes back on. In Tokyo, they were met at the airport by a delegation armed with flowers and a motorcade to escort them to the Imperial Hotel. People called out their names from the streets, and they were continuously pelted with blossoms and confetti through the avenues of Tokyo. This reception was completely unexpected. Franklin said, "I thought there must be some mistake."[74]

The company was supplemented with Japanese dancers, selected by audition and rehearsed for only three days. Franklin staged Act II of *Swan Lake* for the Japanese girls and quickly learned how to count to eight in Japanese. The rest of the offerings were small in scale — the "Black Swan Pas de Deux" for Mia and Freddie, the Waltz from *Le Beau Danube* for Choura and Freddie, excerpts from *Coppelia,* and Slavenska's *Portrait of a Ballerina.* Accompanied by members of the Tokyo Symphony, the dancers got wonderful notices and nightly standing ovations. On June 13, the company opened a week's engagement in Manila and then returned to Tokyo for another round of sold-out performances. The United States Army had made arrangements to fly the dancers to Seoul for two weeks of performances for the armed forces. However, plans were cancelled as the situation in Korea grew more dangerous. Overall, though, the tour had been an enormous success.

When the company returned to the States, they took a vacation and embarked on another cross-country tour. According to Franklin, this last tour was "just badly managed. One moment, there wasn't any more money left. It was very sad."[75] The company dissolved early in 1954. When it folded, Franklin and Slavenska owed thousands of dollars to the government, and Slavenska even had to sell her house. Freddie was in debt as well. Slavenska and Franklin parted on the best of terms: "There were literally no scrubbings, no fights, nothing like that."[76]

Later in her career, Slavenska became an influential teacher, opening a ballet studio in New York in 1960, then teaching at UCLA from 1969 to 1983 and at the California Institute for the Arts from 1970 to 1983. She died of natural causes on October 5, 2002, at the age of eighty-six in an assisted-living residence in Los Angeles, surrounded by family and friends. In an obituary notice, Franklin stated that she was "a very beautiful ballerina, and she was fearless, on stage and in life. She was exceptional in the fact that she was something more than just a ballerina. She managed her own company. She choreographed. She designed costumes. She was quite unique. No other ballerina at the time did all that."[77]

The Ballet Russe de Monte Carlo began a new period of full-company operation under Columbia Artists Management on October 1, 1954, when it opened a tour in Baltimore. Franklin claims that Denham called him and said, in effect, "Well now that you've had your little folly, are you ready to come back and give me back my Ballet Russe de Monte Carlo?"[78] Since he was in financial straits, Franklin accepted the offer. Although there were no New York engagements, the reconstituted Ballet Russe attracted enormous attention, garnering 179 completely sold-out bookings. The lengthy tour closed in Montreal on April 16, 1955. Because of the increasing costs and complications of rail travel, the company now toured in buses, while scenery and costumes were carried in trucks as they had been for the Concert Company. Despite the rigorous schedule, the company was put up every night in hotel beds, never having to sleep in transit, as had often occurred in the era of rail travel.

According to Franklin, Denham asked him to return in order to partner Maria Tallchief, who had been lured away from New York City Ballet with a salary previously unheard of for ballerinas, however "prima." When George Balanchine and Tallchief had met in 1942, she was only nineteen and he was twenty years older. Despite this difference, they had one strong bond besides dance itself— both were dedicated, skilled musicians. Miss Tallchief, who had studied ballet with La Nijinska, had been torn between pursuing a career as a concert pianist or as a ballet dancer. Her rich cultural background, her strong technique, and her exciting stage presence caught Balanchine's eye at once when he arrived at the Ballet Russe. Looking back, Tallchief said, "I didn't know he was courting me. It never occurred to me it was anything beyond his interest in my dancing. He obviously thought I had talent, he knew I was a trained musician, and I think he was intrigued also by the half-American Indian."[79]

Tallchief and Balanchine married in August 1946, and she accompanied him when Balanchine went to Paris to stage his ballets for the Paris Opéra. Tallchief became the first American dancer since Augusta Maywood in 1839 to dance with the Paris Opéra Ballet. When they returned, Tallchief was his prima ballerina for Ballet Society and, later, the New York City Ballet. However, the marriage broke up in 1951. With his multiple wives, Balanchine had the reputation of a Lothario, but it is generally believed that he was too involved in creating ballets to be much of a husband. However, Balanchine's obsession with the young dancer Tanaquil LeClerq and Tallchief's divorce from the choreographer may well have made Tallchief uncomfortable enough to prompt a request for a leave of absence from New York City Ballet.

As part of the strategy of Denham and Fleishmann to provide stability for the nomadic company, the Ballet Russe School was established in March of 1954. The school was taken over from the respected Maria Swoboda School on West 57th Street.

Franklin was appointed faculty head of the school, which was fashioned after such famous ballet schools as the Imperial, Paris Opéra and Sadler's Wells. In its first year of operation, some six hundred students enrolled in the school. Faculty for the first term under Ballet Russe ownership included Franklin, Maria Swoboda, Igor Schwezoff, Anatole Vilzak, Valerie Bettis, Leon Danielian and Duncan Noble. The school survived until June 30, 1967, when it lost its lease.

Franklin's first performance with the reorganized Ballet Russe was in *The Mikado*, which premiered in Washington on October 1, 1954. It was choreographed by Antonia Cobos to the well-known score of Arthur Sullivan, arranged by Vittorio Rieti, with settings and costumes by Bernard Lamotte. Franklin danced the role of Katisha, and the other leading roles were danced by Leon Danielian, Joseph Savino, Irina Borowska, Gertrude Tyven, Yvonne Chouteau and Victor Moreno. Audiences seemed to enjoy *The Mikado*, and it remained in the repertory for several seasons, although P. W. Manchester and other critics complained that the story was not well told. Miss Cobos, however, never intended to retell the intricate plot of the Gilbert and Sullivan *Mikado*, nor did she try to match lyrics with choreography. She merely hung amusing, stylized numbers on the highly danceable music. *The Mikado* had only a mixed success. In his review on the strengths and weaknesses of the reorganized company, John Martin decided that *The Mikado* "must be listed on the debit side."[80]

Harold in Italy premiered at the Boston Opera House on October 14, 1954. This was a symphonic ballet by Léonide Massine, set to Hector Berlioz's *Harold en Italie*, op. 16. The story is that of a poet (the "Childe Harold" of Lord George Gordon Byron's poem) who travels in Italy in the early part of the nineteenth century. He comments on and reacts to what he sees while remaining a comparatively static figure himself. The first movement is "Harold in the Mountains," featuring the Happy Couple (Irina Baronova, Ian Howard). In the second movement, "Harold Meets the Pilgrims," Harold (Leon Danielian) comes upon a pilgrimage (led by Yvonne Chouteau). The third movement, "Pastoral Scene," is led by the Young Shepherds (Nina Novak, Deni Lamont). The last movement is "Orgy of the Brigands." Here, ten brigands and their Leader (Victor Moreno) molest a band of maidens. Harold and the male soloists appear in the nick of time, and they banish the brigands. The ballet ends with Harold atop a high pyramid, flanked by the Happy Couple and the Young Shepherds.

Bernard Lamotte's five backdrops were too diminutive for the scale of a theatre and were considered the weakest designs for any of Massine's symphonic ballets. P. W. Manchester spoke highly of Massine's choreography, but she noted some outdated touches such as the "blowing leaves" and "that ubiquitous pair of deer." The fourth movement was by all accounts the weakest. Massine did not resist the temptation to "resolve" a four-movement symphony, and the intrusions of the leading figures of the previous movements seemed out of key. Although Ann Barzel also gave Massine a positive review, *Harold in Italy* was not to everyone's taste. Doris Hering called *Harold* "a hopelessly outdated ordeal of plushy plastique."[81] *Harold in Italy* disappeared from the Denham repertory after only one season. A company touring one-night stands could not afford the union-labor costs of hanging five backdrops for just one ballet. *Harold* proved to be the last of Massine's symphonic ballets. As Franklin noted, "It was sad for him [Massine] to come back and not have a success."[82]

It is discouraging indeed to give one's all to a role, only to watch a last-minute replacement go down in the history books as the creator of record. Franklin, cast as Harold, developed a bad toothache and had to have a root canal. This was his second such misfortune: on the opening night of Balanchine's1946 *Night Shadow*, Franklin had to be hastily replaced as the Poet when he hurt his back. Nicholas Magallanes went down in the books as the original Poet. Because of his tooth, the scheduled opening of *Harold* was cancelled. Two days later, Leon Danielian stepped in, although Franklin danced the role occasionally in subsequent performances.

The biggest excitement of the 1955–56 season was the presence of Alicia Alonso and Igor Youskevitch. By 1955, they were the most famous couple in ballet, as had been the case with Danilova and Franklin a decade earlier. Alonso was a Cuban ballerina who began her American career with the Ballet Caravan in 1939 and joined Ballet Theatre in 1941. After a year in Cuba, she returned to Ballet Theatre in 1943. Alonso's vision was severely impaired by the time that she switched allegiance to the Ballet Russe, and members of the corps were required to assist her to ensure that her entrances and exits were made without collisions. Thus, dancers posted offstage would snap fingers to indicate the direction of an exit or hold up their Wili skirts so that she could see a white blur where the exit was.[83]

People were flabbergasted by the May 12 announcement that Alonso and Youskevitch would not return to Ballet Theatre. According to *Dance News*, no reason for the switch was given by the dancers or the management.[84] Youskevitch, who was discharged from the navy in December of 1945, had joined Ballet Theatre in the autumn of 1946. Although nothing was said publicly, Youskevitch did indeed have a strong motivation for returning to his alma mater.

Speaking of his business negotiations with Denham, Youskevitch said, "When Denham drank vodka he could be very nice. But when talk turned to money, he wasn't so nice."[85] The real lure for Youskevitch was that he wanted to do more than just simply dance. Since he wasn't prepared to budge an inch on salary, Denham tempted him by offering him the title of artistic advisor.

Franklin has acknowledged that there was definitely a rivalry between Youskevitch and himself, especially when it came to *Giselle*. For instance, according to Freddie, Igor's first project as artistic advisor was to overhaul *Giselle*, perhaps because it was Franklin who had staged the existing version. Igor's first rehearsals didn't go too well:

> Rachel Chapman was at the piano, and he got mixed up, and he started singing something, and Rachel said, "Igor Ivanovitch, that tune you're singing is from *Aurora's Wedding*." And I thought, "Oh dear, is it going to be like this?" He gave up, but Alonso took over, and it was fine ... I insisted on doing a performance of Albrecht in *Giselle*. I didn't care where or how. So there was a program in Chicago, and I danced *Giselle* with Alonso. He [Youskevitch] went out front and he hid — he was all made up, and he came back. We were sharing a dressing room, and he said, "Freddie, you will never dance with Alonso again. Danilova was your partner and she's mine. I will see to it that you never dance with her again." Well, the press the next day was wonderful, and he was very upset. And suddenly, there it goes up on the board: Alonso and I are doing the "Don Quixote Pas de Deux."

Franklin feels that the rivalry largely stemmed from the fact that they were such different dancers: "I think that the trouble was that my range went from *Streetcar* to *Giselle*. He was strictly in the classical mode and was dying to get out of it. He and

Nora [Kaye] did *Streetcar* for Ballet Theatre. He was a disaster. They both were wrong. Mia was a faded blonde beauty, and Nora was very dark and dramatic, but not at all a southern belle."[86]

Igor's return to the Ballet Russe was hardly a happy homecoming. Perhaps Youskevitch should have reminded himself that Franklin was already ballet master and that he was likely to be frustrated in this new position. Years later, he acknowledged his mistake:

> My post as artistic advisor for the Ballet Russe turned out to be strictly for the birds. I was very conscientious and tried very hard to do my job. I felt that the entire repertoire had to be overhauled.... Denham didn't go for the idea. In fact, he didn't go for any of my ideas. He wanted things to stay exactly as they were, and as usual, he didn't want to spend a penny for anything.... All in all, I would say that my return to Ballet Russe was something of a disaster. Finally, I had a talk with Denham and told him that my job there was totally useless — that whatever I tried to do met with no response whatsoever.[87]

After the 1956–57 season, Youskevitch went down to Alonso's company in Havana to help her organize her troupe more fully. He appeared with the Ballet Russe in every subsequent season up through 1960–61, but only in the capacity of guest artist.

On July 9, 1955, the Ballet Russe de Monte Carlo made its first New York appearance in five years, drawing a record audience of 17,000 to the Lewisohn Stadium. At the end of August, the company began rehearsals for its fall cross-country tour. The 1955–56 tour began on October 9 and finished on April 14. There were two new offerings in the fall; both premiered in Toronto. Balanchine's "Minkus Pas de Trois" made its appearance on October 12, 1955. It was a virtuoso showpiece that could be conveniently added to a mixed bill.

The other Toronto premiere was *La Dame à la Licorne,* first seen on October 14, 1955. Danced to a libretto by Jean Cocteau and based on troubadour songs, the ballet derived from the legend that unicorns eat only from the hand of a virgin. Cocteau drew his inspiration for *La Dame à la Licorne* from the series of fifteenth century tapestries of the same name in the museum at Cluny, France. When a Lady (Irina Borowska) becomes enamored of a Knight (Igor Youskevitch), her Unicorn (Nina Novak) dies. Rueful, the Lady spurns the Knight and is left alone.

Out of the blue, Nina Novak suddenly told *Dance News* that she was going to resign from the company in mid–October of 1955. The reporter related, "People close to the dancer said that the reason for her decision is dissatisfaction with the quality and quantity of her roles." Lo and behold, in the January issue of *Dance News*, it was announced, "Miss Novak will not resign after all. Whatever differences there were between her and the management have been amicably resolved."[88] Looks like Nina got her way again: the strategy worked. But for the past two or three seasons, critics had begun to comment that Novak was miscast. Doris Hering wrote, "The major classical roles fall to Nina Novak, despite the fact that she is not a classical dancer."[89] There was resentment in the company that so many of the choicest roles were falling to Novak and to make matters worse, she little-by-little began to take over the casting and supervision of rehearsals. By 1959, after Franklin's departure, she was ballet mistress as well as leading ballerina. Her monopoly on the company caused great resentment among the dancers.

On June 18, 1956, Leon Danielian made his choreographic debut with *Sombreros* in Washington, D.C. It was a Mexican suite which offered romantic and humorous dances in a blending of ballet and Mexican folk styles. *Sombreros* was a pleasant work, a good first effort. From August to September of that summer, Franklin joined his former colleagues Danilova, Sonja Taanila and Robert Lindgren on a South African tour that took them to Johannesburg, Durban and Capetown.

With the 1956–57 season, the Ballet Russe parted company with Columbia Artists and the tour, which began on October 21, 1956, was booked by the company's old friend David Libidins in collaboration with Kenneth Allen Associates. Freddie was increasingly disillusioned with the Ballet Russe. He didn't really want to go back and said that he "did it for Choura" (Danilova had agreed to return to the Ballet Russe as guest artist).[90] The company's lack of a discernable artistic framework, direction, and distinctive style, which had been detectable for years, was now impossible for critics to ignore. As Terry put it, "There is nothing which says, 'we are the Ballet Russe and this is our special quality.'"[91] Unwilling to commission new works, Denham wanted to use only those which had always proven successful. In so doing, he perpetuated a cycle of sameness, which in turn did not attract anyone who might underwrite or sponsor new ballets. The repertoire was becoming increasingly threadbare, and "Ham and Eggs" was on the menu for a high percentage of the tour engagements. Although he would return as a guest artist, Franklin officially left the Ballet Russe after the 1955–56 season.

There were two premieres in December of 1956: Boris Romanoff's *Harlequinade* and Salvador Juarez's *Tragedy in Calabria*. Both featured the stock characters of Harlequin and Columbine, and Ann Barzel noted that *Tragedy in Calabria* "suffered from being another commedia dell'arte episode in a season bursting with Harlequins."[92]

It was during this tour, in Canada, in the spring of 1957, that a scandal was aroused by a deplorable practice. At 11:30 p.m., halfway through *Le Beau Danube*, the curtain suddenly came down. It was lowered midway through the ballet because if it had stayed up one minute longer, Denham would be required to pay the dancers, musicians and stagehands overtime. Outraged, Youskevitch attracted the attention of Canadian newspapers and American dance publications by threatening to resign from the company and by divulging that, far from being an isolated incident, the cutting off of ballets occurred at least once a month. Few practices of the Ballet Russe have earned it more justifiable disdain than the compulsory 11:30 lowering of the curtain.

In Denham's defense, however, it is true that he was sometimes helpless to see to it that performances started on time. Out in the provinces, many audiences saw a ballet performance primarily as a social event, and they expected the curtain to be held until some local dignitary or another had taken his seat. In one city, the curtain was held for more than half an hour until the arrival of the mayor, who, all the while, was fully visible having a leisurely dinner in a restaurant across the street from the theatre.[93]

From April 21 to May 4, 1957, the Ballet Russe returned to New York for its first season at the Metropolitan Opera since 1950 — and what would be its last season there ever. For the occasion, the company was supplemented with prestigious guest artists, including Franklin, Alonso, Danilova, Danielian, and Youskevitch. Danilova and Franklin (who were getting a paltry $125 per performance) were featured in their famous roles in *Gaîté Parisienne*. Ballets new to New York were *La Dame à la Licorne*, *Harlequinade*, *Sombreros* and *The Mikado*.

On April 30, 1957, Denham ordered the curtain down on *Gaîté* before the ballet had ended, although the Met was crowded to standing room with an audience that had come to see Danilova and Franklin. As usual, the reason was reluctance to pay overtime, but at the Metropolitan Opera of all places! The company became the laughing stock of the Big Apple. Denham tried to convince reporters that he had used an "alternate finale" that was "artistically sound" and that he had even heard some audience members say that the short version constituted a "good ending."[94]

The company had reached a low ebb and seemed no longer worthy of New York. John Martin wrote, "At present, the company is definitely a road-show company; it has cut everything down to the irreducible minimum. The physical productions with few exceptions are poor and shoddy. The general style of dancing is coarse-grained and appears to have been scaled to Yankee Stadium."[95] Franklin was fed up with current company practices, and he never again performed with the Ballet Russe after 1957.

When he left the Ballet Russe, Franklin signed a six-month contract with Ballet Theatre. He stayed for only six weeks, and didn't even get paid for three of them. The year was 1957, and Ballet Theatre's financial situation was bleak. Franklin reported that "there was hardly a soul in the house"[96] for the fall 1957 season. By 1958, the company would be forced to disband for the second time since 1948. In the meanwhile, Franklin received an offer from Juan and Anna Garcia Anduze, artistic directors of the Ballet de San Juan, to stage *Les Sylphides*. He said to Lucia Chase, artistic director of Ballet Theatre, "Lucia, look. This is ridiculous."[97] Off he went to Puerto Rico. His stagings for the Ballet de San Juan would continue for the next ten years.

In the same year, Franklin, Danilova, Taanila, and Lindgren banded together once again for Franklin's second tour to Japan. They did excerpts from *Coppelia*, *Raymonda*, and a short piece by Lindgren called *L'Heure bleu*. It fell to Franklin to teach the Japanese girls the Mazurka from *Coppelia*. This dance was beyond the pale of anything the girls had ever experienced:

> They had never seen the mazurka and they couldn't get it, and I showed it and showed it. I broke it down, everything. Madame Tachibana, our employer, said through the interpreter, "Mr. Franklin, you're very tired, you go home. Tomorrow, they will do it." They worked all night, and the next day, she was grinning, and the dancers were all grinning from ear to ear, and they had it down pat. The whole incident is so typically Japanese.[98]

Unfortunately, their sponsor ran out of money to pay the troupe, and it was lucky that they already had their airline tickets back, as far as Hawaii, at least. When they reached Hawaii, they didn't even have enough money to buy a meal, but they went downstairs to the restaurant anyway, prepared to wash dishes if it came to that. By an act of providence, a man approached them and said, "Oh, Madame Danilova and Mr. Franklin, I just saw you in Tokyo, and it was all so beautiful! May I invite you to dinner?" Not surprisingly, Franklin said, "'Of course!' And it was after dinner that I discovered I had a fifty-dollar traveler's check at the bottom of my suitcase."[99]

This windfall provided for a little playtime, a chance to "go Hawaiian." Mitzi Gaynor, who had been in the chorus of *Song of Norway*, was in Hawaii filming the role of Nellie Forbush with Rozano Brazzi in *South Pacific*. The dancers had a wonderful time on the set with them. Fortunately, the little troupe was able to arrange for a performance at one of the local theatres. It sold out, giving them the money to get back to the United States.

After 1957 occurs the steady decline of the Ballet Russe de Monte Carlo. Their annual American tour got underway on October 18, 1957, in Hartford. Except for two performances at Brooklyn Academy of Music a year later, there was no New York season. In her review of the BAM performances, Doris Hering wrote, "Economics and the vicissitudes of touring — persuasive elements both — have made the Ballet Russe de Monte Carlo lose sight of the fact that ballet is a theatre art. The physical elements of their two New York performances were neglected to the point of drabness."[100]

The 1960–61 tour was supposed to begin on October 24, 1960, but it was delayed until December 27 because the Ballet Russe and AGMA failed to agree on terms of a new contract. This put the Ballet Russe on an even shakier financial footing than it already was.

The 1961–62 season was the company's twenty-fifth, silver, anniversary. To celebrate, Denham decided to commission three new works from three former company members — Franklin, Danielian and James Starbuck. Franklin's *Tribute*, danced to César Frank's *Symphonic Variations*, premiered at the Boston Arts Center on July 20, 1961. A plotless work, it employed the same score and the same casting of three couples as had Frederick Ashton's acclaimed *Symphonic Variations*. Yet it was altogether different in mood, and while in no way equal to the Ashton work, balletgoers found *Tribute* enjoyable. For Doris Hering, it "manifested an unusual facility with the vocabulary of the *danse d'école*" and "gave that facility a disciplined and meaningful shape." *Tribute* has proven to be a durable ballet, for it was later produced by the National Ballet of Washington, Milwaukee Ballet and Pittsburgh Ballet Theatre. However, some critics could not resist making comparisons. Clive Barnes felt that *Tribute* "chances its luck against Frederick Ashton's masterpiece to the same score and loses the gamble."[101]

The tour ended with performances at Brooklyn Academy of Music on April 13–14, 1962. These were to be the last performances ever given by the Ballet Russe de Monte Carlo. The company was not drawing as large an audience on tour as it once had, and production costs were soaring. The September 1962 issue of *Dance Magazine* contained the terse announcement, "Because of substantial loss last season, the Ballet Russe has decided not to tour in the season 1962–63."[102] The dancers dispersed, and the company vanished into thin air without fanfare.

However, Denham never stopped dreaming about a new ballet company. Early in 1966, he paid two visits to Monte Carlo to discuss re-establishing a Ballet Russe there. He succeeded, and Denham's new Ballets de Monte Carlo gave its first performance on November 19, 1966, at the Théâtre de Monte Carlo.

Denham envisioned a company that would have regular seasons in Monte Carlo and tour the rest of the year, but not in America, where touring expenses and trade unions made it so difficult for a company to survive. However, many of the dancers in the new company were American, and several were veterans of the Ballet Russe.

The opening night program featured *Les Sylphides*, the "Flower Festival at Genzano Pas de Deux," a revival of *Bacchanale* and *Gaîté Parisienne*. Stagings of *Ballet Imperial*, *Swan Lake* (Act II) and *Raymonda* were also in the repertory. The company was not a good one, and there was a high turnover. Classes were infrequent, and a stream of transient teachers prevented the company from acquiring a consistent style. After Monte Carlo performances in the spring of 1967, the company went on a tour of Spain, then disbanded.

But the wily Denham still continued to scheme. Remembering that Chicago had always loved the Ballet Russe, he called Ruth Page on January 30, 1970. Denham sounded her out on the prospect of becoming involved in the founding of a new Ballet Russe with headquarters in Chicago. [103] Within an hour after making that call, Denham was run over by a bus and killed at Madison Avenue and East 57th Street. His passing seemed to symbolize the last breath of a great era in ballet history.

· 5 ·

A Company in the Capital: The National Ballet

Franklin next embarked on his Washington phase. In a speech titled "Is Washington Really a Hick Town?," the Hon. Harris McDowell, a member of the House of Representatives, made special mention of the "Washington Ballet, which has just acquired Frederic Franklin as its Co-Director and should show steady improvement."[1]

Franklin began his association with the Washington Ballet in 1957.

The Washington Ballet was formed in 1956 under the direction of Lisa Gardiner and Mary Day. This company sprang from their Washington School of Ballet, which they had established in 1944. Mary Day was a pupil of Gardiner, who had danced with Adolph Bolm's Ballet Intime. With the aid of Jean Riddell, one of the most committed patrons of the arts the city had ever seen, Day and Gardiner joined forces with the National Symphony Orchestra to present *Hansel and Gretel* and *Cinderella* for two successive Christmases in 1954–55. From these first successes grew a resident company of thirty-five dancers that was sponsored by the Washington Ballet Guild, with Jean Riddell as chairman of the board.

For many years, the Ballet Russe had performed for one week in Washington, D.C., in a big open-air theatre called the Carter Baron. It was there that Franklin made the acquaintance of Mary Day. In 1957, Day asked him to teach and rehearse her dancers in *Les Sylphides*. Subsequently, he staged *Swan Lake* (Act II), *Raymonda* and the *Polovetsian Dances* for the Washington Ballet.

At first, Franklin commuted between New York and Washington, spending four days a week in the capital and the other three in New York at the Ballet Russe de Monte Carlo School. But when Lisa Gardiner died in 1958, Mary Day appointed Freddie co-director of the Washington Ballet. Franklin lengthened his weekly stay with Mary, teaching at the Ballet Russe School only two days per week. Then he would dash down to Washington to teach from Wednesday to Saturday, with rehearsals on Saturday and Sunday. Within a year after joining forces with Day, Franklin gave the Washington Ballet a new luster and importance that attracted such guest stars as Alicia Markova, Alexan-

141

dra Danilova, Maria Tallchief, Melissa Hayden, Alicia Alonso, Mia Slavenska, Igor Youskevitch and André Eglevsky. Franklin choreographed two original works for the Washington Ballet: *Etalage* and *Homage au Ballet*, to the music of Liszt and Gounod, respectively.

In a 1960 interview, Franklin said, "We are working towards a resident company in the nation's capital."[2] However, Franklin's association with Mary Day proved to be short-lived and acrimonious. On the way back from an engagement in Puerto Rico, Franklin stopped over in Miami to see the closing night of Ballet Theatre before it suspended operations for the second time. He met Mrs. Riddell at that performance, and she offered him $10,000 to be artistic director of a new company. Franklin claims, "She wanted her own company and she didn't want Mary Day."[3] Franklin turned down the money, but he ultimately accepted the position.

In April of 1961, Franklin resigned as co-director of the Washington Ballet as a result of a dispute with the Ballet Guild and Day about the future direction of the company. He felt that the performing group was good enough to flex its muscles and become a professional company, but Miss Day resisted the suggestion, preferring to keep her dancers within the scope of a small regional company.[4]

Franklin spoke of "a great falling out with Mary," and the reasons were personal as well as professional. In 1981, Freddie related, "She was very emotionally involved with me and she told me so, and I said, 'Look, this is not going to work. Please, I can't have anything like this in my life at the moment. I don't want anything like this. I've got lots of work to do, Mary.' And a woman scorned … well that was it."[5]

The National Ballet, Franklin and Riddell's new company, was officially founded with financial assistance from the Ford Foundation and the generous support of Mrs. Riddell, who was estimated to have spent $2 million on its upkeep over the years. Riddell was named president of the sustaining organization: the National Ballet Society, Inc. Franklin and Riddell announced to the press their determination to become one of the best professional dance troupes in the country. Franklin said, "The school and company are for America and for all of the good dancers that we can find and develop. Our intention is to establish a national company in the nation's capital based on artistic policies similar to those of the New York City Ballet and the original policy of the Sadler's Wells." "The National Ballet," declared Mrs. Riddell, "is the only logical name for this company — it's designed not only for Washington, but also for growth."[6]

Ballet Russe veteran Oleg Tupine, who now had his own ballet school in Maryland, was appointed ballet master. Among the National's principals were Andrea Vodenhal and Eugene Collins, formerly of Ballet Russe de Monte Carlo, and Roderick Drew of the Metropolitan Opera Ballet. Vodenhal was one of Franklin's discoveries. She was his student at the Ballet Russe de Monte Carlo School, and he got her into the Ballet Russe over Nina Novak's vehement objections. Franklin "yanked her out of the company"[7] to enlist her in the National. Twenty-five other soloists (including Roni Mahler) and corps members were on the roster as well, most of them drawn from the School of American Ballet. Wags predicted trouble for the National because none of the SAB dancers had professional status, or even much stage experience, but Franklin was committed to developing these dancers, seeing their enormous potential. Economically, these dancers were given as much security as could be found in most other professional ballet companies at the time. Although they started with only a twenty-four-week contract, that number had increased to thirty-two by the end of the decade. By the '70s, the guaranteed contract was up to thirty-eight weeks.

Riddell supplied nearly all of the first season's working budget, which amounted to $108,000. But she was also taking a long-range look at finances: "There is no set subsidy that assures our future," she said. "We are dependent on support from the city."[8] Accordingly, she announced annual fund-raising and membership drives.

Riddell was adamant that there should be no canned music for local performances. Concerts were accompanied by the Baltimore Symphony Orchestra, with Elyakum Shapiro conducting. Franklin and Riddell's ambitious enterprise also included the formation of a new National Ballet School on Connecticut Avenue. The school soon had an enrollment of 250, with classes limited in size to fifteen students. Promising boys were put on scholarship, provided they would commit to taking two classes daily. Franklin saw the school as a resource for company recruitment: "The real idea is to take the dancers from the School into the Company."[9]

After three months of rehearsal and a tryout performance in Baltimore, the National Ballet had its Washington debut on January 3, 1962. At the end of the evening, the troupe received thirteen curtain calls. Lincoln Kirstein and National Ballet board member George Balanchine were among the opening-night enthusiasts. When the final curtain rang down, Mr. Balanchine was among the first backstage to offer his congratulations and a great honor: after viewing this first performance, Balanchine put the repertoire of New York City Ballet at Franklin's disposal.[10] Freddie had another reason to be grateful to "Mr. B." Based largely on the recommendations of Balanchine and Lincoln Kirstein, the National Ballet received a matching grant of $450,000 from the Ford Foundation. Said Franklin, "The Ford Foundation had suddenly come into view, and they were giving a lot of money to Balanchine, and the idea was that Mr. B was given permission to choose certain ballet companies or groups that deserved the money, and he chose us."[11]

In 1963, the Ford Foundation had made the stunning announcement that dance, always a stepchild in the artistic hierarchy, was to be a major object of its philanthropy. Of a ten-year, $7.7 million grant, the largest private sum ever earmarked for dance, $2 million was awarded to Balanchine's company and almost $4 million to his school: in Ford's view, these institutions offered the most stable base for audience development and the upgrading of dance instruction. The remainder of the grant money went to smaller companies — San Francisco, Pennsylvania, Boston, Houston, Ballet West and the National. All of these ballet companies were directed by those who had had professional contact with Balanchine to one extent or another. Naturally, there was much resentment regarding this policy on the part of such overlooked major dance companies as American Ballet Theatre and the Martha Graham Dance Company.

The National Ballet's first performance made it crystal clear that the new company had a broad view of dance. From the beginning, its artistic policy called for modern dance works and contemporary classical works as well as traditional ones. In a scant two weeks, Valerie Bettis created a new work called *Early Voyagers* to a modern score by Ned Rorem. Franklin's *Homage au Ballet*, mounted to Gounod's Symphony no. 2, was a sort of *exercise de style* for twelve female corps, three ballerinas and three male principals. Accomplished with grace, charm and invention, it proved that the corps de ballet was young, fresh, beautifully disciplined and in possession of a distinctive style. Like his earlier *Tribute*, it was no masterpiece of choreography, but it was well-crafted and crowd-pleasing. Franklin also did a "praiseworthy"[12] restaging of *Swan Lake*, Act II.

Franklin was now on a fifty-two-week contract, which left no time for engagements with other companies. Typically, he had put all his eggs in one basket: "I never knew how to give only part of myself— it has always been all or nothing with me!" he commented. He gave up his New York apartment and moved himself "lock, stock and barrel" to Washington. Admittedly, it was a wrench to leave friends and a way of life that he had been cherishing for many years. "But I knew that if I hoped to make something of a Washington company I would have, henceforth, to make Washington my home."[13]

He literally lived in the National Ballet's school, having a flat on the second floor with the studios, dressing rooms and the school's office on the first. Freddie has always loved to cook, and he recalls, "The kids would come up from rehearsal and say, 'Mr. Franklin, what are you cooking tonight?'"[14]

One of the stipulations of the Ford Foundation grant was that the company present lecture-demonstrations in the inner-city schools. Franklin is certainly not a racist; in fact, in his subsequent work with Dance Theatre of Harlem, he proved himself to be one of the great champions of African American ballet dancers. Nevertheless, an all-white (excepting one black female) *ballet* company was not apt to feel itself on friendly turf in the mid-sixties when its dancers went prancing into those inner-city gymnasiums:

> I've never been so frightened in my life. Not that they would have molested us, but it was the attitude, and then, of course, the boys were in tights and the girls were in tutus, and they'd never seen anything like this. But the thing was, when I opened my mouth, they roared with laughter at my English accent — they'd never heard an accent like mine. Then they'd yell at me, "Where do you come from?" [I responded,] "Well, if we'd all get on with what we're here to do..." "Yeah!" they'd all scream, and we'd get going. I was a nervous wreck.[15]

By the end of 1962, the repertory was growing, and Franklin felt the need for another ballerina. He hired Sonia Arova, who was then in Paris. This Bulgarian ballerina began her professional career with London's short-lived Metropolitan Ballet. While there, she fell in love with Erik Bruhn, the celebrated Danish Bournanville dancer. They became engaged in 1947; however, the pair finally called off their five-year engagement after Arova became aware of Bruhn's homosexual tendencies. As part of the package for dancing with the National, Arova insisted on bringing over her own partner, Steven Grebel.

By December 28, the National Ballet had given itself a big birthday present with a full-length production of *Coppelia*, with Arova and Grebel in the leading roles. Franklin had always wanted to do this ballet. Quoting Massine, he said, "It's got mime, pathos, drama, everything. It's a wonderful ballet to take people to for the first time: no strange ladies or swans, or people falling asleep for one hundred years."[16]

The scene is a town square in central Europe. A high dwelling with a balcony projecting from the second floor faces the audience. The mysterious old Dr. Coppelius, who dabbles in magic and alchemy, hobbles out of this house. Coppelius looks up at his balcony, where a lovely young woman is seen reading a book, and steps back inside.

Swanilda enters the square and dances. She waves at the charming young girl on the balcony, and is annoyed when the girl does not respond. She also knows that her fiancé Franz has often waved at this strange girl, whom everyone calls Coppelia and who is said to be the old man's daughter. When Swanilda sees Franz coming down the street, she hides and observes him secretly.

Franz strides over to the house of Coppelius and blows Coppelia a kiss. Swanilda's worst suspicions of Franz's infidelity seem to be confirmed. Swanilda comes out of hiding and accuses Franz of being unfaithful to her, although Franz sincerely denies that he loves anyone else. Swanilda leaves the square, and Franz joins a party of peasants in a rollicking mazurka.

The burgomaster arrives and tells the assemblage that on the next day, the village will receive a great new bell for the town clock as a gift from the lord of the manor. He tells them that the gracious lord will also present handsome dowries to the girls who marry on this day. He turns to Swanilda and asks if she will be wed tomorrow. Swanilda resorts to fate and takes up an ear of wheat, which she shakes near her ear. According to custom, if she hears nothing, then her lover "loves her not." The wheat is silent. She throws it to the ground and announces that she and Franz are no longer engaged. Franz stomps away in a huff.

Dr. Coppelius totters out of his house and locks it. He is accosted by a gang of pranksters, who shove him about, and he unknowingly drops his key. When Coppelius is out of sight, Swanilda and her friends pick up the key, unlock the house and step inside. Coppelius rushes back to find his key. When he discovers that his door is wide open, he runs inside anxiously. Next, Franz comes on, armed with a ladder, which he places against the house to climb up to the window of the mysterious girl.

Act II is set in the workshop in the house of Coppelius. Various dolls can be seen — a Chinaman, a one-man-band doll, an astronomer, a juggler, a Harlequin, a king, and a dancing skeleton. Swanilda looks in the curtain alcove and finds Coppelia. She runs back to her friends and makes mechanical movements: Coppelia is only a doll! Swanilda laughs with glee at the notion of Franz paying court to a lifeless, automated toy. The girls run to the dolls and set them all in motion.

Coppelius runs in, speechless with rage. Swanilda sneaks into Coppelia's booth while Coppelius chases the other girls outside. Franz climbs through the window into the room, whereupon Coppelius pounces upon him. Suddenly, Coppelius becomes quite friendly and invites Franz to sit down and have a drink. However, Coppelius has poured a potion into his drink, and Franz falls fast asleep.

Coppelius finds a secret formula in his huge leather volume and goes to Coppelia's alcove. The scheming Swanilda sits rigidly holding her book. Now the toymaker runs to Franz and pulls the life force out of his body like a magnet. He then goes back to the doll and endows her with it. Swanilda raises her head and stands up, her body still bent at the waist. The delighted Coppelius straightens her up. Then she begins to try out her arms and legs and proceeds to a stiff-legged walk. At the command of Coppelius, her legs move less mechanically, and soon she is dancing a graceful waltz, followed by a bolero and a highland dance.

Swanilda grows tired of her ruse, and Coppelius puts her back into the alcove. Franz awakens and escapes out the window. Swanilda, no longer a doll, pushes the curtains aside and turns on all the real dolls before she too escapes. Coppelius draws the curtains to the alcove and beholds the naked Coppelia.

In Act III, the festival day has arrived. The lord of the manor awaits the presentation of dowries to those who will marry. Swanilda and Franz, in wedding regalia, approach the lord. Franz has learned his lesson and now has no thought for any woman but Swanilda. The irate Coppelius marches on and demands reparations for the damages to his dolls and workshop. Swanilda steps forward and offers him her dowry, but the lord of the manor motions Swanilda away and offers Coppelius a bag of gold, which he ungratefully accepts.

The pageant of the day now commences. Children perform the "Dance of the Hours." Dawn and Prayer appear and dance two variations. There follows a spirited Hungarian czardas for the villagers. Swanilda and Franz arrive and perform a grand pas de deux that symbolizes their reconciliation and their sacred vows. Next, the villagers join the couple in a fast, accelerating dance as the curtain falls.

Franklin's staging was derived from the 1933 version of Nicholas Sergeyev, and thanks to his prodigious memory, it was breathtakingly close to the original. While staying close to his source, Franklin did make a few changes, however. Danilova advised him to "put some juice in it,"[17] so he re-emphasized the mime and gave both the corps and the soloists bigger, more complicated movements. He changed a passage in the "Prayer" solo, which he found too languid. On the advice of Danilova, a third-act variation was added for Franz, using music from Délibes's *Sylvia*.[18]

Franklin also tried to enhance the ballet's visual appeal for children. For instance, he gave the second-act dollmaker's scene more action. For beginners, his production had a dancing skeleton. The 1938 Ballet Russe *Coppelia* had a skeleton in the second act, but it was painted on the drop. For the National production, Freddie opted for a real one hanging from the flies. It jiggled around, much to the delight of the kiddies. In addition to Mr. Bones, Franklin set all of the dolls dancing. In other productions, they had posed stiffly on stage with heads and arms moving, but Franklin set them all running, turning, tearing the place apart. He said, "Children love seeing Coppelius coming back into his doll shop and seeing his dolls running amuck."[19]

In Franklin's genial reading, Swanilda is blessedly unpetulant, as much puzzled as made jealous by the attention of Franz to the indifferent Coppelia. She is heedless rather than malevolent in Act II, when she wreaks havoc in the shop of Dr. Coppelius, and she's instantly repentant in Act III when Coppelius demands retribution. Franklin took Franz at face value: after all, here we have a guy who falls in love with a *doll*. In Franklin's version, he is slightly goofy, childlike, and a tad compulsive when he can't stop fiddling with a sheaf of wheat. Still, he is appealing for his boyish high spirits.

Clad in a suit that was all on one side and made him appear to be leaning, Freddie gave a touch of poignancy to his Coppelius: "You see, I love the doll. And oh, that dreadful Swanilda coming in and messing it all up!"[20] A *New York Times* critic reported that he was "brilliant in the part of the eccentric old dollmaker." However, he added, "the energy of his own acting may have to be toned down somewhat." The critic's main reservation about the ballet was its low-budget production values. For instance, the same

Frederic Franklin as Doctor Coppelius in *Coppelia*. 1963. National Ballet production, Washington, D.C. Staged by Frederic Franklin after Saint-Leon. Music: Delibes. Set: James Waring. Costumes: Joseph Lewis. Photograph: Collection of Frederic Franklin.

costumes were used for the Polish mazurka and the Hungarian czardas.[21] Nevertheless, Franklin's *Coppelia* was a great success and became the National's "bread and butter" ballet.

Year by year, the company's tours were getting longer, and the National was presenting more large-scale works. The troupe gave sixteen performances in its debut season; a dozen were on tour, four were in Washington. Ten seasons later, of its 179 performances, 125 were on tour, and fifty-four in Washington. In 1963, Jean Riddell and Ralph Black, the company's general manager, went to Europe and purchased Ballet Rambert's productions of *Giselle* and *La Sylphide* for a mere $4,000. (Ballet Rambert had changed its focus to modern dance, and the company was eager to get rid of them.) At its height, the National's repertoire was upwards of fifty works with full-length productions of the *Nutcracker, Cinderella, Sleeping Beauty*, and *Coppelia*, in addition to the two ballets above.

In the 1960s, Washington was ludicrously bereft of theatres, considering that it was the nation's capital. In a 1966 review, Clive Barnes stated, "It is a disgrace that the enterprising Washington National Ballet should have to make its performing home at the Lisner Auditorium."[22] Before the construction of the Kennedy Center, Lisner was the only facility the company could feasibly use. It had a small and very shallow stage, similar to that of New York City Center. Dressing room accommodations, storage facilities, lighting, and orchestra pit arrangements were all primitive and inadequate. The seating in the house was cramped and uncomfortable. Right from the beginning, Franklin admitted, "It's going to take the ingenuity of all of us to overcome the technical problems."[23] In spite of these difficulties, the National still managed to mount its full-length ballets at the Lisner.

Early in 1963, Washington, D.C., found itself in the extraordinary position of having three ballet companies. In addition to the Washington Ballet and the National Ballet, American Ballet Theatre (which had added the word "American" in 1957) suddenly arrived on the scene. They came to Washington under the auspices of the Washington Ballet Guild and used Mary Day's facilities for their new headquarters. In 1961, a new wing had been added to the Washington School of Ballet, providing spacious new classroom and rehearsal spaces.[24]

Franklin could not have been pleased by the appearance of this company, especially when American Ballet Theatre began billing itself as "America's National Ballet Company." In an address to a Washington ladies' group Franklin stated, "I don't think that Ballet Theatre can be considered a national company just because it's being housed here for rehearsals."[25] Although it was essentially a touring company, ABT began to increase its number of Washington performances and became a source of competition for the National.

For all of these years, American Ballet Theatre had been very much an itinerant troupe, still without a permanent New York home. The arrangement was that the Washington School of Ballet would be its new home for eleven weeks each year, thus giving the company sorely needed geographic stability. But the bubble quickly burst in the late spring of 1963. Overruling Mary Day, the Washington Ballet Guild voted to "back" but not "subsidize" the company.[26] Again the dancers became nomads. The company did not have a permanent theatre in New York until it finally acquired an official home at the Metropolitan Opera in 1977.

It was in 1964 that Fred met William Ausman, who had taken a part-time job as a stagehand for the National while completing his graduate degree at George Washington University. Bill left Washington in 1969 to work as an international marketer for Tanberg, Inc., in Oslo, Norway. Even so, Bill and Fred remained fast friends, visiting one another whenever possible. In 1972 they bought a lovely apartment on New

York's West Side, and this has been "home" to them ever since, despite their constant traveling. When Ausman first began working backstage for the National, he had no background whatsoever in dance. Over the years, he acquired a vast knowledge of this art form. Asked how he became such an astute dance historian, he replied, "By living with one."[27]

Throughout its existence, the National had a high rate of turnover, especially in 1965. Consistently poor reviews led to Franklin's decision to let Steven Grebel go. Since Grebel was Sonia Arova's fiancé as well as her partner, she was very bitter about this decision and left with him. Recognizing the need for a new ballerina, Franklin went to London and found Marilyn Burr, a principal with London Festival Ballet, who was preparing to leave that company.

In the same year, an invitation to Franklin from the Bulgarian Embassy to represent America at Varna led to the discovery of another future principal, a handsome Hungarian named Ivan Nágy. There were eighteen nationalities among the judges. One of them was the legendary Bolshoi ballerina, Galina Ulanova. Franklin represented the United States, although he forgot that momentarily: "Arnold Haskell represented England. And it was a huge amphitheatre. And there was this big round table with all of the seats for all of the panelists, and instinctively, I went and sat behind the Union Jack. And Arnold Haskell said, 'Fred, no! You've got to find America. That's where you are now!'"[28]

Franklin went back to Varna for a second time in 1966, where he renewed his ties with Ulanova:

> I got along so well with Ulanova. She was so nice. Alicia Alonso was also there, and she got up and said, "My dancers [from Cuba] are better than most of the rest of them here, and we're not getting any gold medals!" This was translated to Ulanova, and Ulanova replied through the interpreter, "Tell her not to worry. We'll have some more made." I swore I'd never go near another competition again, and I didn't.[29]

Marilyn Burr and Franklin's Varna discovery, Ivan Nágy, were frequently paired at the National, and they developed an intimate personal partnership as well. Matters got awkward when Jean-Paul Comelin, another former principal with London Festival Ballet, was invited to Washington to stage his pas de deux, *Idylle*. The problem was that Comelin was Marilyn Burr's husband, and Burr and Nágy were now living together. One day during rehearsals, Comelin walked into Franklin's office and asked, "What's happened to my marriage?"[30] According to Bill Ausman, Comelin "couldn't be around them without seeing it. We carefully kept them apart. So Fred and I had him over for Christmas dinner, and there he was at our house, crying his eyes out."[31] The upshot was that Ivan and Marilyn got married. Comelin joined the National in the next season and partnered Marilyn in his *Idylle*. He also fell in love with one of the girls in the company and got married again himself. Life goes on.

The National had two particularly important performances in New York in 1966 and 1967. For both, Clive Barnes gave the company excellent reviews, a real boost to company morale. The company appeared at the Brooklyn Academy of Music for a single performance on March 5, 1966. Barnes declared, "There are fewer than a dozen ballet companies, probably markedly fewer, able to match the National Ballet's level of technique and artistry. With troupes like this, the idea of first-class American ballet companies outside New York is no longer a pipe dream, but a happy reality." Franklin presented two of his own pieces, his *Homage au Ballet* and *Pas de Trois*, danced to the music of Glinka. Although he dismissed *Homage* as "a slight Balanchinian essay of more fluency than originality," Barnes saw both pieces as "manifestos" by Franklin stating that "he has produced, discovered and developed some of the best girl dancers in the country."[32]

Also on the program were Francisco Moncion's *Night Song* and a revival of *Night Shadow* (*La Sonnambula*) staged by John Taras, with new designs and costumes by David Hayes. Barnes went into a tirade over the neo–Balanchine Moncion piece. What he detected was not snippets from Balanchine's great works but rather "that standard, all-purpose Balanchine ballet that exists only in the minds of his stupidest critical opponents and his most fervent creative disciples." *La Sonnambula* was much more to his liking:

"'La Sonnambula' is fine; so fine in fact, that in many ways it can offer the New York City Ballet a run for its money." Franklin appeared as the Poet once more in an "unsurpassed" performance.[33]

The National Ballet opened its first Broadway season at the City Center on March 27, 1967. They did Franklin's *Homage* and *Tribute*, Balanchine's *Four Temperaments*, Anna Sokolow's *Night* and George Skibine's modernized version of *La Péri*. For Barnes, *Tribute* was "pallid yet elegant, conventional yet sprightly ... the ballet as a whole possessed more style than substance." But he praised the buoyant style of the dancers. Of the performance as a whole he said, "It is not a major company — but is an awfully good minor company."[34]

The company's next New York appearance was in November of 1967 at Brooklyn College's Whitman Auditorium. This time the company played it safe in a program of four tried and true classics: *Les Sylphides*, *Concerto Barocco*, *Raymonda* and the "Don Quixote Grand Pas de Deux." Walter Terry termed Franklin's staging of *Les Sylphides* "a very fine one," and he had much praise for ballerinas Andrea Vodenhal and Marilyn Burr. In reference to the "safe bill," he remarked, "If you could dance, you couldn't lose, and the resident company in our nation's capital made the grade nicely."[35]

In seven seasons, the National Ballet had built a strong foundation in Washington. It was home, and the audience was marvelous. On tour, they were getting more and more engagements in the bigger cities. But the Ford Foundation grant was only for four years, and funding ran out in 1966. Said Franklin, "We have a lot of plans and ideas. All we need is money. Was ballet ever any different?"[36]

In the fall of 1969, Franklin scored a coup when he persuaded Dame Margot Fonteyn to appear with the National in Elsa Marianne von Rosen's restaging of August Bournanville's *La Sylphide*. This historical 1832 work (given in a new version by Bournanville in 1836) launched the Romantic Age of ballet, and made dancing en pointe an essential for the female ballet dancer. Dame Margot, at fifty, was dancing this role for the first time. Walter Terry made some perceptive comments:

Dame Margot is no jumper, less now than a few years ago, and the leg-beats are not as sharp or as shimmery as Bournanville dancers achieve. Yet, Fonteyn has her own remarkable elevation, for when she is merely standing on pointe she has moved herself to a new plane — she seems not to be placed on toe-tip, but pausing there with the aura of flight in her body. There is, furthermore, an elevation of spirit that young dancers rarely achieve.

Andrea Vodehnal as the Sleepwalker carrying Frederic Franklin as the Poet in *La Sonnambula*. 1966. National Ballet production, Washington, D.C. Staged by John Taras. Sets and lighting: David Hayes. Costumes: Patricia Zipprodt. Photograph: Collection of Frederic Franklin.

Terry concluded, "At fifty, then, one of the greatest ballerinas of our time has added yet another classic to her repertory — and triumphed."[37] After *La Sylphide*, Dame Margot became a frequent guest artist with the National. Franklin said, "This is marvelous for the company, not simply as a box office attraction but, more importantly, for the example Margot sets our young dancers."[38]

In 1970 Ben Stevenson arrived to set *Cinderella* for the National Ballet. Stevenson had danced as a principal with the Sadler's Wells and London Festival Ballet. Later, he began a career in the commercial theatre and returned to the Sadler's Wells to mount a successful version of *Sleeping Beauty*.

In the late 1960s, Stevenson had accepted Rebekah Harkness's invitation to come to America to direct the Harkness Youth Dancers. Stevenson maintains that Mrs. Harkness was always good to him and never tried to interfere with his work. Yet Stevenson's rivals, working close to her, influenced her against him. The situation was tense, and Stevenson found himself sitting around for months with nothing to do. Knowing what the inevitable outcome would be, he resigned. Immediately, twelve of the young Harkness dancers left in protest. "That was why the Harkness experience was special," said Stevenson. "Those kids chose leaving with me, though I couldn't offer them work for six months."[39]

It was at this discouraging crossroad in his career that Stevenson accepted the National's offer to mount *Cinderella*, and the ballet proved to be a landmark for the Washington company. When it was first created, it was unequaled in the company's history for splendor and panache. Most impressive was the magical quality of Stevenson's staging, particularly in the transformation scene at the end of Act I. Stevenson was ably assisted in this regard by set designer Edward Haynes and costumer Norman McDowell. Cinderella and her Prince were danced by alternate casts: Gaye Fulton with Desmond Kelly, and Marilyn Burr with Ivan Nágy. The two rambunctious Ugly Sisters were danced by Freddie and ballet master, Larry Long.

Stevenson received only qualified praise for his choreography, however. Although he has always had a knack for spectacular and entertaining story ballets, his choreography for them has not been in the genius class. His movement invention for *Cinderella* did not have the magic of Haynes's spectacular stage effects, and some moments in the ballet were banal or downright awkward. Nancy Mason pointed out that the Ugly Sisters "hadn't fully explored their roles to give each sister a substantive personality, independent and thriving on individual idiosyncrasies." She also complained, "Who ever heard of everyone wearing identical dresses to a ball? Perhaps some variation would lure the eye away from the thin choreography."[40]

When the production was taken to New York for performances at Brooklyn College, Stevenson and Franklin persuaded Margot Fonteyn to return to the National to dance the title role. For Mason, Fonteyn's "characteristic clarity and musicality were wasted on choreography that didn't really allow her to dance.... On the whole, Stevenson created as though he were saving her for a tour de force which never came."[41]

However, not everyone reacted to the ballet as did Mason. For Jean Battey Lewis it was "the greatest success in its [the National's] eight-year history."[42] So popular was this venture that Stevenson received an offer to join the National as co-director. In the meanwhile, the people who had made trouble for Stevenson back at Harkness had been let go, and Mrs. Harkness invited him back. By then he had received invitations from the Berlin Opera as well as the National to act as director-choreographer. Stevenson chose the National, bringing with him the defectors from Harkness, among them, Dennis Poole, Stuart Sebastian and Kirk Peterson. All three were quite promising, although none had ever danced a lead in a big classical ballet.

Franklin welcomed these additions because he had recently lost two of his male principals — Desmond Kelly joined the Royal Ballet (formerly the Sadler's Wells), and Ivan Nágy (after a brief stint with New York City Ballet) joined American Ballet Theatre. Predictably, though, not everyone in the company was happy with the infusion of newcomers. Several National dancers were fired to make way for the Harkness "whizkids." One remaining National dancer groused, "We just stand by and watch. None of the old-timers are given major roles any more, and a lot of promises are broken."[43] Nonetheless, an augmented company enabled Stevenson to choreograph and produce lavish versions of the classics.

Naturally, there were rumors that Franklin was uneasy over the flurry of attention channeled toward Stevenson, but this does not appear to be the case. The two had an apparently relaxed partnership, and Franklin knew that his company needed a resident choreographer. He was also aware that the school was being neglected and that he could

Cinderella. Edward Meyers (left) and Franklin (right) as the Ugly Sisters. Marilyn Burr as Cinderella. 1971. National Ballet production, Washington, D.C. Choreography: Ben Stevensen. Music: Proko?ev. Décor: Peter Farmer. Photograph: Collection of Frederic Franklin.

no longer manage both the school and the company alone. Asked whether his directorial duties would interfere with his choreographic output, Stevenson replied, "I doubt it. That's the marvelous thing about sharing the directorship with Freddie Franklin. He can take over when I'm choreographing."[44]

Stevenson's next project for the National Ballet was to set his *Sleeping Beauty* on the company for the inaugural season of the John F. Kennedy Center for the Performing Arts in September of 1971. The ballet won more Washingtonian fans for the National; unfortunately, when it was taken to New York for performances at Whitman Hall of Brooklyn College in October of 1971, Jack Anderson ripped the production to shreds. In Brooklyn, part of the trouble was the small stage, which made the action look pinched, but for Anderson, the theater's deficiencies could not fully explain the company's lackluster style. He wrote that "the production seldom comes alive," that "like the mime, the dancing is monochromatic," and that "the members of the National Ballet seldom seemed to be having fun as they danced."[45]

For the 1971 Christmas season, Stevenson continued his efforts by revamping the *Nutcracker*, changing the first act from the usual bourgeois milieu to a more rural, informal one. As with his previous full-length ballets, there were some moments of banality and awkwardness in an otherwise serviceable production. In this case, lack of time was partly responsible. With some annoyance, Stevenson pointed out, "most of the time we are on the road, and then AGMA contracts interfere. You have to give the dancers two hours' rest before the performance. Still, you can't kill the dancers."[46]

Stevenson's comments to the dancers in rehearsal were often biting and acerbic. He would say to a girl with less-than-perfect posture, "I see a big hump on your shoulder blades. You'd make a fortune in the zoo." To another girl with a distorted arabesque, he would remark, "Your back leg looks like a coat hanger. Have you just gotten back from the cleaners?" Once, after a two-hour rehearsal, he reportedly told the company dancers, "That wasn't too bad — considering you haven't danced it since yesterday."[47] Yet, despite his sarcastic humor, or perhaps even because of it and because of the concern it represented, the dancers enjoyed and appreciated Stevenson.

In the 1971–72 season, Dame Margot danced more often with the National than with any other company, including her own Royal Ballet, where she was still involved in her celebrated partnership with Rudolf Nureyev. She gave over forty performances with the National this year, dancing the leads in *Sleeping Beauty, Swan Lake, La Sylphide* and *Cinderella.*

Franklin told an interviewer, "I can't say enough about Fonteyn."[48] She was no coddled, pampered star but a hardened trouper who had spent more than her share of time in the trenches. She had suffered untold deprivations with the Sadler's Wells during World War II, dancing in freezing theatres with no food in her stomach. During these days of severe food shortages, she and her colleagues mixed Knox gelatin with water in the wings, which gave them protein, but no food energy.

The toughness and iron will thus engrained in Fonteyn did not abandon her as the years went by. She proved her extraordinary perseverance more than once in her association with the National. Incredibly, there were no first-floor dressing rooms at the Kennedy Center when it opened in 1971. This astounding goof was especially problematic for Fonteyn, who had to make a lightning-fast costume change in *Cinderella* and certainly didn't have time to take the elevator to the second floor. Margot perused the backstage area and found a tiny storage room. She called Franklin over and said, "Just bring me a table and a light bulb and a mirror, if you can find one."[49] He did so, and Margot made do, without a word of complaint.

On another occasion, Margot had appeared as Aurora in a Saturday matinee performance of *Sleeping Beauty* in Philadelphia. This role is one of the most exhausting ones in the ballet repertory, and Margot was looking forward to a relaxing dinner with her friends. As she was dressing for dinner, general manager Ralph Black stopped by and asked her if he should send out for something to eat between shows. When signing her contract, Margot had unwittingly agreed to do two performances of *Sleeping Beauty* in one day. Not even a twenty-year-old in her right mind would have knowingly agreed to such a punishing test of stamina. As Franklin pointed out, "Now one is enough for a week!" Margot stayed calm and decided that she must honor her contract, regardless of the circumstances. She cancelled her dinner plans, sent out for steak and oysters, and took a one-hour nap. "And she was better than ever in the evening performance," Franklin recalled.[50]

Fonteyn became quite irritated when people spoke of her "dedication." She once told Franklin, "I love dancing, but I'm not dedicated to it." Remembering this, Franklin told his interviewer, "I'm not either. I've loved it. It's been my life. But I'm not like a monk. I'm not dedicated at all, and I think it's rather a foolish thing to say one is.... I'm doing it because I want to. But I've got a life also."[51]

By the 1971–72 season, Margot was beginning to feel that the National was her home. She told Ralph Black, "I want to be the head of this company. I really want it." Franklin's initial reaction to her request was not surprising: "To be frank, it was then that I got to be a bit nervous, because I thought, 'We can't go on just being a vehicle.' On the other hand, I told myself, 'Well, if you want to keep the company going, this is the best way to do it. Of course, engage her. Let this be her company.'" However, the board of directors had strong reservations about Fonteyn's proposal, and she understood. As she told Freddie, "I know the young dancers won't have a chance because I will be here." According to Franklin, "We parted so amicably, and we're the best of friends today, and she even came back after that and did some more performances with us." He continued, "She is a real lady of the theatre. I would say very much in the tradition of Danilova, who went on no matter what."[52]

Fonteyn continued to dance until the age of sixty, twelve years before her death in 1991. Some wondered why she didn't retire from performing sooner, but it wasn't as if she didn't need the money. Just as she decided to divorce her habitually unfaithful Panamanian husband, he was shot in the neck by a political rival in 1964 and became a quadriplegic. Fonteyn responded magnificently, sustained by her generosity, her compassion and a steel core of physical and mental discipline. She was forty-five when her husband's medical bills started to arrive, and it was fifteen years before she finally returned to her farm in Panama—a four-roomed bungalow with a corrugated roof, no air-conditioning, no telephone—and no pension to allow for improving these conditions. Her last years were sad ones. She lived in near-poverty and grew more isolated with the death of cherished colleagues, her mother and her husband, Tito. Finally, she had to face the cancer that killed her, using the presence of a visiting Nureyev, himself fatally ill with AIDS, to restore her old fighting spirit.

In the spring of 1974 Franklin realized a long-held wish, to engage Valerie Bettis to remount *A Streetcar Named Desire* on his company. Looking back, Franklin regarded *Streetcar* as his "Swan Song ... I never did another big dancing part." He showed not a whit of envy to see the role of Stanley pass to a younger dancer. "Why should I be jealous, my dear? Life is in phases—in some, we receive; in others, we give."[53]

Like most companies, the National Ballet existed through the whims of fate, persistent management and unending hope. The National depended upon extensive touring for survival. One of the company's problems was the enormous union labor expense of taking three huge productions—*Coppelia, Sleeping Beauty* and *Cinderella*—on the road. Franklin assumed that the National would be named the company-in-residence at the newly-constructed Kennedy Center, since American Ballet Theatre planned to be at the center for short seasons only. The National Ballet became the capital's little gem, only to have the rug pulled out from under it in 1969, when American Ballet Theatre was selected over the National to be the resident company at the Center, even though Lucia Chase had no intention of moving her company to Washington. Roger Stevens, executive director of the center, told Franklin and Riddell that the National Ballet was too small to fill such a large opera house.

The Kennedy Center opened in September of 1971, and its overall effect on the

National was eventually devastating. Now that there was a gorgeous, spacious, state-of-the-art theatre in the area, audiences were less willing to attend events at the Lisner. To maintain large houses, the National was almost forced to perform at the Kennedy Center, but rental fees were astronomical. In 1971, the rental fee was $15,000 per week, and that was just for the four walls. Such things as ushers, musicians, union-scale technical staff, and even heat were not included. Moreover, the center was bringing in heavy competition, such as two weeks of the New York City Ballet, up to six weeks of American Ballet Theatre and glamorous visitors from abroad, such as the Royal Ballet, the Kirov, and the Bolshoi.

Franklin's troubles at the time were exacerbated by an extraordinary string of accidents and illnesses, some of which may have been stress-related. First, he got a hernia and had to have an operation. He was out for six weeks while the company was on the road. Shortly thereafter, he fractured his left foot and before he had fully recovered, he contracted viral pneumonia and developed a clot in his lung. He spent three days in the hospital in serious condition, but he survived. However, he had to remain at home during his recovery. This gave him plenty of time to worry: "I felt something was going to happen to the company. I thought something dire was — because the Kennedy Center wasn't working out."[54]

Many Washingtonians had expected the center to provide for resident companies. They hoped that permanent ballet, opera and theatre companies would enable the city to hold up its head, at least culturally, among the great cities of the world. At first plans for the center were rather amorphous, but as they crystallized, it became evident that the center's board of directors did not regard it as their civic duty to promote community arts organizations. They did not make the slightest concession to the National Ballet, not even to the extent of giving them a small break on the rent.

Franklin's dancers were his pride, and he was not a little gratified that six of them were prize winners at the 1972 Varna ballet competition, "the first time that so large a contingent of American dancers swept the boards."[55] But by the winter of 1973, a falling off of company standards was evident. In early November, the National gave a short season at New York City Center. Although she was quite impressed with the company's revival of Doris Humphrey's *Water Study*, Pamela Gaye's review was harsh:

> Notwithstanding a nervous opening night, the company looked under the weather. There are soloists and principals (including some of the winners at last year's Varna, Bulgaria, ballet competition) who are simply mis-ranked. The corps dancers suffer from anemic technique and projection. New works by resident choreographer Ben Stevenson are lackluster. And half of the sets and costumes are unimaginatively dull.[56]

The dip in company morale that can be caused by reviews of this sort was only exacerbated by rumors that the company was on the verge of financial collapse. In June of 1974, the executive committee of the National suspended operations, the company's eleven-year career ended by inflationary production costs and "insufficient community support." The company had grossed more than $25,000 in advance sales for the coming season at the Kennedy Center, but outstanding debts outweighed foreseeable income. At the time of suspension, the National owed approximately $150,000 to the Internal Revenue Service and had other debts as well.[57]

Franklin and his supporters did not give up without a fight:

Frederic Franklin, 1973. National Ballet, Washington, D.C. Photograph: Collection of Frederic Franklin.

There was a hue and cry in Washington. We called the Congressmen. We were out on the street, knocking on doors. But it was useless in Washington. I could see it, and I had known it. And no matter what, [after] the editorials in the paper, and people who had written from here [New York], they didn't want their own ballet. They didn't want it. They had the symphony, they had a very peculiar opera. Ballet Theatre was coming in, and they were happy.... No matter how, no matter what we did, not one soul in Washington lifted a finger to save us. Not one. And this was the most awful thing.[58]

About three dozen dancers suddenly found themselves on the job market; however, two of the company's brightest new stars — Kirk Peterson and Kevin McKenzie — were snatched up immediately by American Ballet Theatre.

In a surprising turnabout, Mary Day arranged for the Washington Ballet to turn professional and invited the then unknown Choo San Goh to be its chief choreographer. After his untimely death in 1987, although unable to replace his personal dynamism, Day continued her original concept, keeping the company to a modest size and presenting new, classically-based experimental works that were not in other repertoires. After her retirement in 1998, Septime Webre became artistic director.

· 6 ·

Franklin and the Rise
of Regional Ballet

After the folding of the National, Franklin chose to work with a variety of regional companies. His strongest affiliations have developed with eclectic companies that have expressed a strong interest in dance drama: Pittsburgh Ballet Theatre, Cincinnati Ballet, Oakland Ballet, and Tulsa Ballet Theatre.

The Pittsburgh Ballet Theatre grew out of an ill-fated liaison with Point Park College. But the story goes even further back. Before the company was formed, there was a ballet school at the Pittsburgh Playhouse, a community theater which was saved from financial ruin in 1966 through the relentless money-raising efforts of Loti Falk, Turkish-born wife of a wealthy cattle farmer. In the early1960s, Duncan Noble and Jayne Hillier came to the school; when they left, they were replaced by Nicholas Petrov, former Ballet Russe dancer, and artistic director of the short-lived Petrov Ballet.

In 1968, the school was made part of Point Park College. Petrov was not content to merely teach, so in the same year he organized an ambitious *Nutcracker* at Point Park. With eighty-five dancers, this highly successful production featured Violette Verdy as the Sugar Plum Fairy. Soon the people of Pittsburgh were clamoring for more. Petrov enlisted the help of Loti Falk and Arthur Blum (president of the college) to lay plans for a permanent ballet company. The company was officially chartered in 1969.

Initially, there was great excitement over the experiment of being affiliated with a college. But in June of 1973, there was an unforeseen disaster when Point Park College went bankrupt. The company announced its break with Point Park and its intention of going it alone. However, the failure of the college dissuaded people from helping Pittsburgh Ballet, for fear that any contribution they made to the ballet would instead go to pay the college deficit. It took a year-long, intense fund-raising campaign, spearheaded by Loti Falk, to convince Pittsburgh residents that the ballet was now totally divorced from Point Park. By 1975 Pittsburgh Ballet Theatre was established as a strong professional company with forty-seven dancers and a promising future.

Since Petrov was taught by Olga Preobrajenska and Massine, the company style at the time reflected this influence and tended more to the Ballet Russe direction than to the neoclassicism of Balanchine. Given Petrov's nostalgic choice of ballets, Franklin was an ideal candidate for brushing up the company in the traditional repertoire.

Franklin first came to Pittsburgh in 1970, when he and Petrov staged a full-length *Swan Lake* for Pittsburgh Ballet Theatre. In the summer of 1974, he followed up with a staging of *Giselle* for the PBT. Jack Anderson noted, "Franklin's revival eschewed some of the embellishments and supposed 'improvements' which producers have inflicted upon the ballet in recent years, with the result that the action moved with poignant simplicity in Pittsburgh." In his concluding remarks he stated, "If this 'Giselle' typifies its [PBT's] efforts, it deserves continuing success."[1]

In October of 1974, *Dance Magazine* announced that Franklin had joined Pittsburgh Ballet Theater as co–artistic director. In his announcement, Petrov said, "Franklin is one of the greatest ballet masters in the country. Knowing how fast he can revive a ballet, I thought he would be a great addition to our company. The sure ticket — the subscriber — is our livelihood, so it is important that we do the classics well."[2]

By 1975 the rep included the ubiquitous *Nutcracker*, Franklin's stagings of *Giselle* and *Pas de Quatre*, the Franklin/Petrov *Swan Lake*, Léonide Massine's *Gaîté Parisienne*, Michel Fokine's *Petrouchka*, Petrov's *Romeo and Juliet*, *Rite of Spring*, and *Steel Concerto*, Ruth Page's *Frankie and Johnny*, and *Winterset*, a new ballet by Stuart Sebastian. Franklin also danced one of the leading roles in Sebastian's *Winterset* and the role of Father Lorenzo (Friar Laurence) in Petrov's production of *Romeo and Juliet*.

By 1976, PBT had increased its number of performances at Pittsburgh's Heinz Hall and had expanded its touring engagements. The season, which opened September 17, featured two world premieres — a version of *Othello* by John Butler and *Arman's Variation*, a classical pas de trois by Alexander Filipov. Franklin revived his *Tribute*.

With two artistic directors, Franklin had time on his hands and became restless to branch out. On November 11, 1975, Loti Falk, now president of the PBT, announced that an agreement had been reached between the Pittsburgh Ballet Theatre and Chicago Ballet to share the services of Franklin on an equal-time basis.[3] The association between Pittsburgh Ballet and Ruth Page dated to the founding of the PBT, when Page was engaged to aid the company in launching its first season. She staged six of her works on Pittsburgh over the next six years. A number of PBT artists had performed as guests with the Chicago Ballet and vice-versa.

In a meeting between the two organizations, the time which Franklin would allocate to each company was determined, so that neither organization was to be deprived of his services during their respective production periods. The reasoning was that the sharing of an artistic director would further strengthen the ties between the two companies, ultimately resulting in economic advantages for both, and would provide the opportunity for mutual exchange of productions. In the fall of 1975, Freddie and Ruth Page got to work on that exchange by setting *Frankie and Johnny* for Pittsburgh. This revival was presented January 23–25, 1976, in Heinz Hall.

After the demise of the National, Franklin had vowed to himself, "I will never be an artistic director of a ballet company again."[4] But in a scant four months, he had gone back on his own word and had become a co–artistic director of PBT. Franklin was more than weary of the administration, management and endless political wrangling that go with such a position. He missed New York as a home base of operations. He wanted to begin freelancing, to reserve his energy for the thing he probably does better than anyone else in the world. There was a demand for his stagings among regional companies, among them the up-and-coming Cincinnati Ballet. He left Pittsburgh at the end of 1976 and headed down to Ohio. But he didn't burn his bridges with Pittsburgh, for he returned to set *La Sylphide* for PBT's 1977–78 season and *Paquita* for their season of 1980–81.

Petrov remained artistic director of Pittsburgh Ballet Theatre until 1977. Afterwards, the company was without direction. Falk guided the orphaned organization until 1979, when Patrick Frantz, former principal dancer and resident choreographer of the Pennsylvania Ballet, was engaged. By 1982, Patrick had been replaced by Patricia Wilde, for fifteen years a principal with the New York City Ballet. Wilde promptly contributed artistic and organizational stability and several Balanchine works. Her tenure saw dramatic increases in both company budget and number of dancers. She was succeeded by Terry Orr when she resigned in 1997, and PBT is still in strong shape.

Franklin has done much to enhance the prestige of the Oakland Ballet. This company was founded in 1965 by Ron Guidi. Over the next decade, East Bay residents came to know the company through its annual Christmas production of Guidi's 1963 *Hansel and Gretel* and his 1972 *Nutcracker*. The company was prospering, but it faced a dilemma concerning repertory. Aside from the ballets above and a Jo Savino/Ann Jenner revival of *Coppelia*, the remaining works were primarily shorter, original ballets ranging in style from classical to jazz. Guidi grew weary of the repertory's eclecticism. He wanted to find a focus that would distinguish Oakland from other regional companies.

A major turning point was *Billy the Kid*, which Eugene Loring staged for the company in 1976. Loring, who was then teaching at the University of California at Irvine, had declined offers from numerous regional companies to restage this ballet. He consented in the case of Oakland because Guidi's dancers were all good actors as well. Oakland's raw and spirited production won extensive press coverage and led to local and national grants. By 1980, the Oakland Ballet had nineteen full-time dancers on nine-month contracts and a budget of $661,000.

Billy the Kid led Guidi to the focus he was seeking. Oakland Ballet quickly gained a reputation for an impressively rich historic repertoire with its Americana and Diaghilev-era ballets, two years before Dance Theatre of Harlem turned to the same genres. In 1978, Massine staged his *La Boutique Fantasque* and *Contes Russes* for the Oakland Ballet in the year before he died. Massine encouraged Guidi in his quest and so in 1979, Nicholas Beriozov came to stage *Schéhérazade*. Guidi realized that of Diaghilev's five choreographers, Nijinska's work was the least seen on the stage. With her daughter Irina Nijinska's guidance and insight, Oakland reconstructed two lost works, *Les Noces* and *Les Biches*. Subsequent revivals included Nijinska's *Le Train Bleu* and *Bolero,* staged by Irina Nijinska and Nina Youskevitch, respectively. By 1985, the company had also staged Fokine's *Petrouchka* and *Le Coq d'Or*, Massine's *Le Soleil de Nuit*, Kurt Joos's *The Green Table* and Anna Sokolow's *Rooms*.

Franklin first became associated with Oakland Ballet with his fine staging of a chamber-scaled *Giselle*, Act II, in October of 1988. Freddie came back to Oakland the next season to stage his *Tribute* for performances beginning in September 1989. His next

Oakland project, a revival of *Gaîté Parisienne*, was performed on January 3–6, 1994, at the Paramount Theatre. Using sets and costume designs borrowed from Louisville Ballet and Tulsa Ballet Theatre, and based on Etienne de Beaumont's 1938 designs, the staging was unusually authentic to the original.

By January of 2002, Oakland had outgrown the chamber version of *Giselle*, and Franklin headed west to rework Act II for a larger cast. This project was a stretch for the company, since they had little experience with the nineteenth century repertory. Franklin obviously coached them meticulously. Critic Sima Belmar wrote, "Franklin worked wonders with the company, producing a corps de ballet that truly looked like one body moving, a testament to Franklin's keen eye."[5]

Ron Guidi retired in 1998, and he was temporarily replaced by acting artistic director Joral Schmalle. When Karen Brown, a former principal of Dance Theatre of Harlem, took over the helm of Oakland Ballet in 2000, she faced a host of financial challenges. Matters worsened when the company's traditionally profitable *Nutcracker* lost $300,000 in 2002. The company was rescued by a matching grant from the William and Flora Hewlett Foundation, but finances continue to be precarious today, and it is predicted that the company will fold for good in 2006.

Franklin had ties with Tulsa Ballet Theatre by virtue of his friendship with the two Ballet Russe veterans Roman Jasinski and Moscelyne Larkin, who married in 1943 when they were dancers with Colonel de Basil's Original Ballet Russe. They later joined Serge Denham's Ballet Russe de Monte Carlo. Jasinski was born in Poland. Larkin (who appeared with the Ballet Russe as Moussia Larkina) was an American Indian of the Oklahoma Shawnee-Peoria tribe. She was one of five Native American ballerinas of the period, the others being Maria and Marjorie Tallchief, Rosella Hightower and Yvonne Chouteau.

The couple settled in Oklahoma and founded Tulsa Ballet Theatre in 1956. The company gained national recognition over the years for its meticulous revivals of major works created during the Ballet Russe era, and company dancers won acclaim for their distinctive Ballet Russe style. By 1980, Tulsa Ballet Theatre had become a well-respected, fully professional regional company with a repertory of forty ballets and thirty-four dancers, twenty of them salaried for forty weeks a year. As a recognition of its growth in stature, the National Association for Regional Ballet named Tulsa one of eight major regional companies for the 1979–80 season.

Franklin was the ideal choice for ensuring the authenticity of Tulsa's Ballet Russe revivals. Freddie's first experience with Tulsa dated from 1979, when he staged his *Sylvia* pas de deux for the company. He returned to Tulsa to stage *Gaîté Parisienne* and the Balanchine-Danilova *Pas de Dix* in 1983, and did a "masterful"[6] restaging of *La Sylphide* in 1985.

When Franklin arrived to work with the company again in 1995, the Tulsa Ballet Theatre was just recovering from a quagmire of internal strife that had threatened its artistic integrity. After the death of Roman Jasinski Sr. in 1991, Roman Larkin Jasinski was appointed to succeed him, and his mother functioned actively as artistic director emeriti. Jasinski Jr. had joined American Ballet Theatre in 1975. Following his wedding in 1980 to Tulsa Ballet principal Kimberly Smiley, the couple joined the Cincinnati Ballet as principals. Five years later they returned to Tulsa at the rank of principal.

Jasinski Jr.'s tenure as artistic director was turbulent. Following his first season as director, Jasinski dismissed eleven dancers, including two veteran principals. Seven of the dismissed dancers then filed a lawsuit against the company, with representation by AGMA. The dancers claimed that TBT neglected to inform them of their dismissal within the time period stipulated in their contract. The company began to implode when subsequent resignations reduced the roster of twenty-eight dancers to thirteen and left the troupe without a ballet master. At that point, Jasinski unexpectedly resigned in November of 1994 and was told not to return to the facility.[7] The situation was complicated by Moscelyne Larkin's attempts to have her son reinstated. Board members fought back, but they did respond to an eleventh-hour plea from Larkin by inviting Jasinski to apply for the job and to be judged by the same criteria used for all candidates. This he never did.

Franklin had worked closely with Marcello Angelini at the Cincinnati Ballet and thought highly of his potential. He wrote a letter to Tulsa's board of directors which strongly recommended Cincinnati Ballet principal Angelini for the vacant position. Marcello recalls:

> When I applied for the position, I was probably the only candidate that did not meet the most important requirement: experience as an artistic director. Nevertheless, the Search Committee was interested in me; they probably felt my ideas were in line with what they saw the company being in the future. But the big question was being raised: would I be able to do the job, to deliver on those ideas. What really made the big difference between being offered the position or not, was a wonderful letter written by Freddie. He is without a doubt the most respected individual in the field in the US, so his assurance ... gave them [the committee] the peace of mind to take the risk. I remain sure that, without his help, I would not be here today.[8]

Franklin concurs: "I was very instrumental in his becoming Artistic Director."[9] It now appears that Franklin and the board could not have made a better choice.

By the time Angelini arrived in Tulsa to prepare for the company's 1995–96 season, he may have been the only person in town who believed that the company had a bright future. Undaunted by those who considered him an interloper who had unseated the company's founding family, Angelini simply went to work, mending fences and even establishing a friendly relationship with his predecessor. His gracious yet fierce tenacity and superior negotiating skills soon earned him the nickname "the Italian Tornado." Under Angelini, technical standards improved so dramatically that he was able to redeem the company's lost rights to perform Balanchine's works.

In his first season, Angelini asked Franklin to stage *Coppelia*, instead of reviving the version created by the Jasinskis. "I considered Franklin's version better," Angelini said, "and it was a way to show that the company was moving into new territory."[10]

Today, the Tulsa Ballet Theatre is prospering. Within a couple of years, Angelini had changed the repertory "dramatically from what it had been in the past, while still staying in line with the mission of the company and the intentions of the founders." He added, "We are in the middle of an endowment/capital campaign to raise nine million and — two years ahead of schedule — we have raised over ten million.... So things are very good in Tulsa."[11]

Franklin has worked more closely with Cincinnati Ballet than with any other regional company. Significantly, Cincinnati is the only regional company that Franklin has ever signed a regular contract with. Franklin's relationship to Cincinnati began decades before it had its own ballet company. The Ballet Russe often stopped in the city, where its benefactor, "Junky" Fleischmann, resided. Franklin was the houseguest of Julius and his family whenever he was in town.[12]

Before 1971, when ten young dancers were first placed on part-time salary, Cincinnati had no professional dance tradition. Its only exposure to professional dance was what it imported. However, German-settled Cincinnati was an important cultural center for music, and that was what attracted the Cincinnati Ballet's first artistic director, David McLain, in 1966.

David McLain studied at the School of American Ballet and at the studios of the Ballet Russe School and Robert Joffrey. Teaching posts with Joffrey in New York and with Barbara Weisberger in Pennsylvania preceded his decision to move to the Midwest, when he was invited to become the Dayton Civic Ballet's charter ballet master. McLain described himself as a "workaholic," and his first few years in Ohio found him shuttling among teaching posts in Dayton, Columbus, and Cincinnati seven days a week. By the time he felt ready to take over the reins of the Cincinnati Civic Ballet, McLain was also choreographing extensively.

By 1969, distinguished critics like Walter Terry were beginning to sit up and take notice:

> It's amazing, that's what it is. I'm referring to the Cincinnati Ballet Company, operated by the College-Conservatory of Music at the University of Cincinnati. I'm also talking about the amazing young man, David McLain, who has made student dancers seem professional, who has provided for a handsome production which would do justice to a major ballet troupe, and who is himself a choreographer of distinction. Amazing![13]

Two keys to the Cincinnati's Ballet's development were its university affiliation and its eclectic attitude toward repertory. From the start, the civic company had based its operations at the Cincinnati Conservatory of Music. Eventually the CCM merged with the University of Cincinnati, and a university dance division was created. The merger was of enormous benefit to the young ballet company: it received three large studios and the free use of Cincinnati University's eight-hundred-seat, state-of-the-art Corbett Auditorium.

From the beginning, the company distinguished itself with an imaginative repertory. McLain wanted to build a varied repertory, what he called a museum of great works, including both classical and modern masterworks, with contrasting original pieces. A sense of history was reflected in the works of the late Lester Horton, one of the West Coast's most renowned dance figures. Staged by former Horton dancers James Truitte and Carmen de Lavallade, this special wing of Horton works gave the company some vivid, highly theatrical pieces. Truitte's early background brought a special brand of professionalism to Cincinnati, as he scrupulously maintained the Horton works and taught rigorous classes that made exacting demands on the dancers. McLain himself created some memorable works in the sixties, among them *Concerto, Antiche, Arie e Danze, Romanza*, and *Clouds*.

In the early 1970s, the company began to acquire classical works: *Pas de Quatre*, staged by Dame Alicia Markova when she held a faculty appointment at Cincinnati University; *Divertissement Classique*, a gift from Roman Jasinski; and George Balanchine's gifts of *Concerto Barocco* and *Serenade*. McLain had a reverence for these works and a meticulousness about maintaining them which he transmitted to his dancers.

While the regular repertory series continued at the university theatre, two spectacle ballets in 1974 marked the company's take-off date in the eyes of the general public. Both were made possible by local business support and were performed downtown at the Music Hall with the accompaniment of the Cincinnati Symphony. *Firebird*, staged after the original Fokine version by Roman Jasinski and Moscelyne Larkin, sold out its two June premiere performances. McLain told Walter Terry that he didn't think the full-length classics were the right direction for Cincinnati Ballet, but he admitted that he was under tremendous pressure to do a *Nutcracker*.[14] Thus, six months later, the *Nutcracker* was staged by Frederic Franklin and the returning Jasinskis. Franklin's "Snow Scene" was considered the highlight of this ballet, and *Nutcracker* was the production that finally put Cincinnati Ballet on the map.

The Cincinnati *Nutcracker* had all the spectacular effects of an opera-scale production, but it also possessed a cozy, whimsical charm and made no attempt to psychoanalyze Clara. It was simply a big-budget, old-fashioned *Nutcracker* in period style with lavish sets by Jay Depenbrock. In this same year, Franklin staged *Les Sylphides* and *Coppelia* for the Cincinnati Ballet. The latter ballet became a repertory staple until Ivan Nágy staged a new version for the CB in December of 1986.

Franklin's first visits in 1974 coincided with a period of unprecedented growth for the company. When the addition of a live orchestra made the smaller university auditorium unfeasible, the company moved its repertory series to the 2,055-seat Taft Theater. Its downtown location also made the CB more accessible to the general public. But growth was always tempered with careful planning regarding touring costs, new productions, number of dancers. Of Cincinnati Ballet, Franklin remarked, "It is absolutely to my mind a company that is thoroughly thought out. They do not do things unless the money is in the bank to back it up."[15]

By 1975–76, dancers capable of handling more challenging repertory had emerged. The corps was ready for the technical demands of Franklin's stagings of *Pas de Dix*, the Balanchine/Danilova arrangement of the last act of *Raymonda*, and *Swan Lake* (Act II), presented in May of 1976. The Cincinnati Ballet began to develop dancers who came to Cincinnati from other professional regional companies.

By 1977–78, the Cincinnati Ballet had more than doubled its season subscriptions. The company was able to move from the Taft to the Music Hall's more sumptuous setting. However, 3,600 seats had to be filled at the Music Hall, and this was bound to influence repertory decisions. Plus, more and more tour sponsors were asking for evening-length works. If these factors seemed to be pushing the company toward traditional works at the expense of innovation, McLain still tried to keep the repertory in a delicate balance. Franklin noted, "David McLain has been wonderful about this. Of course, the box office is important wherever one works. But the great hue and cry in this land is, 'Where are the choreographers? Who is giving them a chance?'"[16]

Cincinnati had to grapple with this problem at an earlier date than most regional companies, but all have had to come to terms with a new fact of ballet life. In this country — and in most European countries as well — audiences now prefer lavish, full-length dramatic works, particularly the classics, to mixed bills. As ballet companies everywhere struggle to stay afloat in these economically troubled times, artistic directors are faced with a dilemma, a choice between pragmatism and idealism; whether to play it safe and present mostly full-length works that will generate bigger bucks or to program diverse evenings of repertoire with the understanding that there will be too many empty seats.

Oddly enough, America's initial exposure to ballet was in mixed bills offered by various touring companies such as the Diaghilev and Pavlova companies, Ballet Caravan, Ballet Theatre and, of course, the Ballet Russe de Monte Carlo. The rise in popularity of the evening-length story ballet in America is a phenomenon of the past twenty-five years.

American Ballet Theatre mounted its first complete *Swan Lake* in 1967. Between 1975 and 1985 the company staged *Sleeping Beauty, Raymonda, Nutcracker, Don Quixote, Bayadère Cinderella* and *Romeo and Juliet.* Clearly, a trend was beginning to take effect. Bruce Marks, artistic director of the Boston Ballet, told an interviewer, "There are choreographers out there, but they need some help; they need a chance to work. When it wasn't so expensive and so 'dangerous' they did. I want to make a commitment to some young choreographers."[17] Cincinnati has also done a commendable job of fostering and supporting emerging choreographers over the years, but practicalities have dictated that the company offer heaping helpings of the classics as well. Franklin's help in staging them has been invaluable, although he has been most vocal in addressing the problems faced by up-and-coming choreographers.

Freddie's intermittent presence in Cincinnati, limited by his responsibilities elsewhere, was a boost for the entire company. In November of 1977, he was appointed choreographer-in-residence through an NEA grant. The next month, he did his own staging of *Pas de Quatre*, a work which had begun to look enclosed and stylistically wooden in the old Markova version. With his lifetime of experience in dance theatre, Franklin injected new theatricality and projection into the dancers. In May of 1978 he staged his *Sylvia* pas de deux, which was subsequently restaged for a number of companies, most notably in 1990 for Dance Theatre of Harlem. As George Jackson noted, this pas de deux "is typical Franklin in being tastefully demanding of the dancers, yet tailored to flatter them."[18] This adagio showed Franklin's awareness of historical precedents by alluding to the noble poses that were prevalent in the nineteenth century French school, making the dancers seem to become statues at selected moments. He staged his beloved *Coppelia* for the Cincinnati Ballet in 1979, and he and Danilova staged *Paquita* in the same year. His staging of *Frankie and Johnny* was first seen in Cincinnati in 1980. A 1983 staging of *Giselle* (Act II) was Franklin's next project for the CB. 1983 also saw a revival of *Billy Sunday*, with a new score by Carmon DeLeone and a new finale choreographed by Franklin. Franklin once again danced the title role, and the revival was aired on public television.

Franklin was so busy freelancing among regional companies that he never considered remaining in Cincinnati for any length of time, but a tragedy changed his plans. Franklin had earlier noticed that David McLain was suffering from very bad pains in his back. McLain died of lung cancer in December of 1984. Larry Keller (president of the CB at the time) asked Fred to come back as interim director. Franklin certainly had no great yearning to be an artistic director again, but he had a strong sense of loyalty

**Franklin demonstrating the Bartender in rehearsal while staging Ruth Page's *Frankie and Johnny*
for Cincinnati Ballet. September 1980. Photograph: Sandy Underwood.**

to Cincinnati. He agreed to serve as interim artistic director until a permanent replacement could be found. While Larry assured him that the search committee would find
somebody within six months, it would be nearly two years before a permanent director was appointed.[19]

Over the next two years, Franklin's biggest project for the CB was his staging of
La Sylphide, first seen by the local public in May of 1986. Based on Elsa-Marianne von

Rosen's setting for the National Ballet of Washington, it was reportedly rich in dramatic detail and sincerely rendered by the dancers. Without dominating the action, Franklin's own malevolent, strangely commanding portrayal of the evil witch Madge was a strong motivating element. Franklin's artistry made of Madge a genuinely frightening character, and this would become the greatest role of his senior career.

The May performances were done as a tribute to David McLain. At the end of the performance, Freddie received a standing ovation in a moving tribute to his exemplary seventeen-month tenure as acting director. Ivan Nágy had accepted the permanent position.

In 1988, Franklin was named artistic director emeritus, after he had staged more than fifteen works for the Cincinnati Ballet. There followed a hiatus in Franklin's association with the CB as work with Dance Theatre of Harlem and other companies took much of his time. During the years of his absence, the Cincinnati Ballet went through a troubling period of instability.

In 1990 occurred the Mapplethorpe scandal, relating to seven disturbing photographs depicting homosexuality (seven in the context of 175 by photographer Robert Mapplethorpe) which were on exhibit at Cincinnati's Contemporary Arts Center. A Hamilton County grand jury actually indicted the Cincinnati Contemporary Art Center and its director on obscenity charges, probably a first in the history of U. S. jurisprudence. The majority of Cincinnati's citizens seemed to support the beleaguered

Frederic Franklin as the evil witch Madge. Cincinnati Ballet production in *La Sylphide*. 1986. This production staged by Franklin after the Elsa-Marianne von Rosen production for the National Ballet in 1969. (Production originally done for Ballet Rambert in 1960.) Choreography: Bournonville. Music: Lovenskjold. Photograph: Philip Groshong.

CAC museum and its courageous director, and the extensive negative publicity may have done serious harm to the community's carefully fostered image of supporting the arts.[20]

The Cincinnati Ballet fell on hard times in the year of the Mapplethorpe incident, posting a record $500,000 deficit on a $3.8 million budget for the 1989–90 fiscal year. Among the contributing factors was a $200,000 plunge in subscriptions and a $150,000 erosion of corporate support. Part of this may have been due to the fallout from the Mapplethorpe furor. New Orleans was also a financial albatross for the company. In 1983 CB had made an innovative dance-share plan with the New Orleans City Ballet, by which the two cities would share the thirty-nine-member troupe of Cincinnati. Cincinnati would provide New Orleans with performances, lecture-demonstrations, seminars and master classes; in return, the dancers would get more paid work weeks. This was the historic invention of the dual-city company. While it was conceived as a cost-cutting measure, this was not the end result. By 1990, New Orleans City Ballet owed the CB $155,000, which further contributed to the cash flow problem.[21]

The loss of top-level staff aggravated the financial situation still further. Ivan Nágy had been named artistic director of English National Ballet beginning in 1990–91 and was now only a spectral presence in Cincinnati. British native Richard Collins, the company's rehearsal coach and a former member of the English National, became artistic director for the 1991–92 season.

Collins resigned as artistic director in 1993 and was replaced by Nigel Burgoine at the end of the 1992–93 season. In July of 1994, Burgoine resigned, and Dennis Poole served as acting artistic director until the appointment of Peter Anastos. Cincinnati Ballet had seen four different artistic directors in the space of four years, hardly a sign of smooth sailing. Anastos was no stranger to Cincinnati — he had staged seven ballets there since 1981. Peter had the charge of bringing stability and vision to this ballet company, a $3.2 million operation that was still on shaky ground.

Peter Anastos, who had been co-founder of the satirical ballet troupe Les Ballets Trockedero de Monte Carlo, never had the intention of turning Cincinnati Ballet into a one-choreographer company. He had already inherited a rich and diverse repertoire; his goal was to expand on this. The company had been producing modest versions of the classics in order to bolster box office receipts, and this was one of the strategies that had pulled the company out of debt in the past. Anastos was aware of this, and it was at this point that Franklin came back on the scene. Anastos asked Franklin to restore *Giselle* for the February 1995 series, remarking that "his 'Giselle' is a great 'Giselle.'"[22]

Anastos himself was a marvelous choreographer who provided the CB with some of its most successful dances over a period of fifteen years. Especially well-liked was his 1994 ballet adaptation of *Peter Pan*. However, there was some discontent with his overall direction of the company. After less than two years on the job, Anastos suddenly resigned in May of 1996 after a board meeting. Cincinnati Ballet president Laura Brunner told a reporter, "There was discussion with Peter regarding some management and leadership issues…. Peter's strengths certainly were on the artistic side vs. the management side."[23]

Victoria Morgan was appointed the new artistic director (the fifth since 1990) in February of 1997. She was a former principal dancer for both Ballet West and San Francisco Ballet and had been resident choreographer and ballet mistress for the San Francisco Opera. When she accepted the position in Ohio, she became the first female director in Cincinnati's history.

Morgan sailed in with her new *Nutcracker*. She called in Franklin to stage the "Snow Scene" for this production, which was well-received by the community and local critics. The 1997 *Nutcracker* stayed in the Cincinnati repertory until 2001, at which time Ms. Morgan staged an entirely new version herself.

By then, Ms. Morgan had established herself as the best artistic director of this company since David McLain. She was providing an interesting and varied repertory with numerous opportunities for emerging choreographers, she was creating fine works herself, and she was showing an acumen for management that some of her predecessors had lacked. Ms. Morgan had a knack for story ballets and did her own highly-reviewed versions of *Cinderella* (2000), *Romeo and Juliet* (2001), *Midsummer Night's Dream* (2003), and *L'Histoire du Soldat* (2004). Freddie came down to dance Friar Laurence in her *Romeo and Juliet*. Franklin has a high regard for Victoria: "We've kept a nice relationship all the way through. She's a lovely woman, and she's very clever."[24]

Kirk Peterson staged a new version of *Coppelia* (replacing Franklin's 1974 staging) in April of 2001 and followed this up with a staging of the full-length *Don Quixote* in October of the same year. Morgan's November 2002 production of *Sleeping Beauty*, also staged by Peterson, was extremely impressive and put the final seal on Peterson's appointment as resident choreographer of Cincinnati Ballet. Imported choreographers were also brought in to set works during this period of artistic vitality. For a regional company, the scope of the repertory has been amazing, and Franklin was destined to give it yet another dimension in the twenty-first century.

For the past several years, Franklin had been intensely involved with the Balanchine Foundation, a significant project to preserve the ballets of the late George Balanchine. In her 1973 collection of reviews, critic Marcia Siegel observed that "dance exists at a perpetual vanishing point." She described a dance performance as "an event that disappears in the very act of materializing."[25] Three decades later, Labannotation and video technology have definitely helped to rescue this frustratingly ephemeral artistic activity. But Leland Windreich points out that while these methods have proved to be invaluable in the staging of ballets, critics of the system note that "the motional content of a dance cannot be fully recorded and that issues relative to interpretation are impossible to state in a diagram."[26]

The Balanchine Foundation was launched in 1994 by former New York City Ballet dancer Nancy Reynolds and funded with $1.75 million by the Donald W. Reynolds Foundation, established by the dancer's father. The essential purpose of the Balanchine Foundation, directed by Reynolds herself, is to document and preserve the ballets of Balanchine. The foundation has two wings: an Archive of Lost Choreography and an Interpreter's Archive, although there is some overlap. The Interpreter's Archive focuses on important Balanchine works of today for which the original choreography is still extant.

Reflecting Reynolds' belief that personal transmission of a dance experience from a veteran exponent to a novice is still the best way to convey the nuances of a dance, the organization sponsors an ongoing presentation of coaching and videotaping sessions in which retired Balanchine dancers who were personally coached by the choreogra-

pher pass on to young artists their unique experiences as creators of ballet roles taught
to them by the master. The transaction is videotaped, and copies are stored in archival
venues in eleven countries.

The earliest performance to be thus preserved is one by Markova, who agreed to
recreate her principal solo from Balanchine's 1925 ballet, *Le Chant du rossignol*, which
she first performed at the age of fourteen for Diaghilev's Ballets Russes. For the tape,
the intricate dance was taught to a Royal Ballet student, and the performance was
filmed. The film included demonstrations of two other excerpts from this ballet and a
commentary on the genesis of its creation. The program runs 116 minutes and provides
a vital insight into the work of the young Balanchine, this piece being the first he was
commissioned to create for Diaghilev.[27]

Balanchine frequently altered his ballets, which raises the question of which version of a particular work is authentic. Reynolds said that research would endeavor to
discover "what various Balanchine interpreters thought of his work at various times,"
adding that "there may be multiple versions of the ballets."[28] She stresses that stagers
should set the versions that they personally learned from Balanchine as accurately as
possible without being influenced by past or subsequent versions.[29]

The first phase of research concentrated on the retrieval of lost ballets such as *Le
Chant du rossignol* and the1945 version of *Mozartiana*. Franklin, Robert Lindgren and
Sonja Tyven all participated in the reconstruction of the latter. In November of 1996,
Franklin and Vida Brown, who danced in the work and later became a ballet mistress
for Balanchine, assisted Tallchief in setting two pas de deux from *Le Baiser de la fée* on
New York City Ballet principals Nichol Hlinka, Nikolaj Hübbe and Lourdes Lopez.
They were not only coaching the finer points of interpretation, but trying to recon-
struct a ballet that hadn't been danced since 1946. For his next Balanchine Foundation
project, Franklin called upon his remarkable memory to recreate excerpts from the 1946
Ballet Russe production of *Raymonda*. He re-created not only the five female solos from
the original American production, but introduced as well the versions that Balanchine
created in three subsequent productions, all made of excerpts from the three-act ballet.[30] Subsequently, he was taped in his reconstruction of the three leading roles — Poet,
Sleepwalker, Coquette — from Balanchine's 1946 ballet, *Night Shadow*. The work was
danced by Cincinnati Ballet principals Kristi Capps, Tricia Sundbeck, and Dmitri
Trubchanov.

The list of former Balanchine dancers who have worked with the foundation also
includes Allegra Kent, Suzanne Farrell, Alicia Alonso, Melissa Hayden, Marie-Jeanne,
Patricia Wilde, Rosella Hightower, Arthur Mitchell, Helgi Tomasson, Violette Verdy,
Conrad Ludlow, Merrill Ashley, Stanley Zompakos, and Todd Bolender. To date, the
George Balanchine Foundation has sponsored the creation of approximately forty
videos.[31] These are available at seventy qualified research libraries throughout the world,
where they can be viewed on site on an unrestricted basis by all who are interested.

Franklin's next project in Cincinnati would involve not only the restoration of a
Balanchine work but two seminal works by Massine and Ashton as well. Cincinnati
enjoyed a special relationship with the Ballet Russe, because Julius Fleischmann, the
city's multimillionaire patron, bequeathed many Ballet Russe costume and set designs
to the Cincinnati Art Museum after his death. When Victoria Morgan wanted to mark

Frederic Franklin recreating the "black" pas de deux from George Balanchine's *Mozartiana* (1945) with Julie Kent and Nikolaj Hubbe for the George Balanchine Foundation. January 2000. Photograph: Brian Rushton for the George Balanchine Foundation. Courtesy of Nancy Reynolds.

the fortieth anniversary of her company on October 18–19, 2002, her mind turned to the lost works of the Ballet Russe. She decided that the company's birthday bash would be both a gala tribute to the eighty-eight-year-old Freddie Franklin and to the Ballet Russe de Monte Carlo.

The Cincinnati Art Museum joined with the Cincinnati Ballet to present "The Golden Age of Costume and Set Design for the Ballet Russe de Monte Carlo:1938–1944." The exhibit, augmented by contributions from the George Verdak Ballet Russe Collection at Butler University, ran from October 10, 2002, to January 12, 2003, and displayed more than one hundred designs for costumes and sets, including works by Henri Matisse, Pavel Tchelitchew, Salvador Dalí, Eugène Berman, Karinska and Christian Bérard. Franklin had worn many of these costumes himself during his stellar career with the company.

Celebrating the completion of two years' work at the New York Public Library for the Performing Arts, and the Balanchine Foundation, recording and filming commentary on the archives of the Ballet Russe de Monte Carlo. Left to right: Bill Ausman, Barbara Horgan, Mindy Aloff, Monica Moseley, Nancy Reynolds, Fred Franklin and Madeleine Nichols. Photograph: Brian Rushton for the George Balanchine Foundation. Courtesy of Nancy Reynolds.

Franklin had had heart surgery earlier in 2002, but that didn't seem to slow him down. As Barnes observed, "Freddie is never simply honored — he always jumps up and does something wonderful."[32] The company's fortieth anniversary in October saluted Franklin with four works in which he danced while he was with the Ballet Russe.

Assisted by Bart Cook, Franklin undertook to reproduce the original Ballet Russe version of Balanchine's *Night Shadow* and also the famous Waltz made for himself and Danilova in Massine's *Gaîté Parisienne*. Not content to stop there, he also recreated hitherto lost fragments from Massine's *Seventh Symphony* and a solo and duet from Ashton's *Devil's Holiday*. The Balanchine Foundation gave permission for the staging of *Night Shadow* and sent a videographer to tape Franklin and Cook's restaging of this ballet.

Morgan was drawn to *Seventh Symphony* after Ohio State University's Dance Film Archive Director, John Mueller, showed her 16mm footage of the Ballet Russe performing it. At first, Morgan thought it would look dated, but she changed her mind as she considered its spontaneity, musicality and its great sense of expression and exuberance.[33] Ballet mistress Johanna Bernstein Wilt, coached by Franklin, restored the third movement of *Seventh Symphony*. Also on the program were vintage Franklin-related excerpts compiled by filmmakers Dayna Goldfine and Dan Geller.

The most tantalizing gems of the evening — the third movement from *Seventh Symphony* and the lost fragments from *Devil's Holiday*— lured balletgoers and over sixty critics from all over the world to this event. The pas de deux from *Devil's Holiday* was danced by Tricia Sundbeck and Dimitri Trubchanov, and Franklin's solo as the Beggar was performed by Andrey Kasatsky. As Clive Barnes noted, "This ballet has for decades been something of a Holy Grail for Ashton scholars. It has been unseen since 1942. Franklin has phenomenal kinetic memory. There is no one around to check on the authenticity of these two gorgeous fragments (though there were some scratchy videos, shown here before the excerpts), but they looked like Ashton, felt like Ashton and danced like Ashton."[34]

There is an interesting story surrounding the discovery of the *Devil's Holiday* excerpts. Donald Saddler was doing a memorial for Danilova at the Library for the Performing Arts at Lincoln Center shortly after her death. Three television monitors had been set up to show film clips of Danilova dancing. Someone came up to Franklin and told him he was on one of the TV screens: "I went, and I looked, and I said, 'Oh, my goodness me. It's the pas de deux from *Devil's Holiday*.' I never even knew it existed. And then there was my solo. We made a tape of the entire ballet in 1940. And this was all that was left."[35]

The film was the property of the Massine Estate, owned by Massine's son, Lorca, and Lorca's daughter, Maria. From them, Franklin got permission to set the pas de deux and solo for the Cincinnati Ballet. Franklin has the score for the entire ballet, though how he got it, he'll never know. Freddie can read music, and he literally sang the score to himself until he had located the pas de deux and solo. Next he made a tape with American Ballet Theatre pianist Nancy Mattville, and the project was off and running.

There is another interesting story surrounding the Cincinnati Art Museum's Ballet Russe exhibit, for it fanned the flames of a decade-old dispute. Butler University claims to own this vast collection of Ballet Russe sets and costumes. It also lays claim to parts of the estate of George Verdak, saying that Ballet Russe properties that were rightfully Butler's have been intermingled with George Verdak's personal collection. But the heirs of Verdak dispute that claim, saying the works belong to the family's estate.

In an arrangement between Serge Denham and his attorney, Watson Washburn, the nearly five hundred sets and costumes were stored in Texas and in a Connecticut farmhouse after the company dissolved in 1962. Eight years later, after Denham died, Washburn looked for a new caretaker for the properties. Verdak, a former Ballet Russe dancer, set designer, collector of ballet memorabilia, and chair of dance at Butler University, seemed the best choice. In a letter of May 1971, Washburn stated vaguely that "the arrangement with Butler University is in the best interest of the Ballet Foundation, which owned the Ballet Russe."[36] That "arrangement" is not spelled out in the letter. And therein lies the root of the problem: who actually owns these treasures?

In 1971, Verdak brought the properties back to Butler in a truck. They remained in storage in outdoor sheds, Quonset huts and leaky basements for years. A 1978 flood reduced the remaining pieces to 175. Despite cursory efforts to catalogue the works, it wasn't until Verdak's death in 1993 and the rediscovery of the stored sets and costumes by current BU chair of dance, Stephan Laurent, that their value became apparent. Meanwhile, Verdak's estate had begun selling some of the collection to dealers. Butler has countered with lawsuits against the representatives of the estate and the dealers, restraining them from further sales, and the controversy is still unfolding.[37]

Franklin next returned to Cincinnati in 2004. On October 8–9 of this year, the Cincinnati Ballet created the world anew (with the aid of Franklin) by reviving the first three movements of Massine's *Seventh Symphony* at the Aronoff Center. The third movement was such a success in 2002 that ballet mistress Johanna Bernstein Wilt and Franklin decided to add the first and second. According to Victoria Morgan, "Johanna set the steps onto the actual studio floor, and Freddie worked with her to infuse those steps with the "essence" of what Massine asked for, reiterating actual comments from Massine."[38] Because no films survive of the finale, they had to delete the fourth movement. But the first three formed a satisfying whole, and the work now ended on a note of euphoria rather than on one of death and destruction.

Franklin's efforts to provide authentic links for the new generation have extended even beyond the studio walls. He had assisted John Mueller of the University of Rochester's Dance Film Archives (now located at Ohio State) in the synchronization of scores to rehearsal films of Massine's ballets *St. Francis* and the three surviving movements of *Seventh Symphony*.[39] It was this film of the *Seventh* which Wilt used in her reconstruction of the work.

The rebuilding of this neglected ballet was no easy choreographic task. First the primitive 16 mm film from the Dance Film Archives had to be transferred onto videotape. But even then, it wasn't always easy to see who exactly was doing what. Fortunately, it was not filmed in costume, which made it a little easier to see the legs and feet. Wilt reported that the easiest movement to decipher was the third, because there were fewer people. But the two-dimensionality of the film became problematic in the first and second movements, which both employed huge casts. In some cases, Wilt said that it was "hard to see whose body part is where.... So, what I did in a lot of places, if I couldn't see people, I made sort of a composite." At some points, Wilt took the most interesting movements from two or more different people and combined them for one dancer. "It's sort of like being a detective," she said.[40]

Local critic Jerry Stein liked the verve and energy of the third movement, "The Sky." He found the first movement, "The Creation," to be "passable." But he objected to the excessive posing, posturing and angst in "The Earth," the second movement: "It's all a bit much for 2004 and keeps Beethoven's dirge in the second movement from being emotionally accessed." Venerated dance critic and historian Jack Anderson looked at this achievement from a broader perspective. "The Company," he wrote, "brought me to Cincinnati to lecture on the historical context of 'Seventh Symphony.' But its exciting performances made history live."[41]

Cincinnati Ballet is among the most distinguished of America's regional companies. While ballet companies don't survive without featuring the traditional classics, the Cincinnati Ballet has not been afraid to take risks. It has consistently fostered emerging choreographers, among them Trey McIntyre, Victor Kabaniaev, Luca Veggetti, Devon Carney and Donald Byrd, to name a few.[42] CB has also revived important twentieth century historical works, and it has created one of the most adventurous and unusual repertories of any regional company in America.

• 7 •

Back to the Big Apple:
Dance Theatre of Harlem
and American Ballet Theatre

Dance Theatre of Harlem

As with Cincinnati, Franklin's association with Arthur Mitchell and the Dance Theatre of Harlem goes back for decades. Earlier in his career, Mitchell made history as the first black star with a major American ballet company, New York City Ballet. He joined the NYCB in 1955, and in his distinguished career with the company, he created two seminal roles — the pas de deux in *Agon* with Diana Adams and Puck in *A Midsummer Night's Dream*. In 1968, the assassination of Martin Luther King moved him to leave the company to start a dance school in the tough, inner-city neighborhood of Harlem, his birthplace. In establishing a ballet company in Harlem, the point he wanted to make was that he, as an African American, was not an anomaly in ballet. Rather, he was given opportunities not available to others.

Dorothy Maynor asked him to start a dance program at her Harlem School of the Arts. She had a garage as part of the property, and Mitchell installed a floor and barres with his own money. He started with thirty children and charged fifty cents a week, for those who could afford to pay at all. Inside of four months he had eight hundred students. Much of this was due to Mitchell's strategy:

> It was so hot in this garage, because it had a tin roof, that we had to leave the door open. The street gangs and the kids walking by would see us at work, and I'd say, "Come in." "Naa-aa." So I'd relate what we were doing to basketball and football. I'd tell them that if you have a good *demi-plié* and more power in the ball of your foot, you can jump higher.... This intrigued some of the boys. And when I said "Come in and have a look," they said, "Well if we do, we're not going to wear any of those things." They meant leotards and tights. So I said they could wear cutoff dungarees or bathing trunks. That's how I got the boys enrolled.[1]

Six months later, the dance component of Dorothy Maynor's school was larger than all the rest of it put together. There was no space for it, and Mitchell had to leave the school and find a new base of operations. He found an unused garage (another garage!) on West 152nd Street and acquired it in 1971 with the help of the Bernard F. and Alva B. Gimbel Foundation. A $375,000 renovation created three studios and spaces for offices and storage. A lecture-demonstration group from the new school took shape almost immediately.

What was shortly to become the Dance Theatre of Harlem was co-founded by Karel Shook. Shook had danced in the corps de ballet of Franklin's National Ballet and served for nine years as the director of the National Ballet of Holland, becoming a renowned teacher with whom Mitchell had studied. Shook terminated his position as director in the Netherlands to help Mitchell develop a school and company. Dance Theatre of Harlem was incorporated in February of 1969 as a nonprofit organization.

The performing wing of the Dance Theatre of Harlem made its formal debut at the Guggenheim Museum in 1971. This was followed by an appearance at Gian Carlo Menotti's Festival of Two Worlds in Spoleto, which gave the company international exposure. After an impressive number of touring engagements in America and abroad, including an auspicious London debut in 1974, extended seasons were held in New York in 1974, 1975 and 1976. The company was now on a firm foundation.

From the beginning, Arthur Mitchell had the blessings of Balanchine, and this was manifested in a core group of Balanchine ballets in the repertory. In the mid-'70s, the Balanchine works were the strength of the repertory. But Mitchell himself had never been a quintessential Balanchine dancer, and it was immediately clear that he was not interested in merely creating a weak imitation of the New York City Ballet.

In building his repertory, Mitchell sought ethnic themes. When working in this genre, reserve was tossed to the winds — the dancers pulled out all the stops and tore the house down, even when the material was not of the highest caliber. Louis Johnson's *Forces of Rhythm* (1972) juxtaposed several forms of dance, but it was rather simplistic, and each form suffered in the mélange. Another crowd-pleaser was Geoffrey Holder's *Dougla* (1973), based on a wedding ritual of the Dougla people of Trinidad. Most of the company's early forays into the realms of ethnic dance were not very potent except in terms of energy. Comments were often voiced that the Dance Theatre of Harlem repertoire, aside from the Balanchine ballets, was not worthy of its dancers.

In 1980, Mitchell raised the stakes by de-emphasizing the ethnic works and embarking on a program of presenting hallowed nineteenth century classics. He decided on a mounting of *Swan Lake* (Act II) and a suite of dances from *Paquita*. Thus began Mitchell's long and memorable association with Frederic Franklin. He asked Freddie to stage *Swan Lake*, and took a calculated risk by opening it in New York instead of breaking it in on tour. While Franklin's staging was fairly traditional, the costuming changes were dramatic. Perhaps as a reminder that this is a black company, the women were artfully arranged in various shades of blue according to skin tone, the darkest wearing an almost midnight blue, the others in various shades of sky blue and blue-gray.

The leading roles of Odette and Siegfried were danced by alternate casts of Virginia Johnson with Eddie Shellman and Lydia Abarca with Ronald Perry. However, it was the ensemble that took the honors, and this was a very good sign for DTH. Tobi Tobias noted that the quality of the corps work was "more promising for the future than a take-your-breath-away performance of a superstar backed by a chaotic corps."[2]

Arthur Mitchell, George Balanchine and Frederic Franklin at City Center on the opening night of Dance Theatre of Harlem's *Swan Lake*, Act II, staged by Franklin in 1980. Photograph © Jack Vartoogian/Front Row Photos.

Overall, the reception given to the Dance Theatre of Harlem's *Swan Lake* was respectful, but no more. Tobias found the production "over-rehearsed and under-performed, with the dancers conscientiously applying everything they'd learned. But what they'd learned was correct in style and now simply needs burnishing and added thrust, or perhaps only the dancers growing confident enough to be less reverent of the ballet's provenance and let the dancing and the music sweep them away." Arlene Croce agreed: "While it isn't the best possible 'Swan Lake,' it is one worth keeping and getting right, which will mean getting it to happen inside the dancers.... there is also a symbolic victory that the company wants to attain. White American dancers have managed to make themselves credible in this 'Russian' classic; black dancers should have no trouble once the exam jitters are past."[3]

Dance Theatre of Harlem had somewhat more success with the sunnier *Paquita*, staged the same year by Alexandra Danilova with the assistance of Franklin. DTH brought a special élan to the hybrid classicism that the Russians refer to as *demi-caractère*, and the Spanish *Paquita* became an ensemble showcase.

A second new track for Mitchell was to infuse the repertory with dramatic ballets from the Diaghilev era and from the subsequent genre of Americana. De Mille's *Fall River Legend*, Jerome Robbins's *Fancy Free* and Eugene Loring's *Billy the Kid* were added to the rep in 1985, 1987 and 1988, respectively. Mitchell's first, 1981, choice for a dramatic ballet —*Schéhérazade*— was a surprising one. *Schéhérazade* has long been considered hopelessly outdated and choreographically jejune, with its melodramatic plot and long stretches of pure pantomime. Even as early as the mid–1930s, it had already become an object of parody for Balanchine, who spoofed the ballet in the musical *On Your Toes*.

The ballet is set in the great hall of the Arabian palace of Shah Sharyar. Shah Zeman, the shah's brother, contrives to convince Sharyar that his favorite wife, Zobeide (Virginia Johnson), has fallen in love with the Golden Slave (Eddie Shellman). He persuades the king to leave for a hunting trip from which they will return unexpectedly early.

Torn between her love for her husband and the Golden Slave, Zobeide succumbs to temptation and bribes the Chief Eunuch (Frederic Franklin) for the keys to the chambers of the African slaves. She and the other harem wives then abandon themselves to a night of revelry with the Africans. Sharyar returns in the midst of their orgy, and his soldiers chase the slaves and the harem wives, killing them mercilessly at the shah's command. Finally, they kill the Golden Slave. Zobeide pleads unsuccessfully for her own life, then grabs her dagger and dies by her own hand. Shah Sharyar despairs at the destruction wrought by his jealous rage.

Franklin had danced the role of the Golden Slave hundreds of times for the Ballet Russe, and he knew the ballet inside and out. The ballet was taught to Franklin by Massine, and so his version can be traced right back to the Diaghilev Ballet. Franklin staged the ballet according to the original, 1910, version. Wisely, he omitted Fokine's own afterthought, the disruptive pas de deux for Zobeide and the Golden Slave that Fokine inserted in 1914 to the third movement of Rimsky-Korsakov's music.

Most revivals of *Schéhérazade* have failed. Rudolf Nureyev and the London Festival Ballet couldn't bring it to life. The Houston Ballet tried its hand at *Schéhérazade* in September of 1980, with the London Festival Ballet version restaged by Vassili Trunoff. Suzanne Shelton wrote, "All the steps were there, all the spatial patterns, the groupings, the entrances and exits. But the ballet was not there. It was a question of style."[4] (The *Fokine* style, one might add.)

Fokine's choreography for *Schéhérazade* is actually much stronger than its reputation would lead one to believe. Spacially, it is built on ever-tightening circles, the most exciting of which is the human wheel at the climax of the ballet's orgy. Odalisques and slaves encircle the Golden Slave in a running formation that builds in intensity, then abruptly unwinds into flat lines as the dancers hurl themselves toward the footlights. Almost as riveting are the waves of laterally moving lines in the final massacre. Shelton gives an excellent description of Fokine's very specific style for this ballet:

> This is choreography built on friction. Bodies writhe like knotted ropes twisting on themselves. The slaves run in a half-crouch, their thighs like taut springs. When they caress the outlines of the women's bodies, they never touch, only electrify. The women are all asymmetry and indirect allure, shielding their eyes with one arm, flinging their bodies into exposed backbends, then quickly covering themselves with an arm thrown across their vulnerable chests. Knotted fists and rotating wrists add to the chewy texture of the choreography.[5]

As stated, Franklin was in a unique position to make sure that all of the details were religiously observed, that neglected nuances of style were finally restored:

Here, he [Franklin] restrained the hearty back bend of one ballerina, gently pulling her backflung head into its proper position so that she might not exaggerate. There, he demonstrated a fall from demi-pointe that added an element of risk to an enchaînement. He urged the men to jump with their chests facing the floor, feeling the pull of gravity that makes this ballet seem full-bodied, full-blooded. It's the idea of the heaviness and the weight.[6]

However, some of the dancers had trouble with the mime sequences and looked rather wooden at times. David Vaughan noticed that a few dancers sometimes fell into the error of mouthing the words, "you," "me," "go."[7] Although Franklin worked hard to finesse the dancers in the art of mime, there was only so much he could do in a short rehearsal period. Filling this gap in their experience would be one of Franklin's ongoing projects, culminating in his magnificent staging of the Creole *Giselle*.

No small part of the original impact of *Schéhérazade* was its daring interracial love-making. An all-black cast in the Dance Theatre of Harlem version removed that angle. With the nullification of the color bar, *Schéhérazade* lost one of its peculiar twists. Franklin, who remembers being forced to remove his black body paint when he performed the ballet in the American South, was quite aware of this. He stated, "There are no special overtones. The ballet will have to stand on its own feet."[8]

The costuming of Carl Michel departed somewhat from the original designs of Leon Bakst. Karel Shook, who performed *Schéhérazade* with the Ballet Russe, defended the new costumes in a program article on the grounds that Bakst's originals were unsuitable for contemporary physiques: "We were not faced with one of Bakst's most pressing problems, that is, covering up less than perfect bodies." In an interview, Carl Michel pointed to a design for an odalisque, a sausage-link configuration of billowing fabric. "That would make a dancer look like 'Two-ton Tillie!'" he snorted. "You can't put that roll of fabric on her stomach!"[9] Michel freely adopted some of Bakst's designs into form-flattering harem costumes in a muted palette of corals, purples and blues. They were replete with exquisite details, from the gold lace frog-closings down the legs of filmy harem pants split at the sides, to Zobeide's pearl-encrusted halter. Bakst's scenic designs were faithfully recreated by Geoffrey Guy, with lighting by Nicholas Cernovitch.

Dance Theatre of Harlem's production of *Schéhérazade* opened in London in December of 1980. Madame de Valois herself came to see this revival. She had danced one of the three Odalisques (with Lubov Tchernicheva and Nijinska) for Diaghilev's Ballets Russes. Freddie remembers that she came up to him and said, "'I could have gone right in. It was just what it was supposed to be.' So I guess we sort of made up."[10]

This ballet premiered at City Center (on the very stage where the Ballet Russe used to dance it) on January 3, 1981. As the Chief Eunuch, Franklin gave a typically stellar performance. The ballet was an undeniable hit, so much so that extra performances had to be scheduled.

Reviews were surprisingly positive, in view of the fact that many critics already had misgivings about this particular choice. David Vaughan wrote, "In the event, it must be admitted that they have succeeded in pulling it off by dint of the sheer conviction of their performance. The dancers, under Frederic Franklin's direction, did not allow themselves to be intimidated by the ballet's reputation, and they resisted any temptation to send it up." For Arlene Croce, "The value of the DTH 'Schéhérazade' is that it colors blanks I didn't know were there. I don't see a company trying to interpret

ancient psychology or dead aesthetics; I do see dancers performing with unaffected good sense."[11]

In 1982, Franklin staged Ruth Page's *Frankie and Johnny* and Valerie Bettis's long-neglected *Streetcar Named Desire* for DTH. The company's *Streetcar* revival was first seen during its season at the New York State Theater at Lincoln Center, March 11–27, 1982. For John Gruen, it "had all the earmarks of a minor classic."[12] But there were the same old objections from some critics over both the ballet's lack of dramatic clarity and its paucity of extended choreographic sequences.

A Streetcar Named Desire is the type of ballet that can benefit enormously from sensitive cinematography. The DTH *Streetcar* was telecast by PBS for its *Dance in America* series in the winter of 1986. For Gruen, the televised incarnation was "even better" than the staged version: "the ballet has cinematic immediacy made palpable through telling close-ups and unusual camera angles that underscore psychological climate and emotional nuance."[13] Since *Streetcar* did not fill the *Dance in America* hour, its producers added a sampling of the Harlem dancers' versatility by including selections from the *Sylvia* pas de deux (created earlier by Franklin for the Cincinnati Ballet) and *Belé,* choreographed by Geoffrey Holder.

In 1994, DTH brought *Streetcar* back to the stage again. In both of these revivals, the role of Blanche was danced by Virginia Johnson. She felt that the passing of years had given her a new perspective on the role. "I'm closer to the age that Blanche was in the play," the ballerina said. "Now I understand the reality of having something to look back on — regrets and beautiful memories."[14]

Johnson studied with Mary Day in Washington, D.C., at a time when black ballet dancers were practically unheard-of. Because of her race, her teachers at the Washington School of Ballet advised her to look for a jazz or modern dance company. "I felt like I was being banished from the world that I knew,"[15] Johnson said. When Virginia joined the Dance Theatre of Harlem in 1969, there were just four dancers in the company, working with its founder in a tiny, inadequate space. Advancing to leading roles in works by Mitchell, George Balanchine, John Taras and Agnes de Mille, this tall and elegant ballerina remained throughout her career with DTH, gaining international status as a major ballerina. In Johnson, Dance Theatre of Harlem possessed a great dramatic ballerina of the Nora Kaye variety, a dancer who always made dramatic emotion visible at the heart of ballet steps.

Another 1982 premiere for Dance Theatre of Harlem was John Taras's version of the 1910 *Firebird*, originally choreographed by Michel Fokine for Diaghilev's Ballets Russes. Whereas Taras based his choreography on Balanchine's later version, designer Geoffrey Holder departed entirely from the Russian aspect of the tale and set the work in a tropical jungle, dressing the dancers in abbreviated, colorful costumes. Both *Schéhérazade* and *Firebird* were popular with audiences. These early twentieth century works were beginning to reshape Mitchell's approach to the classics of the nineteenth

Opposite: Franklin rehearsing principal dancer Virginia Johnson in his revival of the Ballets Russes de Serge Diaghilev production of Michel Fokine's *Schéhérazade* for Dance Theater of Harlem. Rehearsal at Lehman College, CUNY, Bronx, New York. 7 November 1980. Photograph ©Jack Vartoogian/Front Row Photos.

century as well. The 1980 production of *Swan Lake* (Act II) had been only a qualified success. Reflecting on this, Mitchell said, "there seemed to be something artificial about it. They were imitating; it wasn't authentic, and it wasn't organic. I kept searching for a way to make the material relevant, plausible for us. And now I've found the key."[16]

In 1984, the company really hit its classical stride with a heartfelt and stunningly beautiful production of *Giselle*, staged for the company by Franklin. The production (with minor emendations) was telecast nationally as *Creole Giselle* on NBC in 1987. Dance Theatre of Harlem's production of the full-length *Giselle* was an important milestone for the company and gave Johnson, in the title role, the greatest success of her career.

Mitchell had flirted with the idea of his company performing this quintessential Romantic ballet for some time, but felt certain changes would have to be made. He knew that there were many people around who simply would not accept a black company as a community of medieval Rhineland villagers. More importantly, he wanted his dancers to be able to connect with the story, to make it personally significant: "We don't live in a country that has a king and queen. So if you're trying to get young artists to dance classical roles, you have to find something they can identify with in their lives, so they can buy into the roles."[17] This was precisely why he had commissioned Geoffrey Holder to set the *Firebird* in the Caribbean.

While touring the southern states a few years before *Giselle*'s premiere, Mitchell came across a setting right out of Hollywood. He was standing near a bayou, with the scent of honeysuckle filling the air and a full moon shining on Spanish moss.[18] That encounter inspired him to do some research, and he discovered that prior to the Civil War, a free black society (*gens de couleur libres*), centered in New Orleans, had thrived in Louisiana. At the top of the hierarchy were wealthy Creoles, educated and cultured industrialists and planters, who were often slave owners themselves. The society had a rigid caste structure, as rigid as that among the noblemen and peasants of *Giselle*'s origin. Status was determined by how many generations one's family had been free and by the purity of one's color. Those divisions made certain unions impossible — and a DTH *Giselle* plausible. Mitchell realized that if Giselle were only one generation free and Albrecht were the scion of a prominent Creole family, she would understand that her love is hopeless when she discovers Albrecht's true identity and learns of his engagement to a woman of higher social class. That would give credence to her subsequent madness and death. Mitchell was able to justify the second act completely because there are many Louisiana folktales of spirits and ghosts who wander the swamp.

Although the harvest may have been sugar cane and not grapes, and although certain alterations were made in the storyline, the choreography and the spirit of the piece remained true to the ballet's historical origins. It was precisely because of his concern with authenticity and continuing tradition that Mitchell asked Franklin, who had staged the ballet many times, to do the same for Dance Theatre of Harlem. Franklin followed fairly closely the original choreography as it has been handed down over the years.[19]

The major changes were in the physical end of the production, in the sets and costumes designed by Carl Michel (who also helped Arthur Mitchell to write the libretto). The ballet occurs in 1841, the year of the original *Giselle*'s premiere in Paris. The first act takes place on the farm of Giselle and her mother. Giselle's home is no longer a

Virginia Johnson dancing the title role in *Creole Giselle*, Act II. Staged by Frederic Franklin after Jean Coralli and Jules Perrot. Music: Adolphe Adam. Décor and costumes: Carl Michel. Photograph: Courtesy Virginia Johnson.

thatched-roof cottage, but a low-slung whitewashed house with a porch and broad wooden shutters. The scene is dominated by Spanish moss with sets and costumes in soft autumn tones. The costumes for the first act are based on clothes of the period, including some elegant riding outfits. The farm girls sport the jackets, shawls and head scarves popular in the era, and Giselle is dressed in her traditional color of blue.

The second act is set in a clearing in a bayou. Giselle's tomb rises high to be seen through the trees. Mitchell explained, "In Louisiana, people had to be buried above

Scene from Act I of Dance Theatre of Harlem's *Creole Giselle* (1984) with Virginia Johnson in the title role and Eddie Shellman as "Albert." Staged by Frederic Franklin after Jean Coralli and Jules Perrot. Music: Adolphe Adam. Décor and costumes: Carl Michel. Photograph © Jack Vartoogian/Front Row Photos.

ground because the water table is so high."[20] Franklin and Mitchell created a distinct atmosphere for Act II. Albert (Albrecht in the original version), grieving after Giselle's death, arrives at her grave in a bayou boat.

In the second act, there were no romantic tutus for the Wilis (girls driven by heartbreak to an early grave, who haunt the churchyard and avenge themselves on male intruders). Franklin decided that the bayou location called for a more mysterious, ethereal look, and Carl Michel designed a pale gray tunic. The bottom was cut for a jagged effect at the ends, which enhanced the costumes' floating quality. "When I get through shredding and dyeing it, and it's opened up and brushed, it should look like cobwebs on the air,"[21] Michel predicted, and so it did. The Wilis wore their hair loose, with leaves and flowers on their heads to suggest that they came out of the earth. Upon Giselle's entrance from the tomb, her veil wasn't torn off by unseen hands, but instead flew upwards, vanishing in the ozone.[22]

All of these flourishes added enormous color to this version of *Giselle* without disturbing the familiar choreography. In his quest for dramatic credence, Carl Michel even went so far as to write individual biographies of each of the characters, basing these on actual people who lived in Louisiana at the time and, for verisimilitude, naming them with the family names also current in that society.[23] For Michel, every prop had to be historically justified: "The sword is such a vital part of the story, but could we explain why this man [Albert] is carrying it? I discovered that from 1830 to 1860, the young men of Louisiana were absolutely insane about dueling. They carried their swords everywhere and fought every chance they got."[24]

Although many people consider *Giselle* sacrosanct, the ballet has actually undergone countless changes and revisions — musically, dramatically and choreographically. It was with Marius Petipa's restaging in the 1880s that the ballet underwent its most drastic transformation. And it is from this production that most twentieth century versions stem. Petipa shortened the ballet and added more technically difficult choreography. He also made some key dramatic changes. Giselle stabbed herself in the original version, but in Petipa's version, the sword was removed before she could harm herself, and she died of madness and a broken heart. In the first production, Albrecht's exit at the end of the ballet made it clear that Albrecht would marry Bathilde. But with Petipa, he collapsed on Giselle's grave, leaving it to the audience to decide whether Albrecht would survive the tragedy or not. As Erik Bruhn wrote, "His going to her grave at night is like a nightmare.... In his nightmares a man's wrong deeds come back to him, carrying a message that he must look at right in the face."[25]

When Nicholas Sergeyev staged *Giselle* for Markova and Dolin at the Vic-Wells in 1934, he based his version on Petipa's. That is the version the pair continued to dance when they formed their own company a year later and the one that Franklin grew up with. He stuck closely to the Sergeyev staging, making occasional changes as required by the altered setting. He kept Petipa's desperate action for Albrecht at the end of Act II, but he made the most significant change by restoring the original first-act ending: "No broken hearts in this production," Franklin told a reporter. "She stabs herself to death."[26]

Both Mitchell and Franklin wanted more realism in the crowd scenes. Mitchell observed that *Giselle* had become primarily a vehicle for a great ballerina, and everything else was secondary. He wanted to "get a feeling of time, of a village, of a group of people who are really celebrating a harvest. So we're adding extra characters who give it credence." Some of the villagers weren't even dancers: "We don't want the audience to say, 'There's Mary Jane. She's not dancing tonight, so they dressed her up as the grandmother, and she's doddering around.'" As Jack Anderson noticed, "When the curtain rose, one immediately sensed that the people on stage were friends and neighbors."[27] In order to achieve a better sense of time and place, Franklin had the curtain rise earlier than at the customary point in the music, to reveal the people of the village interacting with each other. "It's like entering into something that already exists,"[28] Freddie explained.

One of Franklin's primary aims was to give the ballet a continuity he felt was lacking in most productions. He was particularly concerned about bridging the gap between the first and second act, where the styles are so different. "Usually it's like watching two separate ballets," he stated. "In the version I knew, we opened the second act with the men of the village playing dice on the outskirts of the cemetery. Hilarion makes his entrance while the men are on. I'm going back to this, because having the men from the first act out there when the second act begins ties things together." Franklin deleted the big overhead lifts from the Act II pas de deux: "They weren't there originally, and I hate them,"[29] he told Sheryl Flatow. He also gave the Wilis an extra touch of violence, as they literally shoved Hilarion off the stage, "presumably to the alligators."[30]

In rehearsals for *Giselle*, Franklin noted that it was difficult to throw a big narrative ballet to dancers unfamiliar with the romantic tradition: "American dancers are not called upon to do much mime. They have no real background in it and are uncomfortable doing it." At one of the DTH rehearsals, Franklin showed the various Giselles the mad scene for the first time, giving a tour de force performance that apparently made the dancers believe for a moment that this seventy-year-old man really *was* Giselle: "I told them that when I show them something, I'm not embarrassed. I'm trying to *be* that person. And I said to them, 'Don't you be embarrassed, either. Don't half do it. Overdo it — we can chip it off.'"[31]

Virginia Johnson observed, "Freddie's very articulate and tells you exactly what he wants you to do. But it's by watching his body, watching his face, that you learn the most. His expressiveness is an enormous help. In watching him, you feel what you need to feel. It's an incredible gift he has."[32]

Giselle was Dance Theatre of Harlem's first full-length ballet and the costliest in its fifteen-year history. It had its world premiere at the London Coliseum as a cultural exchange with the English National Opera company in July of 1984. It was seen by American audiences for the first time in August at New York City Center. In the first cast were Johnson as Giselle, Eddie Shellman as Albert, Lorraine Graves as Myrtha and Lowell Smith as Hilarion. The ballet was an instant success. After the New York premiere, Tobi Tobias reported, "The story sweeps forward as if propelled by character and fate, and the viewer is passionately involved in its outcome." Three years later, at a March 1987 Creole *Giselle* performance at City University of New York, Anderson said simply, "What a wonderful ballet. And what a wonderful production.... what made this 'Giselle' so absorbing was the dedication of the entire company." Anderson reported that Johnson "danced as if swept along by the sheer thrill of being in love." In the Mad Scene, "she appeared to shatter before our eyes." In Act II he noted that her dance steps "always possessed emotional significance," [33] a quality on which she and Franklin had worked exhaustively.

NBC network telecast the *Creole Giselle* on December 27, 1987. Bill Cosby appeared as host for the special. Cosby also played a leading role behind the scenes by calling his boss about the ballet: "It was wonderful to hear my boss say that his wife was in love with DTH. That made it easier — he wanted to make her happy and show that he had a little class."[34] The telecast was seen by ten million viewers, about two and one-half times the number likely to tune in to PBS at that hour.

Following a Glasnost-inspired tour of the Soviet Union in mid–June, initiated under the joint U.S.-Soviet cultural exchange agreement, the Dance Theatre of Harlem returned to New York with only two weeks to prepare for a 1988 June 28–July 3 engagement at City Center as part of the first New York International Festival of the Arts. This occasion saw the company premiere of Franklin's staging of the *Polovetsian Dances* from *Prince Igor*. This ballet by Michel Fokine was choreographed in 1909 for the first Paris season of Diaghilev's Ballets Russes. The ballet originally had a choral as well as an instrumental accompaniment. Franklin struck a compromise. He began the ballet with singer Carol Sebron alone on stage. She remained onstage without singing while the dancing took place, which gave these dances of unbridled passion a useful theatrical distance.

Like Fokine's *Schéhérazade*, this ballet is an old warhorse that runs the risk of looking corny to a contemporary audience. Franklin used exactly the same approach he had used in *Schéhérazade*— namely, to have his dancers pull out all the stops. For most critics, this method worked. As Tobi Tobias remarked, "The ballet [*Polovetsian Dances*] is bound to seem hokey today, but as DTH discovered, to its honor, with other works of bygone eras that now appear naïve, the only way to tackle the material is full-out, with complete imaginative conviction."[35] Under the guidance of Franklin, the DTH dancers demonstrated their growing ability to invest whole-hearted belief in the dramatic situations they portrayed.

In 1989, Franklin officially joined the Dance Theatre of Harlem as permanent artistic advisor. In that year, DTH presented an all–Nijinska program at City Center from June 21 to July 2. The Creole *Giselle* and Franklin's *Sylvia* pas de deux were also revived for this season. All three of the Nijinska works — *Les Noces, Les Biches* and *Rondo Capriccioso*— were staged by Nijinska's daughter, Irina. The Nijinska revivals were of enormous interest to dancegoers, and they were highly-reviewed. However, they were very expensive to produce, and the company was falling on hard times. The all–Nijinska bill was repeated at the company's Kennedy Center season of March 13–25, 1990. This was to be the company's last engagement for some time to come.

As Lynn Garafola noted, "DTH was born at the height of the dance boom, when grants were plentiful and touring earned a big chunk of the company's income. Then came the Reagan years. Government and foundation funds dried up, costs rose steeply, audiences, hit by recession, downsizing and rising ticket prices, declined."[36] In 1990, faced with a projected $1.7 million deficit, DTH laid off all fifty-one of its dancers for six months. In response, Chase Manhattan offered a $50,000 challenge grant, as did the New York State Council on the Arts. Then, in June, the company was saved by grants from American Express and the Lila Wallace — Reader's Digest Fund, who came to the rescue with $1 million each. But even with the strict economizing subsequently practiced, financial stability continued to elude the DTH.

In August and September of 1992, the DTH went to South Africa, two years before Nelson Mandela's election and the abolition of apartheid. "I was hesitant about going," says Mitchell, "but Mr. Mandela called me and said that it was very important at the time to show the children there that opportunities to excel did exist."[37] Franklin accompanied Dance Theatre of Harlem to South Africa in his capacity as artistic advisor. When they arrived, the troupe made it clear to every political faction that they didn't want any trouble. They came simply to share their art, and what was supposed to be a three-week visit turned into a six-week sojourn.

Performances were only a small part of this visit. The company's many-sided activities in South Africa reflected its desire to reach a wide range of people in a politically and socially traumatized country. Before 1994, South Africa was artistically isolated by a ban on cultural exchange, one way in which many nations expressed their disapproval of the country's institutionalized racism. DTH outreach activities were conducted both in cities — chiefly Johannesburg and Pretoria — and in the townships, the segregated areas designated for blacks, Indians, and people of mixed race.

Whatever the South African students wanted to know, a DTH staffer reported, from how to get a visa, to how to do a pas de deux in the style of Fokine, was shared with the youngsters via master classes from Franklin, Mitchell and Virginia Johnson, lecture-demonstrations and open dress rehearsals. As they worked their way through the townships and cities, Mitchell realized that they were dancing through barriers: "I don't mean just political barriers," he said, "I mean psychological and social barriers as well."[38]

The culmination of the outreach program was a two-week season at Johannesburg's Civic Theatre. The last major overseas ballet company to have performed in Johannesburg was the Royal Ballet, way back in 1960. The onus on Mitchell was to introduce thousands of black South Africans to ballet as a theatrical form in a formerly taboo setting. At the same time, the Johannesburg performances also had to reach a highly critical white audience. Both groups responded with great enthusiasm.

From this experience came Mitchell's new outreach program in America, "Dancing Through Barriers." Since he left New York City Ballet to establish DTH in Harlem, Mitchell's dedication to youth has been extraordinary. He stated, "I believe that if you teach a child how to dance, you teach that child how to live."[39]

The "Dancing Through Barriers" project began in Washington, D.C., in 1992. At its peak it had programs in the capital, all of New York City's boroughs, Detroit, and Miami, introducing sixty thousand children yearly to the art and discipline of dance. DTH members worked with local schools, colleges, and universities via classes and lecture- demonstrations. In lec-dems, Mitchell would often ask the children to come onstage and do the dances they were familiar with — usually some style of hip-hop. Much to their surprise, he then broke the steps down to their essential components, showing them how similar the steps are to those of classical ballet. With its determined efforts in arts education, the Dance Theatre of Harlem played a major role in drawing new audiences to dance.

Franklin's next work for Dance Theatre of Harlem was done for their 1996–97 season. He staged the Balanchine/Danilova *Pas de Dix*, done earlier for Cincinnati, for DTH performances at the Kennedy Center from April 3 to May 12, 1996. At the time of this season, the troupe hadn't danced much Balanchine in a while. They rectified that situation by presenting *Serenade*, *The Prodigal Son* and *Concerto Barocco*. For critic George Jackson, only the latter was performed with the proper attack and finesse. Jackson was more impressed with *Pas de Dix*: "The company gave this divertissement a lush touch to distinguish its nineteenth-century Petipa origins from the rigorousness of full Balanchine."[40]

DTH had already been forced to shut its doors for six months in 1990 because of a lack of cash, and it fell on hard times again after the National Endowment for the Arts cut its funding in the mid–1990s. By 1995, DTH was forced to reduce its fifty-two dancers to thirty-six, not enough to perform its popular *Giselle* or *Firebird* without being augmented by students from the school. Finances prohibited the company from presenting new or revived story ballets because of soaring production costs. There was less and less call for the type of staging that was Franklin's forté, and he became less of a presence at DTH.

Franklin noted, "He's difficult with the kids. He's hard on them and sometimes too much. They all call him Mr. Mitchell. And people like Virginia and Lorraine [Graves], they were with him from the very beginning." In an earlier interview he said that the Harlem dancers "work till they drop. And Arthur rules them with a rod of iron.... I don't know of any other ballet company that works as hard as they do."[41] But there are limits to such dedication, and in 1997, Dance Theatre of Harlem's thirty-five performers became the first unionized dancers in U.S. history to go on strike. They walked out on January 22.

A settlement was reached on February 9, two days after the dancers forced Mitchell to cancel auditions for apparent replacement dancers by throwing up a picket line at DTH's Harlem headquarters. Later in the morning, Mitchell emerged from company headquarters and announced that the replacement auditions had been cancelled. He continued, "I'd like to bring you my checkbook and my bank account [which has] nothing but the names of all the dancers.... I've paid for their schooling. I've paid for their first suit."[42] Mitchell undoubtedly cared for his dancers over the years, but there was still a sense that he cared more for the survival of the institution itself. Among the dance cognoscenti, this perception resulted in some strong criticism of Mitchell.

In September of 2000 the company presented Act II only of the Creole *Giselle* for its City Center fall season. For Gus Solomons Jr., the performance was "brittle," "technically precarious," and "tense." The full-length *Giselle* was revived for a season beginning in May 2001 for the DTH's season at Kennedy Center. Critic Sarah Kaufman noted that DTH had not danced the full-length *Giselle* in eight years, "and it shows." For her, "the dancing was tentative, the emotions never felt real, and the whole ballet came across as a sketch rather than as the richly detailed dance-drama it should be."[43]

The company had last performed the complete ballet for their City Center season in 1993. Kaufman recalled that these performances "left a warm and lasting impression of community that made you care about the dancers and their story." She attributed the eight-year absence of *Giselle* from the active repertory to finances. *Giselle* was a big, expensive ballet to pack up and transport. And, after the reduction in company size, it required a bigger cast than DTH could muster without bringing in students. It therefore suffered a lamentable amount of attrition over the years. As Kaufman saw it, "The ballet had the look of being rushed into production without adequate rehearsal and, most especially, without adequate coaching of the principals as to the story they are telling." Five years earlier, George Jackson had made the observation, "Dance Theatre of Harlem dances best when working directly with a choreographer."[44] Unfortunately, Franklin could not supervise the 2001 revival because he was swamped with work on four Ballet Russe revivals for the Cincinnati Ballet.

The DTH works of most recent vintage have been created mostly by black choreographers for a black audience. Typical are Robert Garland's *Return* (2000), set to funk-rock by James Brown and Aretha Franklin, and *South African Suite* (1999), choreographed by Mitchell, Augustus Van Heerden and Laveen Haidu with live music from Soweto Swing. Other black choreographers who have recently set works in this flashy genre include Garth Fagan, Alonzo King, Louis Johnson, Geoffrey Holder, Dwight Rhoden, and Billy Wilson.

Over the years, DTH has developed a substantial black audience. While this is a praiseworthy achievement, the changing cultural tastes of the DTH audience have made it increasingly difficult for the company to maintain a classical identity. While the Balanchine repertory remained, the nineteenth century classics, the Diaghilev ballets and the Americana works had all but disappeared. Mitchell's original vision was to found and develop a company of magnificent black classicists. Franklin can take much of the credit for turning that dream into a reality. Over thirty years after its founding, however, the mission of DTH is now very much up in the air.

Dance Theatre of Harlem was a ballet company that gave its audiences much to think about over the years. Never having strong (or secure) financial backing, and even after thirty years lacking a home theatre, it nevertheless survived to become one of America's cultural treasures. Mitchell himself was honored with a 1993 MacArthur ("genius") Award, a 1994 Kennedy Center Honors award and the 1995 National Medal of Art, along with dozens of honorary degrees from colleges and universities. Long after the novelty value had worn off, and social activists had moved on to other causes, the Dance Theatre of Harlem held its own.

Twenty-five years after its founding, Anna Kisselgoff labeled DTH "a company still in search of a repertory," settling for "hand-me-down" ballets."[45] It is true that Mitchell embraced and then abandoned one repertory focus after another. Yet it is also true that a narrow repertory focus is expensive and can pose a risk at the box office. No doubt driven at least in part by severe and recurring financial problems, Mitchell was often unable to define his artistic aspirations beyond mere survival.

By 2003, the company was more than a million dollars in debt. Arthur Mitchell even mortgaged his own apartment to bring in the funds for *St. Louis Woman: A Blues Ballet*, which opened the Lincoln Center Festival in the summer of 2003. In 2004, Dance Theatre of Harlem should have been celebrating its thirty-fifth anniversary. At a press conference in September of 2004, Mitchell made the shocking announcement that he was putting his company on hiatus once again because DTH faced a $2.5 million debt. Suddenly, the company's forty-four dancers, left with no salary or health benefits, were scrambling to find employment until the company could reconvene.

After a flurry of phone calls seeking help, Mitchell and his staff worked long hours to produce an emergency financial restructuring — the brainchild of Michael Kaiser, president of the Kennedy Center for the Performing Arts. He agreed to act as pro bono advisor to the company and to come up with a strategic plan that would pave the way for the re-opening of the company. He spearheaded a major fund-raising effort and worked with people from the Harlem business community to get big names on the board of directors. Exuding excitement over what he called "the miracle of 152nd Street,"[46] Arthur Mitchell announced plans to reconstitute the company by June of 2005, but over a year and one-half later, this still had not occurred.

There are some interesting points of comparison between the vicissitudes of Mitchell and Franklin in their careers as artistic directors. Mitchell mortgaged his apartment to save the company; Franklin poured his own personal savings into the National Ballet and nearly lost his shirt. In this sense, at least, both men were dedicated to their missions, whether Franklin likes the word "dedicated" or not. There is another parallel in that both Harlem and the National suffered from insufficient community support; however, the reasons for this lack are pointedly different. Washington is a cosmopolitan city which has habitually looked to New York, Europe and Russia for imported cultural attractions. A deeply-rooted sense of civic pride, while not entirely lacking, is less in evidence than it is in most other large American cities. Washingtonians looked the other way while a cultural treasure slipped from their hands. In Franklin's case, the community was simply apathetic. Harlem, by contrast, takes great pride in the achievements of Mitchell and his company, but sufficient community funding for DTH is still a long way in the offing. Kaiser pointed out that while all arts organizations are having a difficult time raising money, organizations in black communities face an extra hurdle. There are fewer individual donors, forcing reliance on dwindling government and corporate money: "Typically money is given to church, education, health care — as opposed to the arts. Building individual donors to arts organizations of color has been very difficult."[47]

The present status of Dance Theatre of Harlem is a grim reminder of the sorry state of funding for the arts in America in general. It will probably be some time before this company reforms again, if it ever does. As Franklin's close friend Bill Ausman points out, "Nobody wants to reconstitute unless they really have an endowment or really have substantial funds."[48] Certainly, Dance Theatre of Harlem will never be the same, with its dancers scattered far and wide and many now employed elsewhere. Fighting back tears, Virginia Johnson said, "Dancing is like writing in the sand. You have to do it every day. Who will be dancing when the company returns?"[49] Whoever returns, one thing is clear — the situation for DTH is quite precarious, but, if Arthur Mitchell has anything to say about it, this will not be the end.

American Ballet Theatre

Franklin first began performing with American Ballet Theatre in 1996. The following year, he was given the opportunity to revive *Coppelia* for ABT. Franklin had already staged his *Coppelia* for the National Ballet, Pittsburgh Ballet Theatre, Tulsa Ballet Theatre, Cincinnati Ballet, Richmond Ballet and Milan's La Scala. Artistic Director Kevin McKenzie, who rose to this position in 1992, had danced in the National Ballet's *Coppelia* and remembered it fondly. Plus, ABT's old version of *Coppelia* by former ABT ballet master Enrique Martinez had gotten stale. "It's a funny thing," Franklin said, "It's been with me all my dancing life and staging it for ABT was like having a career starting all over again."[50]

When Franklin and McKenzie were talking about casting, the latter said, "You know Fred, all the principals want to do it." Franklin took this as a "great compliment,"[51] but he may have had second thoughts when McKenzie assigned him six casts of principals to rehearse! He could never rehearse the six couples all together, because their schedules were so complicated. With more energy than many people half his age, Franklin simply rolled up his sleeves and got to work: "It was awful. You get them for half an hour. Then you get your corps de ballet separately, and then you try putting it all together. And that was hilarious."[52] Franklin had less than ten days to set the entire ballet. He impressed these casts with his good nature and stamina while coaching them in such a limited period of time. "He's very patient, very fun," said soloist Yan Chen. "He knows exactly what he wants; he remembers everything."[53] During rehearsals, Martine van Hamel, McKenzie's wife, asked, "'Fred, do you think you'll ever get it together?' I said, 'I don't know.' But the 'Ballet Theatre Miracle' happened. That is what they call it — the 'Ballet Theatre Miracle.'" As Ausman points out, no small part of the miracle is due to the quality and caliber of the dancers: "It's not like you've got to hammer it in. They see it, they do it. Extraordinary."[54]

The ABT season ran from May 12 to July 5, 1997. Also in this season were four full-length ballets: David Blair's *Swan Lake*, Lar Lubovich's *Othello*, Kenneth MacMillan's *The Sleeping Beauty*, and *The Merry Widow* by Ronald Hynd. The company offered only nine performances of mixed bills this season.

The coveted opening-night performance of *Coppelia* was danced by Angel Corella and Paloma Herrera. Other casts included Susan Jaffe with Jose Manuel Carreno, Amanda McKerrow with Vladimir Malakhov, and Martha Butler with Ethan Stiefel. Franklin used his virtuosic dancers to good advantage. Describing rehearsals, he said, "Male dancers in my day were completely different dancers — our kind of movement was up and down. Now, they're all over the place, doing steps that don't even have names. 'Do something at the end,' I told them when I was teaching the *manège* — and that's what they did."[55]

Coppelia opened at the Metropolitan on May 30 with candy-colored, dollhouse sets by Tony Straiges, costumes by Patricia Zipprodt and lighting by Brad Field. Jennifer Dunning found it to be a "glowing gem," and she noted, "This 'Coppelia' is a warmer, gentler production than the one created by Danilova and Balanchine for the New York City Ballet. The Ballet Theater version packs fewer steps into the music." Sylviane Gold wrote, "Franklin hasn't given 'Coppelia' new clothes. It's an 'I'm OK, you're OK' version of the E. T. A. Hoffmann story. Franklin keeps the spirit light and the humor front and center." Rose Anne Thom noted, "The Company performed 'Coppelia' with obvious affection and understanding."[56]

Balanchine and Danilova's 1974 staging of *Coppelia* for New York City Ballet had downplayed the mime, but Franklin told an interviewer he "wanted to see some of the original theatricality again."[57] He objected to the New York City Ballet production on the grounds that it was "crammed with choreography" and "had nothing to do with the period of the piece."[58] But, of course, his approach was bound to rub some critics the wrong way. For Rhonda Garelick, "the production lacks oomph ... the dancing feels too gentle and low to the ground, too dependent upon pantomime." In his review of *Coppelia*, Thomas Disch wrote, "It's as authentic as you're going to get. Along with this authenticity comes much humdrum and frequently inexplicable mime, long stretches of balleticized folk dancing and a recital number performed by children."[59]

While its tone is certainly light-hearted, *Coppelia* is not devoid of philosophical content. The ballet's subject, the tension between the real and the ideal, is as pertinent as ever in our image-soaked society. Dunning noted, "Mr. Franklin's 'Coppelia' falls somewhere between simple comedy and the dark grandeur of Hoffman's tale."[60] And this was exactly the balance that Franklin was seeking.

The saddest event of this ABT season was the death of Danilova on July 13, 1997, at the age of ninety-three. She had become a permanent member of the School of American Ballet faculty in 1964, a post she held until 1989. Danilova was a familiar figure at ballet performances until she became too frail to attend. It is extremely ironic that she was last seen in public at the May 30 opening of Franklin's *Coppelia*.[61]

Coppelia was performed by ABT once again at the Kennedy Center in Washington on April 7–12, 1998. Franklin's next project for ABT was a 1999 restaging of *Gaîté Parisienne*. Massine himself had set this work for the company in 1970 with his daughter, Tatiana. ABT subsequently did a more controversial revival in 1988, staged by Massine's son, Lorca, and Susanna della Pietra. The furor revolved around the wacky costumes of trendy fashion designer Christian Lacroix. Lacroix clothed the dancers in zesty cartoon couture which was actually a thinly disguised reworking of his 1987 collection. Massine was never one to shun fussy designs and loud colors, but Lacroix's relentless ruffles, flounces, garters, plumes and baubles obscured the choreographic line and made a travesty of the ballet by emphasizing the characters' vulgarity. Ann Barzel was not alone in decrying "the atrocious spectacle to which ABT has reduced this ballet." Lorca's staging was also lambasted as well. John Percival wrote, "to those of us who saw them [Massine's ballets] mounted by his father, it seems sadly apparent that he has not much idea of what they are about.... Add the dreadfully misconceived new designs and you have a recipe for disaster." Franklin remarked that Lorca Massine "would not accept help from a soul that had been in the ballet before."[62] Naturally, when Freddie came in to stage *Gaîté*, it was as close to the original as could be had.

In May of 2000 Franklin appeared with American Ballet Theatre for its May 8–July 1 season, which celebrated ABT's sixtieth birthday. The most important new productions were McKenzie's controversial new staging of *Swan Lake* and a restaging of John Cranko's *Taming of the Shrew* by Cranko expert Reid Anderson and Benesh choreologist Jane Bourne. Although Erik Bruhn's staging of *La Sylphide* was not a new one, it had been absent from the repertoire since 1994, and its restoration was welcome. There were three different casts of leads, the opening-night performance being danced by Nina Ananiashvili and Angel Corella. The three Madges in this production were Martine van Hamel, Victor Barbee, and Franklin. Comparing the three, Clive Barnes wrote, "the palm must go to the 86-year-old celebrated star of the old Ballet Russe, Franklin."[63] Franklin had danced Madge with the National, and his version of the role differed from what Bruhn had staged. So McKenzie said, "'All right, Fred, you do it your way.' And I did. And it was all so much easier to see and very much better."[64] Said Sylviane Gold, "Franklin is — well, Franklin is going to be eighty-six in two weeks. How much longer could we have waited? He is amazing to watch. Even buried under Madge's long gray wig and tattered brown dress, this veteran of the heyday of the Ballet Russe de Monte Carlo bristles with star power. He gives Madge a fiercely determined hobble and a manic glee, and his long fingers seem to emit a malevolent charge into the air."[65]

Freddie took a break right in the middle of ABT's 2000 spring season to attend one of the most momentous gatherings in his life. "The Legacy of the Ballets Russes in the Americas" was a four-day symposium held in New Orleans on June 1–4, 2000. It drew participants from four continents, including nearly one hundred surviving dancers from the de Basil and Denham Ballet Russe companies. Some of these veterans had disabilities, which made travel difficult. Others, like Franklin, were hale and hearty and appeared to have ignored the passage of years.

The reunion was organized in conjunction with the fourteenth international conference of the *Conseil International de la Danse*. It centered around three distinct periods in the company's history: the Diaghilev, de Basil and Denham eras. Two days of panels, lectures, and film presentations dealt with the artistic objectives of the companies, as well as the nitty-gritty of extensive touring. Alonso and Franklin discussed the company's impact on ballet's development in a symposium titled "The Ballets Russes in America," illustrated with motion picture footage from the dancers' careers. Master

Frederic Franklin taking curtain calls after restaging *Gaîté Parisienne* for American Ballet Theatre. April 1999. Left to right, front row, Veronica Lynn, Joaquin De Luz, Franklin, Julie Kent and Guillaume Graffin. Originally staged by Lorca Massine. Scenery: Zack Brown. Costumes: Christian Lacroix for an earlier production. Photograph: Nan Melville, courtesy of American Ballet Theatre.

classes were taught by Franklin, Irina Baronova, Tatiana Leskova, Moscelyne Larkin, George Zoritch, Nathalie Krassovska and Nina Novak. Dancers well into their seventies and eighties demonstrated variations from the Ballet Russe repertoire, giving the younger generation a fleeting glimpse of the performances they had missed. Freddie gave a public coaching session of the Waltz from *Gaîté Parisienne*, using two teenaged dancers.

The conference featured an exhibition of ballet memorabilia, including backdrops created by Dalí, Gontcharova, Berman, Benois and Matisse from the George Verdak Collection at Butler University. But the exhibit, fascinating though it was, couldn't compete with living history, and star-struck balletomanes spent most of their time at the Sheraton Hotel, adjacent to the city's French Quarter, listening in rapt attention to tales of hardship and adventure told by the company's surviving dancers. Though there was frequent mention of the grueling itineraries and the lousy pay, many also called it the best job they ever had. At panel discussions, they spoke movingly and often hilariously of the multinational company that became their family. There was plenty of laughter. "The first time I saw George, I thought he was the most beautiful man I'd ever seen," said Alan Howard of fellow panelist George Zoritch. "You wouldn't believe it now," Zoritch sighed. "I look like the remnants of Louis XIV.... I bend down and I see breasts."[66] Panelist dancers swung from admiration to disapproval in describing de Basil and Denham as "creative accountants."[67] "Baby Ballerina" Irina Baronova, who toured with her mother in tow, recalled that mama used to hide money in her knick-

Frederic Franklin as Madge in American Ballet Theatre's production of *La Sylphide*. 2000. Version by Eric Bruhn. Scenery and Costumes: Desmond Heeley. Metropolitan Opera House. Photograph: Nan Melville, courtesy of American Ballet Theatre.

ers, and that when de Basil needed some, "they would go out in the alley and she would lift her skirt and oblige him." When the audience guffawed, Baronova corrected them: "I mean, she would give him the money."[68]

Panelist Lynn Garafola spoke of a phenomenon that has been mentioned and that all of these veterans have experienced firsthand. She pointed out that innovative one-act ballets have been largely replaced by the return of the evening-length classics. She noted that ballet seems to have come full circle in this respect and suggested that, at the beginning of the twenty-first century, the art form is in a static situation comparable to the one that heralded the innovations which Fokine initiated in the early 1900s.[69]

At a gala performance at New Orleans's Orpheum Theatre on June 2, a coterie of internationally known dancers performed variations created by the company's renowned choreographers: Massine, Balanchine, Fokine, Nijinska and Nijinsky. But the highlight of the performance occurred at the very beginning, when the curtain rose on a half-moon of nearly seventy-five original company members — all formally dressed, most white-haired. The audience rose as one person with thunderous applause and shouts of "Bravo!" Tears were shed on both sides of the proscenium. Heather Wisner reported, "Guest artists from around the world danced, but nothing matched the visceral power of that first tableau and its emotional response, a testament to the company's widespread and enduring influence."[70]

At a formal dinner on June 3, the Vaslav Nijinsky Medal was awarded, posthumously, to de Basil, Massine and Denham, as well as to the alive-and-well Franklin, Nina Novak, Alan Howard, Marc Plattoff, Mia Slavenska, Irina Borowska, and critic

Jack Anderson for their work in advancing Nijinsky's artistic ideals. The conference drove home to the veterans that theirs was an extraordinary era beyond compare. Beyond its obvious ballet trailblazing, the company most likely enjoyed such widespread popularity because, as Franklin stated simply, "We were good and people liked us."[71]

So riveting had Franklin been as Madge that ABT wasted no time in contracting him to appear both in especially commissioned works and a series of character roles in the classics. On October 23–November 4, 2001, American Ballet Theatre did a season called "A Tribute to the American Spirit" at the City Center. The opening night was dedicated to the heroes and victims of the tragic events of September 11. Choreographer Robert Hill created *Reverie* for this occasion. The piece brought three generations back to the stage: '70s star Martine van Hamel, longtime ABT ballet mistress Georgina Parkinson and octogenarian Franklin. They danced together and apart to Schubert songs sung onstage by Camille Zamora, with David LaMarche at the piano. Doris Hering observed, "When you get on in years, you give up jumping and lifting, but there's still a lot to be said by arms." Jennie Schulman concurred: "His beautifully rounded arms, presence and stature were still in evidence," and she noted that Parkinson and van Hamel "looked glamorous and performed with the artistry and warmth that come with maturity." Hering concluded her remarks on *Reverie* as follows: "Franklin is eightyseven. Let's not count the women's years."[72]

The 2003 spring season in New York was highlighted by director Kevin McKenzie's sumptuous *Swan Lake*, which had been the source of much contention when it premiered in May of 2000. The ballet took its second dip in May of 2003. David Blair had set this ballet for ABT in 1967, and McKenzie retained part of his staging, including the Lakeside Act, Petipa's Act I pas de trois, czardas, Spanish dance and mazurka in Act III, as well as a standardized version of the "Black Swan Pas de Deux." McKenzie's changes included a brief scene during the overture showing Odette being abducted by Baron von Rothbart and the bifurcation of the Baron into two roles — the first a half-naked spirit of the lake, the other a smartly-dressed courtier who flirts with the Fiancées in Act III. On opening night, Gillian Murphy and Angel Corella gave extraordinary performances, but they didn't walk away with all the laurels: Jean Battey Lewis wrote, "Standing out in the performance was Frederic Franklin as the Prince's tutor. At eighty-eight he brings a zest to the stage that would be remarkable at any age."[73]

ABT held its 2004 season at the Met from May 10 to July 3. For this occasion, Kevin McKenzie created a "Suite for Freddie" in honor of Franklin's upcoming ninetieth birthday, and the legendary dancer himself graced the stage, gently partnering Amanda McKerrow and Ashley Tuttle for this *pièce d'occasion*. But the high point of the birthday festivities occurred in the actual month of Freddie's birth. On June 21, the company revived *Coppelia* to officially ring in Freddie's new status as a nonagenarian. After the performance, the ebullient Franklin stood center stage at the Metropolitan Opera House with his arms wide open, soaking up the love from a wildly applauding audience. Balloons rained from above, and bouquets of flowers landed at his feet. Critic Kate Lydon wrote, "Franklin is a living legend, ballet royalty, a golden thread woven through dance history."[74] Victor Barbee, who danced the role of Dr. Coppelius on this occasion, told Lydon, "Freddie is what we all hope we'll become when we grow up."[75] As usual, Franklin was unwilling to sit around and simply be honored. He coached

Frederic Franklin as the Tutor and Georgina Parkinson as the Queen Mother after a perform-
ance in American Ballet Theatre's production of *Swan Lake.* 2003. Choreography: Kevin
McKenzie after Marius Petipa and Lev Ivanov. Sets and costumes: Zack Brown. Lighting: Duane
Schuler. Metropolitan Opera House. Photograph: Courtesy of Donald Saddler.

Frederic Franklin as Friar Laurence in American Ballet Theatre's production of *Romeo and Juliet* with Julie Kent and Marcello Gomes as the doomed lovers. 2006. Choreography: Sir Kenneth MacMillan. Staging: Julie Lincoln. Scenery and costumes: Nicholas Georgiadis. Lighting: Thomas Skelton. Metropolitan Opera House. Photograph: MIRA, courtesy of American Ballet Theatre.

three sets of leads for this revival: Ashley Tuttle with Angel Corella, Gillian Murphy with Marcello Gomes, and Xiomara Reyes with Herman Cornejo. *Coppelia* was given eight performances that season.

In July of 2004, Kenneth MacMillan's *Romeo and Juliet* highlighted the ABT's season at the Met. MacMillan's version of Prokofiev's famous ballet is only one of many,

Frederic Franklin as the Charlatan in American Ballet Theatre's production of *Petrouchka*. 2006. Choreography: Fokine. Music: Stravinsky. Staging: Gary Chryst. Sets and costumes: Alexandre Benois. Metropolitan Opera House. Photograph: Courtesy of William Ausman.

but it ranks as one of the greatest ballets of the twentieth century. He created it for the Royal Ballet in 1965, and the production was first staged for ABT in 1985. The sumptuous, heavily realistic scenery and lavish period costumes by Nicholas Georgiadis for that production remained intact, and the 2004 revival boasted a cast of ninety, offering such pairings in the title roles as Marcelo Gomes with Paloma Herrera, Angel Corella with Ashley Tuttle, Ethan Stiefel with Xiomara Reyes, and Maxim Beloserkovsky with Irina Dvorovenko. Franklin danced Friar Laurence (as he had in Petrov's 1975 version for Pittsburgh and Morgan's 2001 version for Cincinnati). Mary Cargill reported, "Frederic Franklin on his knees, pleading for peace, made a profound Friar Laurence." Critic Alexandra Tomalonis claimed, "The great performance was by Frederic Franklin (ninety and the most intense man on stage) as Friar Laurence, who created a world in six seconds while making a simple sign of the cross."[76]

In 2006, Franklin celebrated his tenth anniversary with American Ballet Theatre. In the summer season he performed as the Charlatan in *Petrouchka* (danced by him first in ABT's 2005 summer season), Friar Laurence in *Romeo and Juliet* and the Tutor in *Swan Lake*.

· 8 ·

Still Going Strong
as the Years Pass Along

In the summer of 2004, Franklin got a phone call from the consulate general of the British Embassy in New York:

> "I would like to inform you that you will be mentioned at the Queen's honors." And I said, "What!" And he said, "You know, you've got a lot of very good friends. And, of course, now you will be a CBE." "A Commander of the British Empire!" I cried. "Yes," he replied. And I said, "Well, you said I had a lot of friends — who are they?" And he said, "We're not allowed to divulge. Eventually, you will hear who they all are." He warned, "This is absolutely private, and until it's announced, which will be in two weeks, you're not to say anything to a soul." I said "fine" and that I understood completely. I immediately called my brother.[1]

That same day, Freddie went downtown for an ABT rehearsal, where he ran into ballet mistress and former Royal Ballet principal Georgina Parkinson:

> I had this look on my face, and she said, "Why Freddie, you look as if you've just been knighted!" And I said, very quietly, "Not exactly." She wheeled around and said, "You've got to tell me!" I said, "Only on one condition. You can tell Roy [her husband] and no one else." I said, "I'm a CBE! Now, nobody is supposed to find out. You and my brother and Bill and Roy are the only ones who know so far."[2]

In November of 2004, Franklin made his debut as a choreographer with Britain's Royal Ballet. Two years earlier, Clive Barnes had observed that it would be a wonderful idea for the Royal Ballet to include Franklin's staging of the solo and duet from *Devil's Holiday* as part of its 2004 Sir Frederick Ashton centennial celebrations. While visiting Wendy Toye in London in the summer of 2003, Franklin met with Peter Wright, artistic director of the Royal Birmingham Ballet. Wright expressed great interest in the excerpts, and that November, when Freddie was back in the States, he received a phone call from Wright and Monica Mason. They wanted to see the Cincinnati videotape of the *Devil's Holiday* excerpts, so he sent it over. They promptly sent back what the dates for the Ashton Centennial would be.[3]

Franklin's debut as a choreographer with the Royal came just after a change in the company's leadership and direction. Ross Stretton, artistic director of the Australian

Ballet since 1997, was appointed artistic director of the Royal Ballet in March of 2001 as a successor to the retiring Anthony Dowell. Stretton was faced with an enormous challenge, as the repertory of the Royal is huge, and it is not easy to find the right balance. As Jenny Gilbert observed, "Sweep in with a barrage of changes and unpronounceable new choreographers and he'd be accused of neglecting the company's treasured heritage. Pander to nostalgia, and there would be howls from those who believe ballet is dying on its feet."[4]

Perhaps, then, it is not surprising that some critics accused Stretton of neglecting the Royal's unique heritage. In truth, the Royal had danced much less Sir Ashton in the decade before he ever even took office, but there was only one Ashton ballet in the 2000–01 season and a paucity of MacMillan works as well. Matters changed when Stretton resigned in September of 2002 and was replaced by Monica Mason.

Born in Johannesburg, Mason joined the company in 1958 and became a principal in 1968. She spent eleven years as assistant director, first to Norman Morrice, then to Kenneth MacMillan, Anthony Dowell and Stretton. After three months as acting artistic director she was appointed to the post permanently on December 18, 2002.

Interestingly, Mason's first executive act was to hang a stern portrait of Ninette de Valois on the wall opposite her desk. She says that it serves as a perpetual admonition and statement of intent, though she claims, "This is by no means reactionary."[5] Mason, like most Royal dancers, had lived in terror of the boss they called "Madam."

Where Mason mainly differed with Stretton was over repertoire. She was the crucible of the company's triumphs and traditions. Long associated with the Sir Frederick Ashton and Sir Kenneth MacMillan repertories, she stated, "I want to see the older works done in the right style because soon there won't be anybody left who remembers how those pieces should be done. I want a really good balance between those and the new work that I'm trying to get."[6] Mason poured an exhaustive amount of work into the Ashton centenary: "I very much want," she said, "for the company to dance Ashton the way he should be danced."[7]

Shortly after arrangements with the Royal had been set, Franklin got another call from the British Embassy, asking where he would like the Commander of the British Empire ceremonies to take place: Washington, New York or London. Freddie promptly responded, "'London.' And the next thing I got was a list of dates in September, October and November. I said, 'Bill, November.'"[8] They arrived in London on November 10.

For the Royal's Ashton celebration, Laura Levene reported, "Ashton worship continued unabated at Covent Garden last weekend with the Royal Ballet's unveiling of a new mixed programme of the choreographer's work." As mentioned, since the 1990s, Ashton's ballets had been neglected by the Royal and were often rusty in performance. But for the centenary, Zoe Anderson believed that the company was dancing Ashton "with new confidence."[9] The centenary's well-balanced menu featured 1948's *Scenes de Ballet* and 1951's *Daphnis and Chloe*, sandwiched around some intriguing divertissements — Ashton's 1971 *Thais*, his 1968 *Sleeping Beauty Awakening Pas de Deux* and, of course, Franklin's staging of the solo and pas de deux from *Devil's Holiday*. Two casts danced the *Devil's Holiday* excerpts: Laura Morera with Martin Harvey and Isabel McMeekan with Viasheslav Samodurov. Zoe Anderson wrote that the divertissements were "gorgeous" and added, "These divertissements are the real news of the programme."[10]

Freddie made fast friends with his British colleagues: "I became very close to them

at the Royal. Such a difference from when Ninette was there, believe me. It's unbeliev-
able, Covent Garden coming back into my life. I thought they'd all forgotten, but you
know those Brits. They're wonderful. Covent Garden and ABT are my two homes now.
They love me, and I love them."[11]

This premiere was on Monday, November 14, and Franklin got a standing ovation
when he took a curtain call that night. Right on the heels of his triumph at Covent
Garden, Freddie was off the very next day to Buckingham Palace to receive his Commander of the Order of the British Empire medal from Queen Elizabeth herself. Accompanied by Bill and Wendy, the three were taken to the palace in a limousine. "I told
the Queen that this was the most wonderful day of my life,"[12] he said. Franklin's long
isolation from his homeland naturally put him at a disadvantage when it came to royal
tributes, and this honor for his service to ballet was long overdue. Queen Mary and
George V, who established the honor, are engraved on this awesome medallion of solid
gold. Freddie has not yet worn this coveted royal necklace in public, not even on a run
to Zabars or Fairway.

Franklin got tremendous press in all of the major London newspapers, both for
the Ashton and for his CBE. He got a four-page write-up in the London *Standard,* and
Bill Ausman believes that the only thing that kept it off the front page was the same-
day death of Yasir Arafat. There was so much interest that BBC made special arrangements for a newscast in the middle of the day, when Freddie was receiving his medal
from the Crown. It was broadcast first in England, and it then went World BBC. Bill
flew home from London shortly after the ceremonies. He recalls, "I walked into the
lobby of our building, and the doorman says, 'I've just seen Fred on BBC.'"[13]

Franklin stayed over to visit his brother in Liverpool. A BBC Manchester director had noticed that Fred was all over the papers, and he called him at his brother's.
He told him that BBC Manchester did a program on people over eighty who are still
active in their lives and said that they'd like to do a documentary. It was Friday, and
Franklin was exhausted from all the excitement earlier in the week, but he agreed to
start filming on Tuesday. They went first to the site where he was born, although the
house no longer exists because of the World War II bombings. Then they went to the
other house where he had moved when he was ten. There followed a tour of Liverpool,
which has greatly improved in appearance since the war years. Today, Liverpool is a
lively cultural as well as industrial center. The city's museums and galleries contain
some of the finest collections in Great Britain, and there is also a well-known orchestra.

The tour's final destination was the Empire Theatre, where Franklin's mother had
taken him to see Diaghilev's Ballets Russes, Anna Pavlova and Fred and Adele Astaire.
The documentary crew couldn't get the stage because there was a rehearsal in progress,
but they found a room on the top floor and set up shop. And Franklin talked from nine
in the morning until eight o'clock that night.[14] The feature, titled *Inside-Out*, was shown
all over England.

By now, the inevitable comparisons were being made between Freddie and the
British lad in the title role of the acclaimed motion picture, *Billy Elliot,* the gritty story
of a coal miner's young son who dreams of becoming a ballet dancer. Both grew up in
North England industrial towns. Like Billy, Franklin went to London at age fourteen

HM Queen Elizabeth II investing Frederic Franklin as Commander of the British Empire. Buckingham Palace. 2004. Photograph: British Ceremonial Arts, Limited.

to take his exam in fear and terror at the Royal Academy of Dancing. Like Billy, he had a father who didn't know the faintest thing about dance and regarded it as an unmanly profession. Freddie's father only saw him dance once and told him that if he was bound on a career in show business, he'd make much more money as a comedian. Shortly after the first airing of the documentary *Inside-Out*, a Liverpool headline read, "It's Frederic Franklin, our own Billy Elliot."[15] (Interestingly, *Billy Elliot the Musical*, with a score by Elton John and choreography by Peter Darling, premiered in London to good reviews in the spring of 2005.)

Franklin returned to the States, but not for long. Early in 2005, he got yet another call from the BBC. This time it was BBC Northern Ireland. They were taping a documentary, and the call was from producer and director Clare Delargy:

> He said, "Well there's an Irish boy about eighteen years old and he's graduating from the Royal Ballet School. And we've read all about you, and it's like the Billy Elliot story, and it's the same thing with him, and we'd love it if you can come over — he's very nervous — and give him some encouragement." And I said, "Oh, my goodness me."[16]

And so it came to pass that Franklin flew over the Atlantic yet again — this time, courtesy of the BBC. When he arrived, he spent an entire day talking with the young man about the ballet and what it was like for him and how he felt. In the course of the taping, Franklin observed a rehearsal: "And there he was, and I could see he was nervous, and he started his solo, and he stopped. And we had long talks, and he was in

At Buckingham Palace, after investiture as Commander of the British Empire. Left to right, William Ausman, Wendy Toye, Frederic Franklin. 2004. Photograph: Courtesy of Charles Green.

tears. And it's all on tape, which is wonderful."[17] One has a deep sense that Franklin's trip to make this documentary was not in the spirit of self-promotion. Rather, he genuinely seemed to want to use his vast experience to help this young man, so talented and yet so riddled with self-doubt.

Franklin's next trip to London was occasioned by the death of Dame Alicia Markova. She died in a nursing home in Bath on December 2, 2004, just one day after her 94th birthday. In 1941 she had left the Ballet Russe and moved over to the newly formed Ballet Theatre, rejoining her former partner, Anton Dolin. The war over, Markova embarked on a series of international tours with Dolin, which culminated in 1949 with the founding of London Festival Ballet, now the English National Ballet. Although she formally left Festival Ballet in 1952, she intermittently appeared with it, and also with the Royal Ballet during the course of an international stage career that ended in 1962. From 1963, the year she was awarded her D.B.E. by Elizabeth II, until 1969, she was ballet director of the Metropolitan Opera House in New York, after which she continued to teach and coach. At ninety-two, she was still skimming across a studio floor demonstrating nuances of phrasing to dancers a quarter her age.

This was Freddie's fifth trip across the Atlantic in eighteen months. The funeral was a magnificent one, and it took place in Westminster Abbey. Freddie had mixed emotions. While saddened, he was gratified to see Alicia so richly honored by the British people. He found it "a wonderful thing, really, and I'm so glad I went."[18]

The latest big event in Freddie's life has been the stir created by the new documentary *Ballets Russes*. Five years ago, San Francisco-based, Emmy-winning documentarians Dayna Goldfine and Dan Geller learned that a friend of a friend was helping organize a reunion of the Ballet Russe veterans in New Orleans. They were intrigued, although their dance experience had been limited to their first film, *Isadora Duncan: Movement from the Soul*. Geller and Goldfine decided to go down and get footage of the New Orleans reunion. The project expanded over the next five years to a full-length documentary involving over 1,150 hours of footage and ninety hours of interviews with the surviving dancers. Invaluable aid was given by Chicago-based critic Ann Barzel, whose incomparable collection of films was made available through the Newberry Library. Help also came from the New York Public Library and Jacob's Pillow. Then Goldfine and Geller found an immense cache of film in Australia which chronicled the de Basil Ballet Russe.[19]

The film premiered in September 2005 at the Toronto International Film Festival to a highly enthusiastic audience. It then went to a much larger Toronto theatre and was completely sold out. It had its sneak preview in New York on October 19 at the Bruno Walter Auditorium at Lincoln Center, followed by a run at the Film Forum in Greenwich Village beginning on October 26. The Film Forum run was only scheduled for two weeks, but due to popular demand, the run was extended until January of 2006. The documentary went into national release in November of 2005 and opened on April 16, 2006 at the International Film Center in London.

Ballets Russes zeros in on the years after legendary impresario Diaghilev's death in 1929 and gives a brisk history of the two companies which emerged in the 1930s. Combining a glorious trove of archival footage and lively interviews with such icons as Franklin, Dame Alicia Markova and Irina Baronova, the documentary details a juicy

story of backstage intrigue. Part of the fun is the very fractiousness of the Ballet Russe —
the rivalries, betrayals and clashing egos.

Even into their eighties and beyond, these Ballet Russe veterans can rivet the audience with their wisdom, wit and sheer joie de vivre. With the colorful personalities that
made them stars, they are the heart of this inspired film. Eighty-six-year-old Nathalie
Krassovska, in a low-cut leotard and filmy ballet skirt, describes dodging advances from
Charlie Chaplin. The film shows former "Baby Ballerina" Tatiana Riabouchinska, at
the age of eighty-three, conducting class in a West Hollywood studio. Asked why she
still teaches, she says, "Well, what else would I do? Sell books? Sell fruit? So that's my
life, you know." Behind the scenes Tamara Tchinarova calls Nijinska a "slave driver"
who "wore white gloves because she didn't like to touch the bodies of the sweating girls"
while teaching. The two surviving "Baby Ballerinas"— Riabouchinska and Baronova —
chat about their precocious teens, followed by a tart assertion by Markova that she was
the *original* baby ballerina by virtue of her fourteen-year-old lead in *Le Chant du rossignol.* Raven Wilkinson, the only African American member of the troupe, recounts how
the Ku Klux Klan stormed the stage looking for "the nigger" during a performance in
the Deep South.[20] (Raven was ultimately forced to quit the company when Southern
sponsors refused to let her perform.)

No dancer is interviewed more frequently than Frederic Franklin, who sat for
thirty hours of interviews. He is a marvelous raconteur throughout. For instance, he
quips, "The Russians aren't very nice to each other. You know how they are."[21] He also
reveals his astounding memory for the literally hundreds of ballets he has danced.
According to Geller, Franklin proved to be an indispensable collaborator. It was he
who paved the way for an interview (one of the last) with the publicity-shunning Alicia Markova in her late eighties.[22] He is the cement that gives this film its sense of
tight unity and form.

The film has a broad appeal which transcends the sometimes stuffy circle of balletomanes and ballet dancers. Geller stated, "It became clear as we got into the film further and further that we really wanted to make a movie that someone might go to, sit
down, saying, 'I don't know about this ballet stuff' and then walk out saying, 'My God,
I'd love to go see ballet and what an amazing story.'"[23]

Goldfine and Geller marveled at how many of the Ballet Russe alumni continued
to perform and teach well into their seventies, eighties, and even nineties. They realized that this film was ultimately as much about aging, of having done something beautiful in one's life, as it was about one particular art form. Geller credits the dancers'
remarkable longevity today to their passion for the art: "One thing I think it does say
is that if you do something that you care about deeply in your life, when you get to be
in your senior years, you will live with a life force and a vitality that is unmistakable."[24]

Ballets Russes celebrates the tenacity of artists who survived almost insurmountable challenges. As Goldfine noted, "'Ballets Russes' is about much more than the history of ballet. It's about the human spirit."[25] Sadly, many of the performers passed away
not long after they were interviewed, among them Tatiana Riabouchinska, Dame Alicia Markova, Mia Slavenska, Alan Howard and, just this year, Nathalie Krassovska. Said
Geller, "We had hoped that a film about people who spent their lives and hearts doing
things they loved so much would be really fabulous to put onto the screen and

Frederic Franklin taking a bow at the Met at a gala performance of his production of *Coppelia* in celebration of his 90th birthday. 2004. Franklin staged the production for ABT in 1966. Photograph: Nan Melville, courtesy of American Ballet Theatre.

share. Boy did we get a bumper crop. That's why I think the film plays beyond the core audience. It's really a film about lives well-lived and lives lived in the art."[26]

This Zeitgeist Films documentary is produced by Robert Hawk, Douglas Blair Turnbaugh, Dayna Goldfine and Dan Geller, with an original score by Todd Boekelheide and David Conte and photography by Dan Geller. *Time Magazine* critic Richard Schickmel has named *Ballets Russes* one of the ten best films of 2005. It is not to be missed.

On Wednesday, October 19, 2005, Franklin faced a dilemma. This was the evening of the sneak preview of the documentary at Lincoln Center, while at New York City Center, ABT was giving its opening-night performance of *Rodeo* after a long absence from the repertory. Staged by Paul Sutherland with assistance from Christine Sarry, the revival premiere celebrated Agnes de Mille's centenary. Since Franklin had been consulted on this revival, he naturally thought it imperative to attend both occasions. He asked Dayna and Dan, "What are we going to do? I've got to be at ABT!" It was worked out so that Freddie greeted all the people as they came in to see the documentary and then made a fast dash to City Center in tie and tails. While talking of this upcoming, momentous evening, Freddie gazed down at his CBE medallion, and said, "You know, I can wear this around my neck on opening night. No ... I don't think so."[27] As of this writing, he has yet to wear it, but he really should relent, perhaps for the next big ABT opening.

Franklin shows no signs of slowing down. On April 9, 2006, he appeared with

Tulsa Ballet Theatre for a gala in honor of prima ballerina Daniella Buson's farewell performance. There, Freddie, Bruce Marks, Ivan Nágy, and Ben Stevenson gallantly partnered Buson as the Four Cavaliers in the "Rose Adagio" from *Sleeping Beauty*. Ivan told Freddie, "I'm a nervous wreck already. You've been onstage all this time. I haven't been onstage in thirty years."[28] And Nágy wasn't the only one in a state of anxiety. Said Tulsa Ballet artistic director Marcello Angelini, "I was a nervous wreck, as you can imagine. I was the one having to tell *them* where to go. All four of them my former bosses ... and pillars of the dance community. But they were very serious about it."[29]

There being scant rehearsal time and space in Tulsa Ballet's studios, the four gentlemen staged an impromptu rehearsal in the gardens of the Tulsa Art Museum, each holding a piece of paper in lieu of a rose and refreshing their memories of the steps and patterns given to them by Angelini and Daniella Buson. Marilyn Burr-Nágy stepped in for Buson as Aurora. Soon, a large and curious throng had gathered to stare at these boys as they pranced through their weird maneuvers.[30]

The performance had a strong impact on Angelini and the entire audience:

> It was the first and probably last time that those four major stars, and contributors to the growth of dance worldwide, were on the same stage at the same time. Their personalities came out loud and clear — there was so much charisma onstage that the stage was shining with the natural light of their own personalities.... It was clear to all of us in the audience that some people are born stars; dance just gives them the tools to get there![31]

According to Angelini, the best quote of the evening came from Ben Stevenson, who said, "This performance will make history as it is the first time in the history of the *Sleeping Beauty* that Princess Aurora has to hold up the four cavaliers rather than the other way around!" Angelini added, "Of course, it's not true, but it was a magnificent quote that tells you about the kind, modest and caring spirit of those wonderful individuals."[32]

The BBC Northern Ireland documentary *A God Given Gift: The Leigh Alderson Story* opened in London in the summer of 2006. Naturally, Fred flew to London again for this occasion. As said, the Royal has now become his second home.

Born in Portadown, Ireland, Leigh Alderson was lost to dance at a very early age. At the age of eleven, after competing with hundreds of children from across Europe, he won a coveted place with the Royal Ballet School in London. Leaving home at such an early age was hard on Leigh and even harder on his mother. When the time came to leave for White Lodge each year, his mother's tears would flow. Leigh said that he felt guilty because it was "*my* dream and I was the one taking myself away from her."

White Lodge was his home for five years. Like most dancers there, Leigh grew up quickly from being asked at a young age to do something so difficult. When the five years were up, many of his best buddies did not pass the exam to get into Upper School, and he never saw them again. He felt lonely but somehow stronger for this loss: "In a way that drove me to be more dedicated because you realize at an early age how competitive it is."

As the documentary begins, Leigh is nearing the end of a two-year course which, for the chosen few, will lead to an invitation to join a professional graduate year and will bring them one step closer to the dream of a place in the Royal Ballet. At this point, Leigh is very apprehensive and nervous: "I'll be really honest. I've been incredibly negative towards my- self. It's very hard for me to see the more positive aspects. The mirror is right in front of you, and not every day is going to be a good day." [33]

Gailen Stock, director of the Royal Ballet School, has vivid memories of Leigh Alderson in his very first year at White Lodge: "He was trying so hard, but it was just this joy of dance that really came through and appealed to me. He had all the right ingredients for a dancer, the right physique. But more than anything else, it was the joie de vivre that I thought was special, and it's very rare in a dancer." [34]

Frederic Franklin, CBE. 1998. Photograph: Courtesy of Roy Round.

The documentary reveals an exceptionally talented eighteen year old who has lost that sense of joy. His teacher and rehearsal coach, Chris Pownes, nailed the problem down quite precisely:

> His perfectionism sometimes comes as a disappointment. It can be very soul-destroying.... We have a problem with Leigh in that he is his own worst enemy. He tends to find the negative in absolutely everything. He becomes analytical to the point where he doesn't seem to like anything he does in the classical studio. The closer you come to being a professional, the more crucial it is to get better, and it *does* become more analytical, but the fun can get drawn right out of the equation. And I think it's important that he tries to find that back again. But he's the only one who can do that. [35]

Franklin makes his first appearance in this film at an Upper School rehearsal, where he is introduced to the young dancers with appropriate pomp and ceremony. During warm-up, he is quick to see the potential in Leigh: "He's a very gifted young man, and pure classical male dancers are rare birds. They don't grow on trees." [36]

The rehearsal scene that followed this remark was intensely emotional. Leigh began his solo variation, hopped out of a pirouette midway through, and quit cold, a look of self-hatred on his face. He told Pownes that he thought his dancing was "awful." Pownes asked, "And if I told you that it wasn't would you believe me?" Leigh shook his head. Pownes responded quietly, but with an air of stern finality:

> You leave me in a position where there's little I can do. Look, I can't take you from *here* to *there* [gesturing to each side]. You've got to take yourself into the next stage. Now the next stage is not technical at all. It's about you stepping over that hurdle and managing to believe in yourself a little bit and allowing yourself to be human, which means it's not going to be perfect.... Pick it up as if nothing's happened, because you have to give that to the audience. You have to give that to yourself . Even if you're fatigued, even if you fall, even if everything's crumbling, can you actually pick yourself up and continue? Because that's the strength of someone.[37]

Leigh started crying. Out of Leigh's earshot, Freddie made the observation that even a rehearsal must always be treated as a performance — "Performance value is everything." After the rehearsal, Franklin spoke with Leigh one-on-one:

> You've been given many gifts, you know. You have a line — don't worry about the silly pirouettes. They'll all be there, that will come. You know the thing is, Leigh, you're an entertainer. Above all, you're an *entertainer*. And that's what it's all about. The beauty of the business is what you've been given and what you make of the lovely things you have. And you're only eighteen, Leigh, and it's all out there, and the road is beautiful, and you must enjoy it.

Leigh teared up again, but this time, they were tears of relief, not those of despair. To the credit of Franklin and Pownes, one senses and hopes that he is finally ready to move on to that "next stage," to regain what he had lost in childhood. Of course, only Leigh can cultivate the capacity to think less about his self-absorption in technique and more about the gift that he is giving to the audience. But he needs some help, and words of wisdom from a legendary dancer were obviously inspirational. By the documentary's end, he seems to be reaching an epiphany. And, by the way, he was accepted for the professional graduate year.

One scene of the film catches Fred and Leigh on a stroll through the park. Fred says, "You know, Leigh, you've been given many lovely things. Don't negate them. There're God-given gifts, they are. Hang on to them."[38] Over the years, Franklin has done just that, and few can claim to have done it so superlatively. In no small part, this feat is due to a quality of the spirit — a quality of richness and joy that he has communicated to everyone he has ever touched. Lord Byron summed up the whole matter in a few simple words: "All who would win joy, must share it: happiness was born a twin." What Franklin has shared will never be forgotten.

Chapter Notes

Chapter 1

1. Franklin, interview with the author, 16 March 2006.

2. Franklin, quoted in Roslyn Sulcas, "Franklin Speaks Frankly," *Dance International,* Fall 1998, 12; Olga Maynard, "Frederic Franklin: A Life in the Theatre," *Dance Magazine,* June 1974, 44.

3. Heather Wisner, "Ballets Russes Reunion: One Last Grand Adventure," *Dance Magazine,* Sept. 2000, 62.

4. Franklin, interview with the author, 14 October 2005.

5. Transcript, interview of Franklin by Peter Conway, 1 May 1979, Jerome Robbins Dance Division, New York Public Library at Lincoln Center.

6. Franklin, interview with the author, 15 October 2005.

7. Franklin, interview with the author, 14 October 2005.

8. Maynard, "Frederic Franklin: A Life in the Theatre," 50.

9. Ibid.

10. Sulcas, "Franklin Speaks Frankly," 12.

11. "An Informal Interview with Frederic Franklin," *Dance Digest,* May 1958, 186.

12. Franklin, interview with the author, 14 October 2005.

13. Wisner, "Ballets Russes Reunion: One Last Grand Adventure," 62.

14. Maynard, "Frederic Franklin: A Life in the Theatre," 44.

15. Ibid.

16. Phyllis Rose, *Jazz Cleopatre* (New York: Doubleday, 1989), 140.

17. Ibid., 143.

18. Mistinguette, *Mistinguette: Queen of the Paris Night,* trans. Lucienne Hill (London: Electra, 1954), 33.

19. Ibid., 51.

20. Mistinguette, *Mistinguette and Her Confessions,* trans. and ed. Hubert Griffith (London: Hurst and Blackett Ltd., 1938), 272–74.

21. *Mistinguette: Queen of the Paris Night,* 133.

22. *Mistinguette and Her Confessions,* 69.

23. Franklin, interview with the author, 14 October 2005.

24. Rose, *Jazz Cleopatre,* 144.

25. Sulcas, "Franklin Speaks Frankly," 12.

26. Franklin, interview with the author, 14 October 2005.

27. Ibid.

28. Sulcas, "Franklin Speaks Frankly," 12.

29. Franklin, interview with the author, 15 March 2006.

30. Legat, quoted in ibid.

31. De Valois, quoted in Clive Barnes, "Frederic Franklin — An Anglo-Russian Prince," *Dance Magazine,* July 1994, 90.

32. Ibid., 46, 48.

33. Dolin, quoted in Maynard, "Frederic Franklin: A Life in the Theatre," 46.

34. Astafieva, quoted in Nadine Meisner, *The Independent* (London, England), 3 December 2004.

35. Anton Dolin, *Markova: Her Life and Her Art* (London: W.H. Allen, 1953), 156–57.

36. Markova, quoted in Mary Clarke, *The Sadler's Wells Ballet: A History and an Appreciation* (New York: Da Capo Press, 1977), 101.

37. Louise Jury, "Sex, Censorship and the Real Mrs. Henderson," *The Independent* (London, England), 12 November 2005.

38. Ibid.

39. Dolin, *Markova: Her Life and Her Art,* 183.

40. Dolin, quoted in Arthur Todd, "Ballet Blossoms in Washington, D.C.," *Dance and Dancers,* Oct. 1960, 19.

41. Dolin, quoted in Sulcas, "Franklin Speaks Frankly," 13.

42. Dolin, quoted in Todd, "Ballet Blossoms in Washington," 19.

43. Maynard, "Frederic Franklin: A Life in the Theatre," 48.

44. Franklin, quoted in Dolin, *Markova: Her Life and Her Art,* 191.

45. Franklin, interview with the author, 14 October 2005.

46. Dolin, *Markova: Her Life and Her Art,* 191.

47. Franklin, interview with the author, 15 October 2005.

48. Franklin, interview with the author, 14 October 2005.

49. "The Markova-Dolin Ballet," *Dancing Times,* Jan. 1938, 508.

50. Transcript, interview of Franklin by Conway, 2 May 1981.

51. "The Sitter-Out," *Dancing Times,* Dec. 1936, 262.

52. Cited in Jury, "Sex, Censorship and the Real Mrs. Henderson," *The Independent* (London, England), 12 November 2005.

53. Alicia Markova, *Giselle and I* (New York: Vanguard Press, Inc., 1960), 17.

54. Danilova, quoted by Franklin, interview with the author, 14 October 2005.

55. Sulcas, "Franklin Speaks Frankly," 13.

56. Ibid.

57. Franklin, interview with the author, 15 October 2005.

58. Transcript, interview of Franklin by Conway, 1 May 1979.

59. Dolin, *Markova: Her Life and Her Art,* 198.

Chapter 2

1. Transcript, interview of Danilova by Peter Conway, 1978–79, Jerome Robbins Dance Division, New York Public Library at Lincoln Center.

2. Arnold Haskell, "Balletomane's Log Book," *Dancing Times,* July 1937, 393.

3. Danilova, quoted in A.E. Twysden, *Alexandra Danilova* (New York: Kamin Dance Publishers, 1947), 107.

4. "Choreography to Court," *Time,* 30 August 1937, 27.

5. Heather Doughty, "The Choreographer in the Courtroom," proceedings, Dance History Scholars, Fifth Annual Conference, Harvard University, February 1982.

6. John Selby, "New Ballet," *Cincinnati Enquirer,* 6 February 1938.

7. "Julius Fleischmann Dies at 68," *New York Times,* 24 October 1968.

8. "Blum Ballet Sold to Company Here," *New York Times,* 20 November 1937.

9. Franklin, interview with the author, 14 October 2005.

10. Transcript, interview of Franklin by Conway, 27 October 1981.

11. Martin, "Massine and de Basil Companies Merged," *New York Times,* 24 April 1938; Richardson, "The Sitter Out," *Dancing Times,* June 1938, 267.

12. "Head of Ballet Russe Must Pay $52, 250 by Court Order," *New York Times,* 18 September 1947.

13. Leo Kersley, "The Ballet Russe," *Ballet Today,* Dec. 1961, 26.

14. Franklin and Massine, quoted in Heather Wisner, "Dressed and Impressed," *Dance Magazine,* Oct. 2002, 52.

15. Menuhin, "Dancing for Balanchine: 1933," *Ballet Review,* Fall 1988, 36; De Mille, *Dance to the Piper,* cited in Pamela Gaye, "A Conversation with Léonide Massine," *Dance Scope* 13, no. 4 (1979): 21.

16. George Zoritch, *Ballet Mystique: Behind the*

Glamour of the Ballet Russe (Mountain View: Cynara Editions, 2000), 109; transcript, interview of Franklin by Conway, 1 May 1979; Wilson, "The Italian Renaissance," *Ballet Annual* 15 (1961): 128.

17. P.W. Manchester, "A Conversation with P.W. Manchester," interview by David Vaughan and Dale Harris, *Ballet Review* 6, no. 3 (Fall 1977–Winter 1978): 82.

18. Lillian Moore, "Frederic Franklin," *Dancing Times,* Feb. 1939, 610.

19. Transcript, interview of Franklin by Monica Mosely and Mindy Aloff, 3 May 2000, Jerome Robbins Dance Division, New York Public Library at Lincoln Center; Franklin, interview with the author, 14 October 2005.

20. Edwin Denby, "Monte Carlo Minus Franklin," *New York Herald Tribune,* 13 September 1944.

21. Transcript, interview of Franklin by Mosely and Aloff, 13 August 2000.

22. Ibid.

23. Martin, "New Work Marks Opening of Ballet," *New York Times,* 13 October 1938.

24. Sulcas, "Franklin Speaks Frankly," *Dance International,* Fall 1998, 13.

25. Walter Terry, "Three Times a Star," *New York Herald Tribune,* 16 April 1942.

26. Franklin, interview with the author, 15 March 2006.

27. Léonide Massine, *My Life in Ballet* (London: Macmillan, 1968), 206.

28. Cited in Jack Anderson, *The One and Only: The Ballet Russe de Monte Carlo* (New York: Dance Horizons, 1981), 19–20.

29. Grace Robert, *The Borzoi Book of Ballets* (New York: Alfred A. Knopf, 1946), 279.

30. "Hands Seen on Scenery Spell Out Words — Gloria!" *Hartford Times,* 9 December 1948, cited in Anderson, *The One and Only,* 27.

31. Martin, "Massine's 'St. Francis,'" *New York Times,* 23 October 1938; Haskell, "Ballet Extremes," *The Bystander,* 10 August 1938.

32. Transcript, interview of Franklin by Conway, 27 October 1981.

33. Ibid.

34. Transcript, interview of Franklin by Mosely and Aloff, 21 December 2001.

35. Franklin, quoted in Sulcas, "Franklin Speaks Frankly," 15.

36. Martin, "Ballet Russe Returns," *New York Times,* 24 October 1941; transcript, interview of Franklin by Conway, 8 May 1979.

37. Transcript, interview of Franklin by Mosely and Aloff, 3 May 2000.

38. "Ballet Dancers' Duel Is Averted as Lifar Sails," *New York Herald Tribune,* 23 October 1938.

39. Franklin, quoted in Anderson, *The One and Only,* 26; Zoritch, *Ballet Mystique,* 87.

40. Dolin, *Markova: Her Life and Her Art,* 214.

41. "Ballet Dancers' Duel Is Averted as Lifar Sails," *New York Herald Tribune,* 23 October 1938.

42. Sol Hurok, *Sol Hurok Presents: A Memoir of the Dance World* (New York: Hermitage House, 1953), 134.

43. Transcript, interview of Franklin by Mosely and Aloff, 3 May 2000.

44. Dolin, *Markova: Her Life and Her Art,* 213.

45. Ruth Seinfel, "Big Man of Ballet," *Collier's,* 17

February 1940, 46; P.W. Manchester, "A Conversation with P.W. Manchester," 87.

46. Massine and Hurok, quoted in "Ballet Dancers' Duel Is Averted as Lifar Sails," *New York Herald Tribune*, 23 October, 1938.

47. Transcript, interview of Franklin by Mosely and Aloff, 9 May 2000.

48. Franklin, interview with the author, 14 October 2005.

49. Ibid.

50. 1939 Press Release, Ballet Russe de Monte Carlo, Franklin Clipping Files, Jerome Robbins Dance Division, New York Public Library at Lincoln Center; Terry, "Three Times a Star," *New York Herald Tribune*, 16 April 1942.

51. Terry, "Dance Is Hard Work," *New York Herald Tribune*, 25 February 1940.

52. Quoted material taken from 1939 Ballet Russe de Monte Carlo program notes, Jerome Robbins Dance Division, New York Public Library at Lincoln Center.

53. Lincoln Kirstein, "Dance in Review," *Dance*, Nov. 1940, 5.

54. Terry, "The Ballet," *New York Herald Tribune*, 29 September 1948.

55. Martin, "Markova Dances in 'Rouge et Noir,'" *New York Times*, 4 March 1949.

56. Léonide Massine, *My Life in Ballet*, 212.

57. Franklin, interview with the author, 14 October 2005.

58. Franklin, quoted in Sulcas, "Franklin Speaks Frankly," 13.

59. Franklin, interview with the author, 14 October 2005.

60. Ashton, quoted in David Vaughan, *Frederick Ashton and his Ballets* (New York: Alfred A. Knopf, 1977), 174.

61. Robert, *Borzoi Book of Ballets*, 108; Edwin Denby, *Looking at the Dance* (New York: Pellegrini and Cudahy, 1949), 217.

62. Vaughan, *Frederick Ashton and His Ballets*, 174.

63. Martin, "The Dance: Ballet Russe Permieres," *New York Times*, 5 November 1939; Terry, "Balanchine's 'Baiser de la Fée' Performed by Ballet Russe," *New York Herald Tribune*, 11 April 1940.

64. Dalí, quoted in Ramón Gómez de la Sena, *Dalí*, ed. Franco Paone, trans. Nicholas Fry and Elisabeth Evans (New York: William Morrow and Company, 1979), 227–28.

65. Transcript, interview of Franklin by Moseley and Aloff, 19 April 2000.

66. Martin, "Surrealism and Americana," *New York Times*, 19 November 1939.

67. Robert Lawrence, *Victor Book of Ballets and Ballet Music* (New York: Simon and Schuster, 1950), 48; Robert, *Borzoi Book of Ballets*, 35.

68. Martin McCall, "Novelties Form Prop of the Ballet Russe," *Daily Worker*, 18 November 1939; Martin, "Surrealism and Americana," *New York Times*, 19 November 1939.

69. Denby, *Looking at the Dance*, 218–19; Martin, "Surrealism and Americana," *New York Times*, 19 November 1939.

70. Robert, *Borzoi Book of Ballets*, 155.

71. "Ballet Theatre Can't Compete; Wants Ballet Russe Unionized," *New York Herald Tribune*, 22 March 1940.

72. Kirstein, quoted in ibid.

73. Denham, quoted in "Dancers of Ballet Russe Get $45 Minimum," *New York Herald Tribune*, 26 March 1940.

74. Platt, quoted in Wisner, "The Ballets Russes Reunion: One Last Grand Adventure," *Dance Magazine*, June 1974, 62.

75. Terry, "Theilade Work, 'Clouds,' Staged by Ballet Russe," *New York Herald Tribune*, 11 April 1940.

76. Franklin, quoted in Anderson, *The One and Only*, 78.

77. Stravinsky, quoted in Lawrence, *Victor Book of Ballets and Ballet Music*, 50.

78. Terry, "Balanchine's 'Baiser de la Fée' Performed by Ballet Russe," *New York Herald Tribune*, 11 April 1940; George Amberg, *Ballet: The Emergence of an American Art* (New York: Mentor Books, 1949), 82; Denby, *Looking at the Dance*, 220; Robert, *Borzoi Book of Ballets*, 41.

79. Press Release, Ballet Russe de Monte Carlo, "Frederic Franklin — Biographical Notes," Jerome Robbins Dance Division, New York Public Library at Lincoln Center.

80. Rosalyn Krokover, *The New Borzoi Book of Ballets* (New York: Alfred A. Knopf, 1956), 38.

81. Franklin, interview with the author, 14 October 2005.

82. Denby, *Looking at the Dance*, 222.

83. Sabin, "'Serenade' and 'Nutcracker' Seen," *Ballet*, Oct. 25, 1940, 15; Terry, "Russian Ballet," *New York Herald Tribune*, 27 October 1940; Albertina Vitak, *American Dancer*, Dec. 1940, 13.

84. Franklin, interview with the author, 14 October 2005.

85. Stravinsky, quoted in Lawrence, *Victor Book of Ballets and Ballet Music*, 324–25.

86. Denby, *Looking at the Dance*, 220.

87. Denby, *Looking at the Dance*, 220; Hering, quoted in Nancy Reynolds, *Repertory in Review: Forty Years of the New York City Ballet* (New York: Dial Press, 1977), 51.

88. Bruce Fleming, "Serenade," *International Dictionary of Ballet*, ed. Martha Bremser (Detroit: St. James Press, 1993), 1273.

89. Vitak, *American Dancer*, Dec. 1940, 13; Sabin, "'Serenade' and 'Nutcracker' Seen," *Ballet*, 25 October 1940, 16.

90. Franklin, interview with the author, 14 October 2005.

91. Ibid.

92. Sabin, "Ballet Russe de Monte Carlo Opens Season," *Ballet*, 25 October 1940, 16; Rhodes, "New York Letter," *Dancing Times*, Dec. 1940, 124.

93. Vitak, *American Dancer*, Dec. 1940, 13; Terry, "Russian Ballet," *New York Herald Tribune*, 27 October 1940; Irving Kolodin, "'New Yorker' Given to Gershwin Music," *New York Sun*, 19 October 1940.

94. Franklin, interview with the author, 14 October 2005.

95. Terry, "Russian Ballet," *New York Herald Tribune*, 27 October 1940; Vitak, *American Dancer*, Dec. 1940, 13.

96. Terry, "Russian Ballet," *New York Herald Tribune*, 27 October 1940.

97. "Tempo!" *Dance*, April 1940, 6.

98. Massine, *My Life in Ballet*, 218.

99. 1941 Program Notes, Ballet Russe de Monte Carlo, Jerome Robbins Dance Division, New York Public Library at Lincoln Center.

100. Cyril Beaumont, *Supplement to the Complete Book of Ballets* (London: Putnam, 1952), 65.

101. Sabin, "Saratoga," *Dance Observer*, Nov. 1941, 124.

102. Franklin, interview with the author, 14 October 2005.

103. Sabin, "Saratoga," *Dance Observer*, Nov. 1941, 124; Terry, "The Week's Debuts," *New York Herald Tribune*, 26 October 1941; Henry Simon, "'Saratoga' Misses the Spitoon," *P.M.*, 20 October 1941.

104. Transcript, interview of Franklin by Mosely and Aloff, 13 August 2001.

105. Terry, "Ballets and Books," *New York Herald Tribune*, 19 October 1941.

106. Chujoy, "Dance in Review," *Dance*, Dec. 1941, 24; Terry, "Ballets and Books," *New York Herald Tribune*, 19 October 1941.

107. Martin, "Monte Carlo Ballet Gives Way to de Basil," *New York Times*, 3 November 1940; Terry, "Season Closed by Ballet Russe de Monte Carlo," *New York Herald Tribune*, 4 November 1940.

108. Hurok, *Sol Hurok Presents: A Memoir of the Dance World*, 137.

109. Terry, "Monte Carlo Case," *New York Herald Tribune*, 19 April 1942.

110. Transcript, interview of Franklin by Conway, 1 May 1979.

111. Terry, "Three Times a Star," *New York Herald Tribune*, 16 April 1942.

112. Danilova, quoted in transcript, interview of Franklin by Mosely and Aloff, 3 May 2000.

113. Twysden, *Alexandra Danilova*, 127.

114. Terry, "Screen Ballet," *New York Herald Tribune*, 11 January 1942.

115. Massine, *My Life in Ballet*, 221.

Chapter 3

1. Carol Easton, *No Intermissions: The Life of Agnes de Mille* (Boston: Little Brown and Company, 1996), 150.

2. Agnes de Mille, *Dance to the Piper* (Boston: Little Brown and Company, 1952), 204.

3. Ibid., 207.

4. Ibid., 212.

5. George Amberg, *Ballet: The Emergence of an American Art* (New York: Mentor Books, 1949), 229.

6. De Mille, *Dance to the Piper*, 217.

7. Ibid., 218.

8. Ibid.

9. Ibid., 208.

10. Zoritch, *Ballet Mystique*, 105.

11. De Mille, *Dance to the Piper*, 208.

12. Ibid., 208–09.

13. De Mille, quoted by Franklin, interview with the author, 14 October 2005.

14. De Mille, *Dance to the Piper*, 219.

15. Franklin, quoted in ibid., 221.

16. Ibid., 227.

17. Ibid., 232.

18. Ibid.

19. Ibid., 233.

20. Martin, "The Dance: A New Period?" *New York Times*, 1 November 1942.

21. Robert Lawrence, "The Ballet," *New York Herald Tribune*, 20 May 1943.

22. Robert Wahis, "The City Center's Ballet Is as Pure as Its 'Snow Maiden,'" *New York Daily News*, 9 March 1945.

23. Denby, "Pleasures of Familiarity," *New York Herald Tribune*, 15 April 1944; Martin, "The Dance: A New Period?" *New York Times*, 1 November 1942.

24. Franklin, interview with the author, 15 March 2006.

25. Martin, "The Dance: Ballet Russe," *New York Times*, 30 May 1943.

26. De Mille, *Dance to the Piper*, 228.

27. Denham, quoted in Anderson, *The One and Only*, 85.

28. Martin, "The Dance: A Flock of Premieres," *New York Times*, 22 August 1943; Sabin, "Reviews of the Month," *Dance Observer*, May 1944, 51; Denby, "The Dance," *New York Herald Tribune*, 11 April 1944.

29. Sabin, "Reviews of the Month," *Dance Observer*, May 1944, 51; Robert Garland, "Ballet Russe Offers 'Red Poppy,'" *New York Journal-American*, 14 April 1944.

30. Martin, "The Dance: A Flock of Premieres," *New York Times*, 22 August 1943; Sabin, "Reviews of the Month," *Dance Observer*, May 1944, 51.

31. Franklin, interview with the author, 14 October 2005.

32. Denby, "Angels and Gypsies," *New York Herald Tribune*, 11 April 1944; Martin, "The Dance: A Flock of Premieres," *New York Times*, 22 August 1943.

33. Franklin, interview with the author, 14 October 2005.

34. Barzel, "Season in Review," *Dance News*, Nov. 1943, 3; Sabin, "Reviews of the Month," *Dance Observer*, May 1944, 51; Denby, "Angels and Gypsies," *New York Herald Tribune*, 11 April 1944.

35. Transcript, interview of Franklin by Moseley and Aloff, 19 April 2000.

36. Franklin, interview with the author, 14 October 2005.

37. Edwin Denby, "Angels and Gypsies," *New York Herald Tribune*, 11 April 1944.

38. Transcript, interview of Franklin by Mosely and Aloff, 2 May 2000.

39. "Youskevitch in Navy," *Dance News*, Feb. 1944, 3.

40. Denby, "The Monte Carlo Now," *New York Herald Tribune*, 25 March 1945.

41. Garland, "Sol and Butch to Vie for Ballet of Ballets," *New York Journal-American*, 27 March 1944; "A Deplorable Situation," *Dance News*, April 1944, 2.

42. Martin, "The Dance: More in Sorrow," *New York Times*, 7 May 1944.

43. Danilova, quoted by Franklin, interview with the author, 14 October 2005.

44. Ann Barzel, "Lancashire Lad to Ballet Master," *Dance News*, Feb. 1946, 36.

45. A.E. Twysden, "Ballet Russe on Tour," *Dance*, April 1945, 16.

46. Zide, quoted in Anderson, *The One and Only,* 206; Arthur Todd, "A New Company Gets a Washington Inauguration," *Dance Magazine,* March 1963, 38.

47. Danielian and Toye, quoted in Arthur Todd, "Ballet Blossoms in Washington, D.C.," *Dance and Dancers,* Oct. 1960, 18.

48. Franklin, quoted in Gary Parks, "Bringing Remembrances of Things Past to Ballet," *USA Today,* 4 June 1997.

49. Martin, "City Center Opens Season of Ballet," *New York Times,* 11 September 1944; Barzel, "The Monte Carlo and Ballet Theatre Compared," *Ballet Annual* 1 (1945).

50. Barzel, "The Monte Carlo and Ballet Theatre Compared," *Ballet Annual* 1 (1945).

51. De Mille, quoted in Sulcas, "Franklin Speaks Frankly," *Dance International,* Fall 1998, 11.

52. Cited in Anderson, *The One and Only,* 201.

53. Olin Downes, "The Dance vs. Grieg," *New York Times,* 29 October 1944; Denby, *Looking at the Dance,* 393.

54. Denby, "Balanchine's 'Danses Concertantes,'" *New York Herald Tribune,* 17 September 1944.

55. Franklin, interview with the author, 14 October 2005.

56. Denby, *Looking at the Dance,* 104; Moore, "Two New Balanchine Ballets," *Dancing Times,* Nov. 1944, 60.

57. Martin, "City Center Opens Season of Ballet," *New York Times,* 11 September 1944; Chujoy, "Ballet Russe de Monte Carlo," *Dance News,* Oct. 1944, 7.

58. Martin, "Troupe Restores Four Dances," *New York Times,* 23 February 1945.

59. Franklin, interview with the author, 14 October 2005.

60. Denby, *Looking at the Dance,* 83–84.

61. Denby, *Looking at the Dance,* 83–84; Chujoy, "Ballet Russe de Monte Carlo," *Dance News,* Oct. 1944, 7.

62. Denby, "Scallions to the Management," *New York Herald Tribune,* 25 September 1944.

63. Chujoy, "The Season in Review," *Dance News,* 9 March 1945, 9.

64. Denby, "The Monte Carlo Now," *New York Herald Tribune,* 25 March 1945.

65. John Martin, *Ruth Page: An Intimate Biography* (New York: Marcel Dekker, Inc., 1977), 111.

66. Zoritch, *Ballet Mystique,* 179–80.

67. Chapman, quoted in Anderson, *The One and Only,* 234.

68. Franklin, interview with the author, 14 October 2005.

69. Ibid.

70. Martin, *Ruth Page,* 111.

71. Ibid.

72. Ibid., 112.

73. Cited in ibid., 113.

74. Franklin, interview with the author, 14 October 2005.

75. Ibid.

76. Denby, *Looking at the Dance,* 106; Martin, "'Frankie, Johnny' Revived by Ballet," *New York Times,* 1 March 1945.

77. Denby, *Looking at the Dance,* 108.

78. Martin, "Balanchine Dance Is Given at Center," *New York Times,* 8 March 1945.

79. Franklin, interview with the author, 14 October 2005.

80. Denby "Lovely Incident," *New York Herald Tribune,* 15 March 1945.

81. Martin, "The Dance: Going and Coming," *New York Times,* 25 March 1945; Denby, "Franklin's New Classicism," *New York Herald Tribune,* 17 September 1945.

82. Chujoy, "Dance in Review," *Dance News,* Oct. 1945, 2.

83. Transcript, interview of Franklin by Mosely and Aloff, 21 December 2001.

84. Balanchine, quoted in ibid., 26 April 2000.

85. Terry, "World Premiere," *New York Herald Tribune,* 28 February 1946; Martin, "Balanchine Dance in World Premiere," *New York Times,* 28 February 1946; Denby, *Looking at the Dance,* 199.

86. Terry, "World Premiere," *New York Herald Tribune,* 28 February 1946.

87. Danilova, quoted in "Ballet's Man of Memory," *Boston Globe,* 6 April 1988.

88. Transcript, interview of Franklin by Mosely and Aloff, 3 May 2000.

89. Martin, "Ballet Russe Finds Spring Very Early," *New York Times,* 17 February 1947.

90. Martin, "'Raymonda' Given by Ballet Russe," *New York Times,* 13 March 1946; Moore, "American Notes," *Dancing Times,* Nov. 1946, 69.

91. Terekhov, quoted in Wisner, "The Ballets Russe Reunion: One Last Grand Adventure," *Dance Magazine,* Sept. 2000, 62.

92. Franklin, interview with the author, 14 October 2005.

93. De Mille, *Dance to the Piper,* 222.

94. Franklin, interview with the author, 15 March 2006.

95. De Mille, *Dance to the Piper,* 223.

96. Franklin, interview with the author, 15 March 2006.

97. De Mille, *Dance to the Piper,* 223.

98. Baronova, quoted in Wisner, "Ballets Russes Reunion: One Last Grand Adventure," 62.

99. Zoritch, *Ballet Mystique,* 92.

100. De Mille, *Dance to the Piper,* 224.

101. Danilova, quoted in Anderson, *The One and Only,* 246.

102. Platt, cited in Wisner, "Ballets Russes Reunion: One Last Grand Adventure," 62.

103. De Mille, *Dance to the Piper,* 221.

104. Larkin, cited in Wisner, "Ballets Russes Reunion: One Last Grand Adventure," 63.

105. Zoritch, *Ballet Mystique,* 94–95.

106. Transcript, interview of Franklin by Mosely and Aloff, 2 May 2000.

107. Franklin, interview with the author, 14 October 2005.

108. Cited in Anderson, *The One and Only,* 248.

109. Franklin, quoted in Norman Wilner, *Eye Weekly,* 8 December 2005.

110. "Ballet's Man of Memory," *Boston Globe,* 6 April 1988.

Chapter 4

1. Denby, *Looking at the Dance,* 198; Amberg, *Ballet: The Emergence of an American Art,* 74.

2. Cited in Martin, *Ruth Page*, 120.

3. Terry, "The Ballet," *New York Herald Tribune*, 24 February 1947.

4. Amberg, *Ballet: The Emergence of an American Art*, 66.

5. Martin, "The Dance: Sampler," *New York Times*, 9 March 1947; Martin, "Dance Experiment at the City Center," *New York Times*, 5 March 1947; Chujoy, "The Season in Review," *Dance News*, April 1947, 5.

6. Anderson, *The One and Only*, 133.

7. Martin, "The Dance: Premieres," *New York Times*, 21 September 1947.

8. Martin, "The Dance: Honor Roll," *New York Times*, 29 August 1943.

9. Martin, "Some Words in Praise of Ruthanna Boris," *New York Times*, 2 March 1947.

10. Transcript, interview of Franklin by Mosely and Aloff, 21 December 2001.

11. Terry, "The Ballet," *New York Herald Tribune*, 11 September 1947; Martin, "The Dance: Premieres," *New York Times*, 21 September 1947.

12. Franklin, interview with the author, 15 October 2005.

13. Cited in Anderson, *The One and Only*, 136.

14. Amberg, *Ballet: The Emergence of an American Art*, 65; Martin, "Miss Boris Stars in Caton Ballet," *New York Times*, 13 September 1947.

15. Robert F. Martin, *Hero of the Heartland* (Bloomington: Indiana University Press, 2002), 84.

16. Franklin, quoted in Ruth Page, *Page by Page*, ed. Andrew Mark Wentink (New York: Dance Horizons, 1978), 131.

17. Danilova, quoted in ibid., 103.

18. Page, *Page by Page*, 131.

19. Janet Light, "Frederic Franklin's Extraordinary Memory," *Ballet News* 1, no. 8 (Feb. 1983): 29.

20. Martin, *Ruth Page*, 131.

21. Terry, "Dance: Ballet Looks Ahead," *New York Herald Tribune*, 13 March 1949.

22. Franklin, interview with the author, 15 October 2005.

23. Page, *Page by Page*, 184.

24. Transcript, interview of Franklin by Mosely and Aloff, 9 May 2000.

25. Terry, "The Dance: A Refreshed Ballet Russe," *New York Herald Tribune*, 10 October 1948.

26. Transcript, interview of Franklin by Conway, 22 October 1981.

27. Martin, "Ballet Russe Opens Its Season," *New York Times*, 20 September 1948.

28. Transcript, interview of Franklin by Conway, 22 October 1981.

29. Martin, "Ballet Russe Opens Its Season," *New York Times*, 20 September 1948; Terry, "The Dance: A Refreshed Ballet Russe," *New York Herald Tribune*, 10 October 1948.

30. Franklin, interview with the author, 15 October 2005.

31. Ibid.

32. Ibid.

33. Shearer, quoted in transcript, interview with Mosely and Aloff, 9 May 2000.

34. De Valois, quoted in transcript, interview with Conway, 22 October 1981.

35. Michael Powell, *A Life in Movies* (New York: Knopf, 1987), 242.

36. Franklin, interview with the author, 15 October 2005.

37. Transcript, interview of Franklin by Conway, 22 October 1981.

38. Franklin, interview with the author, 15 October 2005.

39. De Valois, quoted by Franklin, interview with the author, 15 October 2005.

40. Shearer, quoted in Meredith Daneman, *Margot Fonteyn* (New York: Viking Penguin, 2004), 236.

41. Nerina, quoted in ibid., 236–37.

42. Transcript, interview of Franklin by Conway, 22 October 1981.

43. Martin, "'Graduation Ball' Revived by Ballet," *New York Times*, 22 September 1949.

44. Terry, "The Ballet," *New York Herald Tribune*, 12 April 1950.

45. Transcript, interview of Franklin by Mosely and Aloff, 9 May 2000.

46. Chujoy, "The Season in Review," *Dance News*, May 1950, 5; Hering, "Ballet Russe de Monte Carlo," *Dance*, June 1950, 4.

47. Transcript, interview of Franklin by Mosely and Aloff, 9 May 2000.

48. Transcript, interview of Franklin by Conway, 22 October 1981.

49. Franklin, interview with the author, 15 March 2006.

50. Franklin, quoted in Wendy Perron, "Fokine Family 'Nutcrackers,'" *Dance Magazine*, Dec. 2002, 42.

51. "Chauviré Great Giselle," *Montreal Star*, 31 March 1932.

52. Transcript, interview of Franklin by Conway, 22 October 1981.

53. Transcript, interview of Franklin by Mosely and Aloff, 2 May 2000 and 21 December 2001.

54. P.W. Manchester, "A Conversation with P.W. Manchester," 114.

55. "News of Dance and Dancers," *Dance*, August 1952, 1.

56. Terry, "Ballet at the Stadium," *New York Herald Tribune*, 21 July 1952.

57. Terry, "Ballet at the Stadium," *New York Herald Tribune*, 21 July 1952; Kastendieck, "Night of Ballet at the Stadium," *New York Sun*, 21 July 1952.

58. "On Tour," *Dance*, Nov. 1952, 6.

59. Martin, "Ballet Company Stages 'Streetcar,'" *New York Times*, 9 December 1952.

60. Franklin, interview with the author, 15 October 2005.

61. Horst, quoted in Herbert M. Simpson, "Valerie Bettis," *International Encyclopedia of Dance*, ed. Taryn Benbow-Pfalzgraf (Detroit: St. James Press, 1998), 54.

62. Franklin, interview with the author, 15 October 2005.

63. Terry, "Slavenska-Franklin Ballet," *New York Herald Tribune*, 9 December 1952.

64. Martin, "Ballet Company Stages 'Streetcar,'" *New York Times*, 9 December 1952.

65. Franklin, interview with the author, 15 October 2005.

66. Martin, "Ballet Company Stages 'Streetcar,'" *New York Times*, 9 December 1952; Terry, "Slavenska-

Franklin Ballet," *New York Herald Tribune*, 9 December 1952; Claudia Cassidy, "On the Aisle," *Chicago Daily Tribune*, 24 November 1952.

67. Krokover, *The New Borzoi Book of Ballets*, 250; Martin, "Ballet Company Stages 'Streetcar,'" *New York Times*, 9 December 1952.

68. Coleman, "'Mlle Fifi' a Delightful New Ballet at Century," *New York Daily Mirror*, 10 December 1952.

69. Terry, "Slavenska-Franklin Ballet," *New York Herald Tribune*, 9 December 1952.

70. Terry, "Slavenska-Franklin Ballet," *New York Herald Tribune*, 11 December 1952.

71. Martin, "Slavenska's Ballet Has Local Premiere," *New York Times*, 11 December 1952; Terry, "Slavenska-Franklin Ballet," *New York Herald Tribune*, 11 December 1952.

72. Franklin, interview with the author, 15 October 2005.

73. Ibid.

74. Franklin, quoted in John Martin, "Slavenska, Danilova, Franklin," *New York Times*, 6 June 1953.

75. Franklin, interview with the author, 15 March 2006.

76. Ibid.

77. Franklin, quoted in "Mia Slavenska — Ballerina Fearless on Stage and in Life," *Los Angeles Times*, 10 October 2002.

78. Transcript, interview of Franklin by Conway, 22 October 1981.

79. Tallchief, quoted in Jean Battey Lewis, "Tallchief: A Ballerina in Step with Balanchine," *The Washington Times*, 1 December 1996.

80. Manchester, "The Season in Review," *Dance News*, Nov. 1954, 7; Martin, "The Dance: Summing Up," *New York Times*, 5 May 1957.

81. Manchester, "The Season in Review," 7; Barzel, "Ballets Down the Drain," *Ballet*, Fall 1963, 78; Hering, "Reviews," *Dance*, Dec. 1954, 57.

82. Transcript, interview of Franklin by Mosely and Aloff, 9 May 2000.

83. Anderson, *The One and Only*, 158–59.

84. "Alonso, Youskevitch Move to Ballet Russe de Monte Carlo," *Dance News*, June 1955, 1.

85. Youskevitch, quoted in John Gruen, "Igor Youskevitch: Part Two," *Dance Magazine*, May 1982, 57.

86. Franklin, interview with the author, 15 October 2005.

87. Youskevitch, quoted in John Gruen, "Igor Youskevitch: Part Two," 58.

88. "Novak to Leave Ballet Russe," *Dance News*, Nov. 1955, 3; "Novak Will Not Leave Ballet Russe," *Dance News*, Jan. 1956, 4.

89. Doris Hering, "Ballet Russe de Monte Carlo," *Dance Magazine*, Dec. 1958, 5.

90. Transcript, interview of Franklin by Conway, 22 October 1981.

91. Terry, "Ballet Summary: Phoenix Premieres," *New York Herald Tribune*, 12 May 1957.

92. Barzel, "Ballet Russe de Monte Carlo," *Dance News*, Feb. 1957, 8.

93. Anderson, *The One and Only*, 166.

94. Denham, quoted in Walter Terry, "Met Curtain Rung Down as Ballet Runs Overtime," *New York Herald Tribune*, 2 May 1957.

95. Martin, "The Dance: Summing Up," *New York Times*, 5 May 1957.

96. Transcript, interview of Franklin by Conway, 22 October 1981.

97. Ibid.

98. Franklin, interview with the author, 15 October 2005.

99. Ibid.

100. Hering, "Ballet Russe de Monte Carlo," *Dance*, December 1958, 25.

101. Hering, "Spring Surge," *Dance Magazine*, June 1962, 34; Clive Barnes, "Dance: Washington's Stage Shortage," *New York Times*, 22 November 1966.

102. "Ballet Russe to Sit Out Season," *Dance Magazine*, Sept. 1962, 4.

103. Anderson, *The One and Only*, 184.

Chapter 5

1. McDowell, quoted in Arthur Todd, "Ballet Blossoms in Washington, D.C.," *Dance and Dancers*, Oct. 1960, 18.

2. Franklin, quoted in ibid.

3. Transcript, interview of Franklin by Conway, 22 October 1981.

4. Janet Mclean, "New Ballet Company — No. 3 — Emerges in Nation's Capital," (Meridean) *Mississippi Star*, 8 August 1962.

5. Transcript, interview of Franklin by Conway, 27 October 1981.

6. Franklin and Riddell, quoted in Arthur Todd, "Ballet Blossoms in Washington, D.C.," 39; and in Arthur Todd, "A New Company Gets a Washington Inauguration," *Dance Magazine*, March 1963, 66.

7. Transcript, interview of Franklin by Conway, 22 October 1981; Franklin, interview with the author, 15 October 2005.

8. Todd, "A New Company Gets a Washington Inauguration," 66.

9. Ibid., 39.

10. Ibid., 38.

11. Franklin, interview with the author, 15 October 2005.

12. Todd, "A New Company gets a Washington Inauguration," 66.

13. Maynard, "Frederic Franklin: A Life in the Theatre," 56.

14. Transcript, interview of Franklin by Conway, 27 October 1981.

15. Ibid.

16. Franklin quoting Massine in Sulcas, "Franklin Speaks Frankly," 15.

17. Danilova, quoted in Valerie Gladstone, "Resetting a Masterwork," *Newsday*, 30 May 1997.

18. Sulcas, "Franklin Speaks Frankly," 15.

19. Franklin, quoted in Jerry Stein, "Classical Fantasy 'Coppelia' Is Ideal Ballet for Children," *Cincinnati Post*, 14 March 1996.

20. Franklin, interview with the author, 15 October 2005.

21. "National Ballet Offers 'Coppelia,'" *New York Times*, 28 December 1964.

22. Barnes, "Dance: Washington's Stage Shortage," *New York Times*, 22 November 1966.

23. Franklin, quoted in Todd, "A New Company Gets a Washington Inauguration," 38–39.

24. "Area News from Washington, D.C.," *Dance Magazine*, May 1961, 71.

25. Franklin, quoted in Judith Martin, "Challenges Ballet Theatre Claim," *Washington D.C. Post and Times Herald*, 7 November 1962.

26. *International Encyclopedia of Dance*, s.v. "American Ballet Theatre," Doris Hering, 70.

27. William Ausman, interview with the author, 7 September 2006.

28. Franklin, interview with the author, 15 October 2005.

29. Ibid.

30. Transcript, interview of Franklin by Conway, 27 October 1981.

31. Ausman, interview with the author, 15 October 2005.

32. Barnes, "Dance: A Visit by the National Ballet," *New York Times*, 7 March 1966.

33. Ibid.

34. Barnes, "Dance: National Ballet Opens City Center Season," *New York Times*, 28 March 1967.

35. Terry, "Ballet from Boston, Washington, New York," *Saturday Review*, 11 Nov. 1967, 80–81.

36. Franklin, quoted in "Franklin In New Role," *The Philadelphia Inquirer*, 6 April 1969.

37. Terry, "World of Dance," *Saturday Review*, 1 Nov. 1969, 46.

38. Franklin, quoted in Maynard, "Frederic Franklin: A Life in the Theatre," 56.

39. Stevenson, quoted in Victoria Huckenpahler, "Give the Public What Sells, But...," *Dance Magazine*, May 1972, 14.

40. Mason, "The National Ballet with Margot Fonteyn," *Dance Magazine*, Dec. 1970, 77.

41. Ibid.

42. Lewis, "The National Ballet in 'Cinderella,'" *Dance Magazine*, June 1970, 22.

43. Anonymous dancer, quoted in Huckenpahler, "Give the Public What Sells, But...," 15.

44. Stevenson, quoted in ibid.

45. Anderson, "Reviews," *Dance Magazine*, Feb. 1972, 22.

46. Stevenson, quoted in Huckenpahler, "Give the Public What Sells, But...," 16.

47. Ibid.

48. Transcript, interview of Franklin by Conway, 27 October 1981.

49. Ibid.

50. Ibid.

51. Ibid.

52. Ibid.

53. Franklin, quoted in Maynard, "Frederic Franklin: A Life in the Theatre," 56.

54. Transcript, interview of Franklin by Conway, 27 October 1981.

55. Franklin, quoted in Maynard, "Frederic Franklin: A Life in the Theatre," 56.

56. Pamela Gaye, "Reviews," *Dance Magazine*, Feb. 1974, 64.

57. "Washington's Money-Troubled National Ballet Folds," *Chicago Sun-Times*, 13 June 1974.

58. Transcript, interview of Franklin by Conway, 27 October 1981.

Chapter 6

1. Anderson, "'Giselle' in Pittsburgh," *Dance Magazine*, Dec. 1974, 22.

2. Petrov, quoted in "Presstime News," *Dance Magazine*, Oct. 1974, 8.

3. Pittsburgh Ballet Theatre News Release, 14 November 1975, Jerome Robbins Dance Division, New York Public Library at Lincoln Center.

4. Transcript, interview of Franklin by Conway, 27 October 1981.

5. Belmar, "Oakland Ballet Broadens Horizons," *Dance Magazine*, Feb. 2002, 70.

6. Lili Cockerille Livingston, "Tulsa Ballet Theatre's Ballet Russe Renaissance," *Dance Magazine*, Feb. 1986, 62.

7. Lili Cockerille Livingston, "Tulsa and the Italian Tornado," *Dance Magazine*, Sept. 1999, 71–72.

8. Marcello Angelini, interview with the author, 8 August 2006.

9. Franklin, interview with the author, 15 March 2006.

10. Angelini, quoted in Livingston, "Tulsa and the Italian Tornado," 72.

11. Angelini, interview with the author, 8 August 2006.

12. Heather Wisner, "Russian Revolution Takes Ohio," *Dance Magazine*, Oct. 2002, 18.

13. Terry, "World of Dance" *Saturday Review*, 10 May 1969, 38.

14. Ibid.

15. Transcript, interview of Franklin by Conway, 27 October 1981.

16. Franklin, quoted in Janet Light, "Frederic Franklin's Extraordinary Memory," *Ballet News*, 1, no. 8 (Feb. 1983): 30.

17. Marks, quoted in Sheryl Flatow, "Full-Length Ballets," *Dance Magazine*, July 1995, 40–41.

18. Jackson, "Dance Theatre of Harlem," *Dance Magazine*, August 1990, 60.

19. Franklin, interview with the author, 15 March 2006.

20. Richard Philp, "Kickoff," *Dance Magazine*, June 1990, 7.

21. Jerry Stein, "Cincinnati Ballet Meets Hard Times," *Dance Magazine*, Nov. 1990, 16.

22. Anastos, quoted in Jackson, "Dance Theatre of Harlem," *Dance Magazine*, August 1990, 26.

23. Brunner, quoted in Jerry Stein, "Anastos Resigns: Ballet Seeks Director," *Cincinnati Post*, 24 May 1996.

24. Franklin, interview with the author, 15 October 2005.

25. Marcia Siegel, *At the Vanishing Point* (New York: Saturday Review Press, 1968), 1.

26. Windreich, "Capturing the Dance," *World and I*, 1 November 2002.

27. Ibid.

28. Reynolds, quoted in Joseph H. Mazo, "Reynolds Endows Balanchine Foundation," *Dance Magazine*, Dec. 1994, 37.

29. Reynolds, interview with the author, 27 June 2006.

30. Windreich, "Capturing the Dance," *World and I*, 1 November 2002.

31. Reynolds, interview with the author, 27 June 2006.

32. Barnes, "Frederic Franklin Honored at the Cincinnati Ballet," *Dance Magazine*, Feb. 2003, 51.

33. Cited in Wisner, "Russian Revolution Takes Ohio," *Dance Magazine*, Oct. 2002, 18.

34. Barnes, "The Devil Returns in Ashton's Lost Work," *The Independent* (London, England), 12 November 2002.

35. Franklin, interview with the author, 15 October 2005.

36. Cited in Marina Brown, "A Legacy in Dispute," *Dance Magazine*, Dec. 2002, 44–46.

37. Ibid.

38. Victoria Morgan, interview with the author, 6 August 2006.

39. Light, "Frederic Franklin's Extraordinary Memory," 30.

40. Wilt, quoted in Jerry Stein, "Ballet Poised for New Season," *The Cincinnati Post*, 5 October 2004.

41. Stein, "Ballet Opens 42nd Season on a High," *The Cincinnati Post*, 9 October 2004; Anderson, "The Cincinnati Ballet," *Dance Magazine*, Jan. 2005, 195.

42. Morgan, interview with the author, 6 August 2006

Chapter 7

1. Mitchell, quoted in Ralph Backlund, "From a Garage on West 152nd Street," *Smithsonian*, 28 July 1988, 31–32.

2. Tobias, "Dance Theatre of Harlem," *Dance Magazine*, April 1980, 57.

3. Ibid.; Croce, "Shuffling Cards of Identity," *The New Yorker*, 28 Jan. 1980, 79.

4. Shelton, "Michel Fokine's 'Schéhérazade,'" *Dance Magazine*, Jan. 1981, 76.

5. Ibid.

6. Ibid.

7. Vaughan, "Reviews," *Dance Magazine*, April 1981, 32.

8. Franklin, quoted in Shelton, "Michel Fokine's 'Schéhérazade,'" 78.

9. Shook and Michell, quoted in Vaughan, "Reviews," *Dance Magazine*, April 1981, 32.

10. De Valois, quoted by Franklin, interview with the author, 15 October 2005.

11. Vaughan, "Reviews," *Dance Magazine*, April 1981, 30; Croce, "Dancing," *The New Yorker*, 26 Jan. 1981, 100.

12. Gruen, "Dancevision," *Dance Magazine*, Jan. 1987, 90.

13. Ibid.

14. Johnson, quoted in Robert Johnson, "DTH Brings a Dramatic Revival to the State Theatre," *Dance Magazine*, March 1994, 15.

15. Johnson, quoted in Marilyn Hunt, "Virginia Johnson As," *Dance Magazine*, Oct. 1990, 40.

16. Mitchell, quoted in Tobi Tobias, "Arthur Mitchell and the Dance Theatre of Harlem," *Dance Magazine*, Jan. 1982, 74.

17. Mitchell, quoted in Valerie Gladstone, "DTH Celebrates the Big 30," *Dance Magazine*, Oct. 1999, 71.

18. Sheryl Flatow, "True to the Spirit," *Ballet News*, Sept. 1984, 11.

19. Ibid.

20. Mitchell, quoted in ibid., 12.

21. Mitchell, quoted in ibid., 12.

22. Jennie Schulman, "DTH in World Premiere," *Back Stage*, 22 September 2000.

23. Peter J. Rosenwald, "Creole 'Giselle,'" *Dance Magazine*, Sept. 1984, 58.

24. Michell, quoted in Flatow, "True to the Spirit," 13.

25. Bruhn, quoted in George Balanchine and Francis Mason, *Balanchine's Complete Book of Ballets* (New York: Doubleday and Company, 1977), 272.

26. Franklin, quoted in Flatow, "True to the Spirit," 13.

27. Mitchell, quoted in ibid., 12–13; Anderson, "The Dance: 'Giselle,'" *New York Times*, 14 March 1987.

28. Franklin, quoted in Flatow, "True to the Spirit," 12.

29. Ibid., 13.

30. Sarah Kaufman, "Harlem's Lifeless 'Creole Giselle,'" *The Washington Post*, 24 May 2001.

31. Franklin, quoted in Flatow, "True to the Spirit," 14.

32. Johnson, quoted in ibid.

33. Tobias, "Love's Young Dream," *New York*, 15 Oct. 1984, 77; Anderson, "The Dance: 'Giselle,'" *New York Times*, 14 March 1987.

34. Cosby, quoted in "D.T.H.," *The New Yorker*, 28 Dec. 1987, 35.

35. Tobias, "Dance," *New York*, 18 July 1988, 47.

36. Garafola, "DTH at 30," *The Nation*, 3 Jan. 2000, 33.

37. Mitchell, quoted in Valerie Gladstone, "Dance Theatre of Harlem; Crashing through Barriers," *Dance Magazine*, March 1997, 72.

38. Ibid.

39. Ibid., 73.

40. Jackson, "Dance Theatre of Harlem," *Dance Magazine*, Oct. 1996, 106.

41. Franklin, interview with the author, 15 October 2005; transcript, interview of Franklin by Conway, 27 October 1981.

42. Mitchell, quoted in Paul Ben-Itzak and Valerie Gladstone, "Presstime News," *Dance Magazine*, April 1997, 48.

43. Solomons Jr., "Passionate Points," *Dance Magazine*, Dec. 2000, 80; Kaufman, "Harlem's Lifeless 'Creole Giselle,'" *The Washington Post*, 24 May 2001.

44. Kaufman, "Harlem's Lifeless 'Creole Giselle,'" *The Washington Post*, 24 May 2001; Jackson, "Dance Theatre of Harlem," 106.

45. Kisselgoff, "Dance Theatre of Harlem," *New York Times*, 14 March 1996.

46. Mitchell, quoted in Zita Allen, "'Anonymous' Angel Saves Dance Theatre of Harlem," *New York Amsterdam News*, 8 December 2004.

47. Kaiser, quoted in Verena Dobnik, *AP Worldstream*, 7 December 2004.

48. Ausman, interview with the author, 15 October 2005.

49. Johnson, quoted in Joseph Carmen, "Harlem Troupe Faces Uncertain Future," *Dance Magazine*, Dec. 2004, 20.

50. Franklin, quoted in Sulcas, "Franklin Speaks Frankly," 15.

51. Ibid.

52. Franklin, interview with the author, 15 October 2005.

53. Yan Chen, quoted in Valerie Gladstone, "Resetting a Masterwork," *Newsday*, 30 May 1997.

54. Franklin and Ausman, interview with the author, 15 October 2005.

55. Franklin, quoted in Sulcas, "Franklin Speaks Frankly," 15.

56. Dunning, "Making a Classic Gentler and Warmer," *New York Times*, 3 June 1997; Gold, "'Coppelia,' ABT's Staging of Guys and Dolls," *Newsday*, 4 June 1997; Thom, "American Ballet Theatre," *Dance Magazine*, Oct. 1997, 89.

57. Franklin, quoted in Gladstone, "Resetting a Masterwork," *Newsday*, 30 May 1997.

58. Transcript, interview of Franklin by Mosely and Aloff, 26 April 2000.

59. Gerelick, "A Comic but Stiff Toy Story," *Newsday*, 22 June 2004; Disch, "The Prince of the Pagodas," *The New Leader*, 11 August 1997.

60. Dunning, "Making a Classic Gentler and Warmer," *New York Times*, 3 June 1997.

61. Lynn Garafola, "Alexandra Danilova," *Dance Magazine*, Oct. 1997, 61.

62. Barzel, "National Reviews," *Dance Magazine*, July 1989, 62; Percival, "In and Out of Favour," *Dance and Dancers*, Jan. 1989, 29; transcript, interview of Franklin by Mosely and Aloff, 3 May 2000.

63. Barnes, "Another Season in the Sun," *Dance Magazine*, Sept. 2000, 97.

64. Franklin, interview with the author, 15 October 2005.

65. Gold, "Enchanted in Nature's Realm," *Newsday*, 24 May 2000.

66. Howard and Zoritch, quoted in Leland Windreich, "The Legend Lives — Ballets Russes Share Notes," *World and I*, 1 January 2001.

67. Ibid.

68. Baronova, quoted in ibid.

69. Cited in ibid.

70. Wisner, "Ballets Russes Reunion: One Last Grand Adventure," *Dance Magazine*, Sept. 2000, 61.

71. Quoted in ibid.

72. Hering, "Autumn Reveries at ABT," *Dance Magazine*, March 2002, 76–77; Schulman, "Opening Night Bravura and Bravos," *Back Stage*, 9 November 2001.

73. Lewis, "Pointe, Counter Pointe," *Washington Times*, 28 June 2003.

74. Lydon, "Forever Freddie," *Dance Magazine*, Oct. 2004, 24.

75. Barbee, quoted in ibid.

76. Cargill, "American Ballet Theatre," *Dance Magazine*, Nov. 2004, 78; Tomalonis, "From ABT, A Doomed 'Romeo and Juliet,'" *The Washington Post*, 24 February 2003.

Chapter 8

1. Franklin, interview with the author, 15 October 2005.

2. Ibid.

3. Ibid.

4. Jenny Gilbert, "A New Broom at the Royal," *The Independent Sunday* (London, England), 10 June 2001.

5. Mason, quoted in Norman Lebrecht, "Byline," *The Evening Standard* (London, England), 22 January 2003.

6. Ibid.

7. Mason, quoted in Nadine Meisner, "Leaping Forward," *The Independent* (London, England), 26 March 2003.

8. Franklin, interview with the author, 15 October 2005.

9. Levene, "Snow Drifters, The Hard Nut, Ashton," *Sunday Telegraph* (London, England), 21 November 2004; Anderson, "First Night: Neglected Ashton Revived," *The Independent* (London, England), 15 November 2004.

10. Anderson, "First Night: Neglected Ashton Revived," *The Independent* (London, England), 15 November 2004.

11. Franklin, interview with the author, 15 October 2005.

12. Franklin, quoted in "Ballet Dancer, 90, Honored by Queen," *Associated Press*, 16 November 2004.

13. Ausman, interview with the author, 15 October 2005.

14. Franklin, interview with the author, 15 March 2006.

15. Cited in ibid.

16. Cited in ibid.

17. Ibid.

18. Franklin, interview with the author, 15 October 2005.

19. Allan Ulrich, "Living History: Recalling the Ballets Russes," *Dance Magazine*, Nov. 2005, 16.

20. Krassovska, Riabouchinska, Baronova, Tchinarova, Markova, and Wilkinson, cited and quoted in *Ballets Russes*, dir. and prod. by Dan Geller and Dayna Goldfine, Zeitgeist Films, 2005.

21. Franklin, interviewed in ibid.

22. Cited in Ulrich, "Living History: Recalling the Ballets Russes," 16.

23. Steve Inskeep, *Morning Edition* (National Public Radio), 23 September 2005.

24. Geller, quoted in Elizabeth Khuri, "Center Stage," *WWD*, 4 November 2005.

25. Goldfine, quoted in Ulrich, "Living History: Recalling the Ballets Russes," 16.

26. Geller, quoted in Norman Wilner, "Ballet Magnifique," *Eye Weekly*, 8 December 2005.

27. Franklin, interview with the author, 15 October 2005.

28. Nágy, quoted in interview with the author, 16 March 2006.

29. Marcello Angelini, interview with the author, 8 August 2006.

30. Ibid.

31. Ibid.

32. Stevenson, quoted by Angelini, interview with the author, 8 August 2006.

33. Leigh Alderson, quoted in *A God Given Gift: The Leigh Alderson Story*, dir. and prod. by Clare Delargy, BBC Northern Ireland, October 2005.

34. Gailen Stock, quoted in ibid.

35. Chris Pownes, quoted in ibid.

36. Frederic Franklin, quoted in ibid.

37. Alderson and Pownes, quoted in ibid.

38. Franklin, quoted in ibid.

Bibliography

This bibliography is restricted to books and lengthy magazine articles. Newspaper and magazine reviews, transcripts and other archival material are cited in the notes to each chapter.

Amberg, George. *Ballet: The Emergence of an American Art.* New York: Mentor Books, 1949.

Anderson, Jack. *The One and Only: The Ballet Russe de Monte Carlo.* New York: Dance Horizons, 1981.

Balanchine, George, and Francis Mason. *Balanchine's Complete Book of Ballets.* New York: Doubleday and Company, 1977.

Barzel, Ann. "Lancashire Lad to Ballet Master — Frederic Franklin." *Dance,* Feb. 1946, pp. 12–13.

Beaumont, Cyril W. *Ballets Past and Present.* London: Putnam, 1955.

_____. *Supplement to the Complete Book of Ballets.* London: Putnam, 1952.

Chamot, Mary. *Gontcharova: Stage Designs and Paintings.* London: Oresko Books Ltd., 1979.

Christie, Ian. *Powell, Pressburger and Others.* London: British Film Institute, 1978.

Clarke, Mary. *The Sadler's Wells Ballet: A History and an Appreciation.* New York: Da Capo Press, 1977.

Daneman, Meridith. *Margot Fonteyn.* New York: Viking Penguin, 2004.

de Mille, Agnes. *Dance to the Piper.* Boston: Little Brown and Company, 1952.

Denby, Edwin. *Looking at the Dance.* New York: Pellegrini and Cudahy, 1949.

de Sena, Ramón Gómez. *Dalí.* Edited by Franco Paone, and translated by Nicholas Fry and Elisabeth Evans. New York: William Morrow and Company, 1979.

De Valois, Ninette. *Come Dance with Me.* London: Hamish Hamilton, 1957.

Dolin, Anton. *Divertissement.* London: Sampson, Low, Marston and Co., n.d.

_____. *Markova: Her Life and Her Art.* London: W.H. Allen, 1953.

Easton, Carol. *No Intermissions: The Life of Agnes de Mille.* Boston: Little Brown and Company, 1996.

Flatow, Sheryl. "Full-Length Ballets." *Dance Magazine,* July 1995, pp. 40–41.

_____. "True to the Spirit." *Ballet News,* Sept. 1984, pp. 11–14.

Franks, A.H. *Twentieth Century Ballet.* London: Burke Publishing Co. Ltd., 1954.

García-Márquez, Vincente. *Massine.* New York: Alfred A. Knopf, Inc., 1995.

Hall, Fernau. *An Anatomy of Ballet.* London: Andrew Melrose, 1953.

Haskell, Arnold. *Balletomania Then and Now.* London: Weidenfeld and Nicholson, 1977.

Hurok, Sol, in collaboration with Ruth Boode. *Impresario.* New York: Random House, 1946.

_____. *S. Hurok Presents: A Memoir of the Dance World.* New York: Heritage House, 1953.

Kirstein, Lincoln. *Ballet, Bias and Belief.* New York: Dance Horizons, 1983.

Krokover, Rosalyn. *The New Borzoi Book of Ballets.* New York: Alfred A. Knopf, 1956.

Lawrence, Robert. *Victor Book of Ballets and Ballet Music.* New York: Simon and Schuster, 1950.

Lifar, Serge. *Histoire du Ballet Russe depuis les origines jusqu'a nos jours.* Paris: Nage, 1950.

_____. *Traité de Chorégraphie.* Paris: Bordas, 1952.

Manchester, P.W. "A Conversation with P.W. Manchester." Interview with David Vaughan and

Dale Harris. *Ballet Review* 6, no. 3 (Fall 1977–Winter 1978): 82–87, 114.

Markova, Alicia. *Giselle and I.* London: Barrie and Rockliff, 1960.

Martin, John. *Ruth Page: An Intimate Biography.* New York: Marcel Dekker, Inc., 1977.

_____. *World Book of Modern Ballet.* Cleveland: World Publishing Company, 1952.

Martin, Robert F. *Hero of the Heartland.* Bloomington: Indiana University Press, 2002.

Massine, Léonide. *My Life in Ballet.* London: Macmillan, 1968.

Maynard, Olga. *American Ballet.* Philadelphia: Macrae Smith Company, 1959.

_____. "Frederic Franklin: A Life in the Theatre." *Dance Magazine,* June 1974, pp. 44–50, 56.

Mistinguette. *Mistinguette and Her Confessions.* Translated and edited by Hubert Griffith. London: Hurst and Blackett, Ltd., 1938.

_____. *Mistinguette: Queen of the Paris Night.* Translated by Lucienne Hill. London: Electra, 1954.

Noss, Luther. *Paul Hindemith in the United States.* Urbana: University of Illinois Press, 1989.

Page, Ruth. *Page by Page.* Edited by Andrew Mark Wentink. New York: Dance Horizons, 1978.

Powell, Michael. *A Life in Movies.* New York: Knopf, 1987.

Quiros, Rod. *Igor Youskevitch.* Chicago: Dance Press, 1956.

Reynolds, Nancy. *Repertory in Review: 40 Years of the New York City Ballet.* New York: Dial Press, 1977.

Robert, Grace. *The Borzoi Book of Ballets.* New York: Alfred A. Knopf, 1946.

Rose, Phyllis. *Jazz Cleopatre.* New York: Doubleday, 1989.

Shelton, Suzanne. "Michel Fokine's '*Schéhérazade.*'" *Dance,* Jan. 1981, pp. 76–78.

Siegel, Marcia. *At the Vanishing Point.* New York: Saturday Review Press, 1968.

Simon and Schuster Book of the Ballet. New York: Simon and Schuster, 1979.

Solway, Diane. *Nureyev: His Life.* New York: William Morrow and Company, Inc., 1998.

Stravinsky, Igor, and Robert Craft. *Conversations with Igor Stravinsky.* London: Faber, 1959.

Sulcas, Roslyn. "Franklin Speaks Frankly." *Dance International,* Fall 1988, pp. 11–15.

Taper, Bernard. *Balanchine.* New York: Harper and Row, 1963.

Terry, Walter. *The Dance in America.* Revised edition. New York: Harper and Row, 1971.

Todd, Arthur. "Ballet Blossoms in Washington." *Dance and Dancers,* Oct. 1960, pp. 18–19, 35.

_____. "A New Company Gets a Washington Inauguration." *Dance,* March 1963, pp. 38–39, 66.

Twysden, A.E. *Alexandra Danilova.* New York: Kamin Dance Publishers, 1947.

Vaughan, David. *Frederick Ashton and His Ballets.* New York: Alfred A. Knopf, 1977.

Walker, Kathrine Sorley. *De Basil's Ballets Russes.* New York: Atheneum, 1983.

Wisner, Heather. "Ballets Russes Reunion: One Last Grand Adventure." *Dance,* Sept. 2000, pp. 61–63.

Zoritch, George. *Ballet Mystique: Behind the Glamour of the Ballet Russe.* Mountain View: Cynara Editions, 2000.

Zorina, Vera. *Zorina.* New York: Farrar, Straus and Giroux, 1986.

The following works have been consulted as general references:

International Dictionary of Ballet. Edited by Martha Bremser. Detroit: St. James Press, 1993.

International Encyclopedia of Dance. Edited by Taryn Benbow-Pfalzgraf. Detroit: St. James Press, 1998.

Index

223